Conference participants in front of the National University of Samoa Fale with Prime Minister Hon Tuilaepa Lupesoliai Sailele Malielegaoi

CHINA AND THE PACIFIC

THE VIEW FROM OCEANIA

EDITED BY MICHAEL POWLES

VICTORIA UNIVERSITY PRESS
for the New Zealand Contemporary China Research Centre

VICTORIA UNIVERSITY PRESS
Victoria University of Wellington
PO Box 600 Wellington
vup.victoria.ac.nz/

Copyright © Editor and contributors 2016
First published 2016

This book is copyright. Apart from
any fair dealing for the purpose of private study,
research, criticism or review, as permitted under the
Copyright Act, no part may be reproduced by any
process without the permission of
the publishers

National Library of New Zealand Cataloguing-in-Publication Data

China and the Pacific (Conference) (2015 : Apia, Samoa)
China and the Pacific : the view from Oceania / edited by Michael Powles.
ISBN 978-1-77656-053-0
1. Pacific Area—Relations—China—Congresses. 2. China—Relations—Pacific Area—Congresses. 3. Pacific Area—Foreign economic relations—China—Congresses. 4. China—Foreign economic relations—Pacific Area—Congresses.
I. Powles, Michael. II. New Zealand Contemporary China Research Centre. III. Title.
327.9051—dc 23

Printed by Printstop, Wellington

Contents
and Conference Programme

Preface — 11

Introduction — 15
Michael Powles
Conference Organiser, former New Zealand ambassador to China; former high commissioner to Fiji

1. Official Opening

Chair: Fui Le'apai Tu'ua 'Ilaoa Professor Asofou So'o
Vice Chancellor, National University of Samoa, Apia

Opening Address — 25
Hon Tuilaepa Lupesoliai Sailele Malielegaoi
Prime Minister of Samoa

Welcome Address — 29
Her Excellency Mme Li Yanduan
Ambassador of the People's Republic of China, Apia

Keynote Address — 33
Tony Browne
Chair, New Zealand Contemporary China Research Centre, Wellington

2. Changing Geopolitics: China and the Pacific

Chairs: Leasiolagi Professor Malama Meleisea, *Director, Centre for Samoan Studies, National University of Samoa, Apia,* and Professor Liu Shusen, *Director of the Centre for Oceanic Studies, Peking University, Beijing*

China's Growing Impact on the Regional Political Order — 41
Dame Meg Taylor
Secretary General, Pacific Islands Forum Secretariat, Suva

The Chinese Pacific: An Historical Review — 46
Dr Paul D'Arcy
Associate Professor, School of Culture, History and Language, Australian National University, Canberra

China's Engagement with the South Pacific: Past, Present and Future   53
Professor Liu Shusen
Deputy Dean, School of Foreign Languages, and Director of the Centre for Oceanic Studies, Peking University, Beijing

A Regional Perspective   62
Ms Fekita Utoikamanu
Deputy Director-General, Secretariat of the Pacific Community, Noumea and Suva

China's New Leadership and its Perceptions of the Asia Pacific Region   67
Professor Bo Zhiyue
Director, New Zealand Contemporary China Research Centre, Victoria University of Wellington

Reflections on the Experiences of the Chinese Community in Samoa   73
Tuatagaloa Aumua Ming Leung Wai
Attorney-General of Samoa

3. Regional Security

Chair: Associate Professor Tarcisius Kabutaulaka, *Center for Pacific Island Studies, University of Hawai'i*

The Pacific Islands in China's Geo-Strategic Thinking   89
Associate Professor Yu Changsen
Executive Director, National Centre for Oceania Studies, Sun Yat-sen University, Guangzhou

Reordering Oceania: China's Rise, Geopolitics, and Security
   in the Pacific Islands   98
Professor Terence Wesley-Smith
Director, Center for Pacific Island Studies, University of Hawai'i at Manoa

Regional Security and the Role of External Actors   112
Dr Jim Rolfe
Director, Centre for Strategic Studies: New Zealand, Victoria University of Wellington

4. Chinese in the Pacific

Chairs: Professor Brian Moloughney, *Pro-Vice-Chancellor, University of Otago, Dunedin*, and Professor Jenny Dixon, *Deputy Vice-Chancellor (Strategic Engagement), University of Auckland*

Chinese–Samoan Interactions – Influences Both Ways: Entangled
   and Intimate Histories   123
Associate Professor Toeolesulusulu Damon Salesa
Head of Pacific Studies, University of Auckland

China in the Pacific: Alternative Perspectives   128
Dr Iati Iati
Lecturer, Department of Politics, University of Otago, Dunedin

China and the Pacific: A View from Tonga   139
Pesi Fonua
Publisher/Editor, Matangi Tonga Online, Tonga

The Drivers of Current Chinese Business Migration to the South Pacific   144
Dr Graeme Smith
Research Fellow, State, Socirty and Governanace in Melanesia Program, School of International Political and Strategic Studies, Australian National University, Canberra

A Pacific Island Student in China – Reflections   150
Dr Rebecca Bogiri
Port Vila, Vanuatu

Non-Traditional Security and Global Governance: China's Participation in
   Climate Adaptation in Oceania   154
Associate Professor Wang Xuedong
Deputy Director, National Centre for Oceania Studies, Sun Yat-sen University, Guangzhou

5. Development Cooperation

Chairs: Associate Professor WANG Xuedong, *Deputy Director, National Centre for Oceania Studies, Sun Yat-sen University, Guangzhou,* and Letuimanuʻasina Dr Emma Kruse Vaʻai, *Deputy Vice-Chancellor, National University of Samoa, Apia*

The Context of Overall Aid in the Pacific – and Its Effectiveness   161
Professor John Overton
Professor, School of Geography, Victoria University of Wellington

Mapping Chinese Aid in the Pacific   173
Dr Philippa Brant
Research Associate, Lowy Institute for Public Policy, Sydney

Soft Loans and Aid: China's Economic Influence in the Pacific   176
Dr Biman Prasad
Leader, National Federation Party, Fiji; formerly Professor of Economics, University of the South Pacific, Suva

China's Aid: A Melanesian Perspective   180
Dulciana Somare-Brash
Deputy Director, Pacific Institute of Public Policy, Vila

The Samoan Experience of China's Aid   184
Mrs Peseta Noumea Simi
Assistant Chief Executive, Ministry of Finance, Apia

China's Development Aid to Fiji: Motive and Method   189
Professor Lyu Guixia
Research Centre for Pacific Island Countries, Liaocheng University, Shandong

The Trend Towards Chinese Triangular Development Cooperation: The Cases of PNG and Timor-Leste   193
Denghua Zhang
PhD Candidate, Australian National University, Canberra

The Tripartite China/NZ/Cook Islands Project in the Cook Islands – a Cook Islands Perspective   201
Hon Mark Brown
Minister of Finance, Cook Islands

The Tripartite China/NZ/Cook Islands Project in the Cook Islands – a New Zealand Perspective   208
Peter Zwart
Ministry of Foreign Affairs and Trade, Wellington

6. Trade and Investment

Chairs: Ms Andie Fong Toy, *Deputy Secretary-General, Pacific Islands Forum Secretariat, Suva*, and Michael Powles, *formerly Chair, WCPFC Preparatory Conference, ambassador to China, high commissioner to Fiji*

The Samoan Experience   217
Auelua Samuelu Enari
Chief Executive Officer, Ministry of Commerce, Industry and Labour, Apia

China and Natural Resource Developments in Oceania:
   Feeding the Dragon   221
Associate Professor Tarcisius Kabutaulaka
Associate Professor, Center for Pacific Island Studies, University of Hawai'i, Hawai'i

Foreign Investments and Local Expectations: PNG's Experience with China   235
Dr Patrick Matbob
Divine Word University, Madang, Papua New Guinea

China's Growing Tuna Fishing Fleet in the Pacific Ocean:
   A Samoan Fisheries Perspective   244
Ms Joyce Samuelu Ah Leong
Assistant Chief Executive, Ministry of Agriculture and Fisheries, Apia

China and the Sea: Potential for Pacific Partnerships?   248
Dr Paul D'Arcy
*Associate Professor, School of Culture, History and Language, Australian National
   University, Canberra*

7. The Final Forum

Chair and Moderator: Jon Fraenkel
Professor of Comparative Politics, Victoria University of Wellington

Co-Chairs: Leasiolagi Professor Malama Meleisea, *Director, Centre for Samoan
   Studies, National University of Samoa*, and Associate Professor Yu Changsen,
*Executive Director, National Centre for Oceania Studies, Sun Yat-sen University,
   Guangzhou*

Overview of the Final Forum – Drawing the Strands Together   259
Michael Powles
Conference Organiser; formerly ambassador to China and high commissioner to Fiji

Editor's Acknowledgements   276

Index   277

'Ava ceremony of welcome. From foreground: Letuimanu'asina Dr Emma Kruse Va'ai, Deputy Vice-Chancellor of National University of Samoa; Fui Le'apai Tu'ua 'Ilaoa Professor Asofou So'o, Vice Chancellor, NUS; Leasiolagi Professor Malama Meleisea, Director, Centre for Samoan Studies, NUS

Preface

This book is based on a conference entitled *China and the Pacific: The View from Oceania,* which was held on the campus of the National University of Samoa in Apia from 25 to 27 February 2015. The idea for the conference and its topic were conceived by the New Zealand Contemporary China Research Centre. Consultations among the Centre and Victoria University of Wellington, National University of Samoa and Sun Yat-sen University of Guangzhou led to sponsorship responsibilities being shared between the three universities. (Notes on the three universities follow at the end of this Preface.)

From the outset, an agreed priority for the conference was to give ample opportunity for both Pacific voices to be heard and for productive engagement and discussion between Pacific Island participants and those from China.

Two-and-a-half days long, the conference was divided into several sessions, and this book follows the order in which topics were discussed at the conference. Following a traditional welcoming *'Ava* ceremony, the Opening Session was chaired by Fui Le'apai Tu'ua 'Ilaoa Professor Asofou So'o. Samoa's Prime Minister, Hon Tuilaepa Lupesoliai Sailele Malielegaoi, opened the conference with a substantive address on the conference topic. He was followed by Welcome Remarks by Her Excellency Mme Li Yanduan, Ambassador of the People's Republic of China to Samoa, and a Keynote Address from Mr Tony Browne, Executive Chairman of the New Zealand Contemporary China Research Centre. The substantive sessions, continuing through to midday on Friday 27 February, were:

- Changing Geopolitics: China and the Pacific,
- Regional Security,
- Chinese in the Pacific,
- Development Cooperation,
- Trade and Investment,
- Final Forum.

The conference was widely regarded as successful in providing both a platform for Pacific voices to be heard and the opportunity for engagement and discussion between Pacific and other participants. Pacific participants included ministers, senior officials and academics from all around the region. Regional organisations were represented by the Secretary-General of the Pacific Islands Forum Secretariat, Dame Meg Taylor; her Deputy, Ms Andie Fong Toy; the Deputy Director-General of the Secretariat of the Pacific community, Ms Fekita Utoikamanu; and the Deputy Director of the Pacific Institute of Public Policy, Ms Dulciana Somare-Brash.

From China there was a strong delegation from the Sun Yat-sen University of

Guangzhou led by Associate Professor Yu Changsen, two participants from Peking University of Beijing and one from Liaocheng University of Shandong. In addition, China's ambassador to Samoa and her deputy participated in the discussions. Recognised Pacific experts from New Zealand, Hawaiian and Australian universities, several of them originally from Pacific Island countries, made major contributions.

To ensure there was ample time for participants to engage in discussion on the issues raised, the morning of the third day of the conference was devoted to a general discussion of issues that were raised earlier in the conference – or that participants thought should have been raised. This Final Forum was chaired and moderated by Jon Fraenkel, Professor of Comparative Politics at Victoria University of Wellington (and formerly of the University of the South Pacific), assisted by Leasiolagi Professor Malama Meleisea, Director of the Centre for Samoan Studies at National University of Samoa, and Associate Professor Yu Changsen, Executive Director, National Centre for Oceania Studies, Sun Yat-sen University, Guangzhou. This ambitious experiment was regarded as successful by the many participants who took advantage of the opportunity to seriously engage on issues. That success was largely due to Professor Jon Fraenkel's skilful organisation and moderation.

Finally, the most significant contribution to the success of the conference was provided by the National University of Samoa, through both its organisation and cheerfully efficient support for participants, and also the unique venue in the University's tremendous *Fale Samoa*.

This book aims to serve as a record of the conference. It is based on the papers presented by participants or, when there were just oral presentations, on the transcript of proceedings. We hope it will serve also as a stimulus for further discussion.

The Sponsoring Universities

The New Zealand Contemporary China Research Centre
The New Zealand Contemporary China Research Centre aims to be a global leader in knowledge acquisition and knowledge sharing on the political, economic and social life of contemporary China among tertiary institutions, the business sector and the policy community for the benefit of New Zealand. It supports research, lectures, seminars, conferences, visitor exchanges and information sharing.

The only nationwide research centre on contemporary China in the world, the New Zealand Contemporary China Research Centre is based at Victoria University of Wellington. In addition to Victoria University of Wellington, it has six other member universities – the University of Auckland, Auckland University of Technology, the University of Canterbury, the University of Otago, the University of Waikato and Lincoln University.

The Centre holds an annual international Conference on Contemporary China: 'China's development' (2009), 'China and India: the end of development models'

(2010), 'China and Japan in modern economic growth' (2011), 'The Chinese model of modern economic development and social transformation' (2012), 'China's global course: the political economy of China going global' (2013) and 'China at the Crossroads: What the Third Plenum means for China, New Zealand and the World' (2014).

The Centre also holds conferences, workshops, seminars and symposiums, often in conjunction with leading Chinese and other universities. 'China and the Pacific' is one such conference.

The National University of Samoa

The National University of Samoa (NUS) is mandated to actively engage in fulfilling its critical role in national economic and social development through provision of quality academic education and training programs, and excellent research opportunities receptive to the development of Samoa.

Vision
The National University of Samoa will be recognised nationally and internationally as a vibrant and innovative centre of excellence in research, Samoan studies and quality learning, teaching and training across all disciplines.

Mission
To create the ultimate environment conducive to superior learning, quality teaching, professional training and robust research opportunities that are responsive to the economic and social development of Samoa.

Goals
- The NUS will be internationally recognised for quality of teaching and training and student's learning outcomes;
- The NUS will be the premiere research institution in Samoa and Centre of Excellence for Samoan Studies;
- The NUS will have staff of the highest calibre;
- The NUS will nurture strategic relationships with local and international partners;
- The NUS will sustain excellence in organisation and resource management.

Values
The following core values underpin all our activities and articulate ideals to which we aspire to hold ourselves accountable:
- Dedication and Commitment;
- Respect for and Preservation of the integrity of the Samoan Culture;
- Collaboration;
- Entrepreneurship;
- Innovation and Creativity;
- Responsiveness;
- Achievement and Excellence.

The Centre for Oceania Studies, Sun Yat-sen University, Guangzhou

Sun Yat-sen University (SYU) is currently ranked within the top 10 universities in China. It is located in Guangzhou, in Southern China, adjacent to Hong Kong and Macao. SYU is fully committed to education and internationalisation and has established extensive exchange cooperation relationships with overseas universities. SYU hosts a number of excellent research institutes on international and area studies that focus on Australia and Pacific studies. In January 2012, the Centre for Oceania Studies was chosen as an Area and Country Study Cultivation Base by the Ministry of Education of China. Professor Wei Ming Hai, Vice-President of the University, was appointed as the Director.

The main tasks of the Centre are research, personnel training and policy consulting. Research fields include: 1) Politics and legal systems; 2) Economic development and trade; 3) External relations; 4) Social, historical and cultural issues in the vast area of Australia, New Zealand and South Pacific countries and territories. The Centre offers graduate and undergraduate courses across all university levels. Recent publications include the 'Bluebook of Oceania' and the 'Dictionary of Who's Who in Oceania'. The mid to long-term goal of the Centre will be to develop it into a well-known think-tank on Oceania affairs.

'Ava ceremony of welcome: Dame Meg Taylor, Secretary-General, Pacific Islands Forum and Ms Andie Fong Toy, Deputy-Secretary-General

Introduction

Michael Powles[1]

This conference on *China and the Pacific: The View from Oceania* was conceived and organised against a background of increasing interest in China's growing role and influence in the Pacific. Over a decade ago, an article published under the alarmist title *Dragon in Paradise: China's Rising Star in Oceania*[2] began what became a heated debate. Initially the alarmists held sway and those who pointed to potential opportunities as well as challenges were in a small minority. Early in the debate, the voices most clearly heard were those of Australians, New Zealanders and Americans, usually warning loudly of the dangers for the region that a more powerful China would bring. Gradually discussion became more balanced[3] and in 2011 Dr Jian Yang, then of Auckland University, published a comprehensive study on the subject, which covered both challenges for the Pacific and opportunities that China's growing presence could bring.[4]

Surprisingly, in retrospect, these discussions paid little heed to Pacific Island views. They certainly existed: while debate continued among outside observers on the best way to deal with China in the Pacific, most Pacific Island governments were quietly developing solid bilateral relations with Beijing or, in some cases, with Taipei. But, reflecting perhaps a paternalism derived from colonial times, no-one thought to give their clear views prominence.

A main purpose of this conference was to change that and to provide a firm platform for Pacific viewpoints to be heard and discussed with participants from China.

The conference, held at *Fale Samoa* on the campus of the National University of Samoa from 25 to 27 February 2015, was the brainchild of the New Zealand Contemporary China Research Centre based at Victoria University of Wellington. A three-way partnership was formed with the National University of Samoa in Apia and Sun Yat-sen University of Guangzhou. It was agreed that the National University of Samoa would host the conference, which would be supported by all three universities.

From the outset, it was intended that the conference would break new ground in three respects:
- priority would be given to views from the Pacific Islands,
- the conference itself would be held within the Pacific Islands region (in Samoa) and
- it would provide opportunities for perspectives to be exchanged between scholars and officials from the Pacific Islands on the one hand and China on the other.

While there was no attempt to reach agreed conclusions or positions, the impressions which most participants took away with them will have included a clear sense that China is in the Pacific to stay, that its influence is likely to increase and that Pacific Island countries need to acknowledge and accommodate that. China's growing role will pose challenges for countries of the region. But Chinese participants were emphatic that China wanted to cooperate with them and they also emphasised the valuable opportunities that China can bring. Inevitably, cooperation between China and Pacific countries has sometimes been difficult. Concerns were clearly expressed by participants. But overall, the sense of participants was that Pacific governments increasingly believe cooperation with China can be valuable for them. A positive atmosphere seemed to be developing between Beijing and the capitals of the region – one participant commented that it was attributable at least in part to a growing confidence on the part of Pacific leaders that they had more control over their nations' destinies than they have had in the recent past. There was increasing 'Pacific Island agency' as one participant put it.

Traditional partners of Pacific Island countries also have no alternative but to adapt to the changes flowing from China's rise; New Zealand has begun to do so, particularly in the field of development cooperation.

The tone for the conference was set by Samoa's Prime Minister, Hon Tuilaepa Lupesoliai Sailele Malielegaoi, in his Opening Address. He agreed that China's strong and increasing influence in the Pacific warranted the conference's dedicated examination of the implications of these changes. He went on:

> The singling out however of a country and its motives sometimes creates an implicit impression that all is not quite what it seems and there are conspiracies afoot. It is a sentiment that would easily attend discussions of 'what China wants' with its growing strength, the ubiquity of its diaspora and not least the often relentless pursuit by the media of perceptions of China's levels of assertiveness in promoting and securing its interests . . . [O]bjectivity is clearly very important to the exchanges and outcomes of your conference to help inform the policy makers not just in Beijing and in the Oceania capitals but in those of all the international actors from outside the region presently active or intending to be so in the Pacific.

> We read and hear of the views of analysts and observers that point to colliding interests and inevitable rivalry between a rising China and the United States . . . with the worrying prospects of confrontation and even conflict. It would be most interesting to receive the objective scholarly and expert examination that your conference will bring to bear on such gloomy forecasts . . .

The Prime Minister went on to speak positively of Samoa's own economic relationship with China.

An equally clear request was made by the Ambassador of China to Samoa, Her Excellency Mme Li Yanduan, in her Welcome Remarks:

Undeniably, the current international studies are dominated by Western literature and theories, whereas the Oriental studies or specifically the Asia studies are far from being adequately represented. So I am happy today to see that many Chinese scholars are invited to this conference, who can offer China's side of the story and make valuable input.

In his Keynote Address to the conference, Tony Browne, Chair of the China Centre at Victoria University and a former ambassador to China (and high commissioner to Vanuatu), reviewed the development of China's growing role in the region – to the point that it has become a global power, 'in many ways the dominant power in the Asia Pacific ... China's role and impact will be a feature of any discussion of the Pacific for the foreseeable future. That is a reality which is here to stay.'

Tony Browne emphasised the importance of the priority accorded the 'View from Oceania' in the conference title:

> It is not an occasion where we gather with security and strategic experts from that global industry to consider other countries' views, other ideological perspectives on where the interests of the region would best lie or how they might best be managed. We are here to ensure that views of this region, of its leaders, its scholars and its public, are heard.

He went on to describe China's approach to diplomatic relations with the countries of the region, particularly its investment of more time and diplomatic energy in the Pacific Islands region than has any other country from outside the Pacific Forum membership:

> China's rhetoric that all diplomacy should be conducted as exchanges between equals, notwithstanding differences in population, military power, geographic size or economic might, has led Presidential and Prime Ministerial doors in Beijing being more readily open to Pacific Island leaders than those in any other major capital. I expect that a diplomatic analyst assessing the political impact of such regular contact would find that it is more profound than many outside the region may want to realise.

This judgement was borne out by the remarks and attitude of many of the participants at the conference.

A Positive Tone

Tony Browne emphasised one aspect of China's involvement in the region that can easily be over-looked:

> The tone of China's engagement with South Pacific countries will be important – as important as the economic or physical legacy its presence and growing involvement may leave.

This reference to the desirability of a positive 'tone' of engagement seemed also to influence discussion at the conference, encouraging its cheerful and positive tone. Privately, one participant wondered whether this upbeat atmosphere might have influenced participants' positive impressions of aspects of China's developing relations with Pacific Island countries.

Chinese Communities in the Pacific and Personal Interaction

Samoa's Attorney-General, Tuatagaloa Aumua Ming Leung Wai, gave a full account of his own Chinese heritage and the history of several generations of his family in Samoa and, particularly, their passage from cruel racial discrimination and segregation in early colonial times to integration and inter-marriage in recent decades. His presentation opened a discussion on the role of Chinese communities on the ground: while most established communities had become well integrated and were accepted as integral parts of society, the role of recent migrants was still a matter of debate and some were more worried by this factor than by the growing regional influence of China itself. One participant summed up these concerns by saying that this was becoming an issue with strategic implications, not just social.

A personal story was also told by Dr Rebecca Bogiri of Vanuatu, who having completed a law degree at the University of the South Pacific recently completed masters and doctors degrees in China. Her account was very positive and it included a number of comments on the way the Chinese system handled overseas students.

Changing Geopolitics

It was suggested that overhanging the discussion on *Changing Geopolitics: China and the Pacific* was the proposition, attributed to then Secretary of State Hillary Clinton at the Pacific Islands Leaders meeting in Rarotonga in August 2012, that the Pacific was 'big enough for all of us'. Many who worried more about the consequences of US/China rivalry than other considerations happily endorsed the suggestion. But several Pacific Island participants disagreed. One questioned whether increased military involvement in the region by outside powers would be welcome to Pacific Island countries. This caution was hardly surprising given the extraordinary history of foreign intervention and domination in the Pacific. Even after eventual independence from colonial rule there was frustration with ongoing constraints on freedom of action. Meanwhile, the ambitious aspirations for their Pacific and Island homes, best articulated by the late Epeli Hau'ofa in his historic *'Our Sea of Islands'*,[5] continue to be held by Pacific peoples and their leaders.

In fact, there was little discussion of the possibility of US/China rivalry impacting on the Pacific Islands region. The focus throughout the conference was on the growing role of China, the likelihood that it would be permanent and the challenges and opportunities this created for Pacific Island countries.

One Pacific participant spoke of the need for Island countries to 'feed the dragon, tame it and then ride it'. He said he was confident Pacific Island countries could do this successfully, reflecting a confidence about the future and Pacific Islanders' likely capacity to achieve their own objectives that was clearly shared by many other participants.

Another suggested that perhaps Island countries should not so much worry about taming the dragon but should instead 'use the dragon to help tame the kiwi, the kangaroo and the bald eagle'. In this regard, there was discussion of 'the China alternative' in terms of geopolitics and aid in particular.

Some felt that deeper issues still needed to be faced. A participant from Melanesia emphasised that Pacific Islands should not be judged according to 'institutional standards that were not designed by or for us'. Current institutions in the region should be regarded as 'transitional'. There was a sense that the geopolitical change brought about by China's increased influence and role in the region could make it easier to reconsider aspects of the status quo.

The geopolitical implications for the countries of the region of the appearance of a 'China alternative' were mentioned by several participants and developed by Professor Terence Wesley-Smith, formerly of New Zealand, now with the University of Hawai'i, and one of the region's most respected commentators. In his paper, *Reordering Oceania: China's Rise, Geopolitics, and Security in the Pacific Islands*, Wesley-Smith saw little evidence from Beijing's activities in the Pacific Islands region of a grand strategy driven by hegemonic aspirations. But China did not support 'the strengthening of the neo-liberal state in island places', which was 'the ultimate objective of Australian aid and diplomacy in the region'.

He continued:

> The major concern for Australia and other established powers active in the region is that the rise of China will disrupt the extensive structures of regional influence carefully constructed over many years to pre-empt non-traditional security risks. At issue is, first of all, Beijing's longstanding practice of providing support to its aid partners without political conditions, except adherence to the 'one China' policy. This provides Pacific leaders at least the possibility of avoiding some of the unwanted pressure associated with the aid-leveraged Western-led reform agenda.

He went on to acknowledge restraint on China's part:

> However, it is worth noting that Beijing's bilateral agreements do not require island states to modify or relinquish their ties with Western powers, and recent multilateral initiatives appear specifically designed not to replace the existing architecture of regional cooperation. Indeed, Beijing has been careful to work within established Pacific regional organisations, and to avoid any direct challenges to existing patterns of leadership.

Moreover, there is no sense that China has held itself out as representing alternative political or economic policy options that Pacific Island countries should follow. Few of the Pacific Island participants articulated specific views on the 'China alternative' but it was clearly regarded by many to be a significant consequence of the changing geopolitics of the region.

A More Confident and Assertive Pacific Leadership?

Several participants believed increasing confidence on the part of some leaders in the region was emerging. This was reflected in a suggestion that Melanesian leaders, through the Melanesian Spearhead Group, were determined to have a hand in setting the standards by which their governments and institutions should be judged. It remained to be seen how far this would be taken in practice but it was based on strong belief that a concept of 'good governance' which contained no indigenous elements was unacceptable.

Another participant, from the Polynesian Pacific, spoke of the need for Pacific governments to be more assertive in negotiations with aid donors, China included, to ensure that development outcomes truly reflected Island country wishes. To this end, Island governments should more often 'act collectively' to achieve their objectives. Hon Mark Brown, Cook Islands Minister of Finance, spoke of the emphasis donor governments placed on projects making 'economic sense' and he argued that it was equally important for projects to make good 'island sense' even if that cost more money.

The Assistant Chief Executive of Samoa's Ministry of Finance, Mrs Peseta Noumea Simi, spoke of many years of dealing with China's aid to Samoa, particularly in negotiating with Chinese officials, and made it clear that Samoans negotiated throughout with confidence and strength – positions that were clearly respected by their interlocutors. Other participants indicated a renewed interest in making greater efforts to ensure their development objectives were better reflected in projects.

Specifically, participants spoke of the disadvantage for Island countries when donors, particularly China, designed projects in their own capitals and then brought in all labour and materials for aid projects from overseas. Clearly these were major concerns. It was suggested that China could be prepared to respond to some of these concerns and indeed had done so on one or two occasions. A likely consequence of the conference is that China's development partners will push more strongly for changes in these areas.

The issue of soft loans from China and the burden of indebtedness being assumed by some Pacific Island countries was discussed at some length. A participant from Samoa indicated determination to push harder for grant rather than loan aid. Tonga's situation was of particular interest. A former Minister of Finance from Tonga reminded the conference that nobody made Tonga accept concessional loans from China. And in his paper, Pesi Fonua, Editor of *Matangi Tonga*, Nuku'alofa, spoke of the crisis he believed Tonga was in:

> It is clear that the increasing role and influence of China in Tonga today . . . is a debt collector's influence, and Tonga has no option but to satisfy the demands of the debt collectors.

None of the Chinese present responded to these comments but indicated that these strong views would be reported back to Beijing. Hopefully the same will apply on the issue of conserving the valuable Pacific tuna fishery. Ms Joyce Samuelu Ah Leong, Samoa's lead fisheries negotiator, spoke of Pacific concerns for the sustainability of the tuna resource and concluded by thanking China for all its generous aid and asking for just one more thing: a more responsible policy on the conservation of the Pacific tuna fishery.

Other messages conveyed to the Chinese present included the strong view that Beijing needed to understand that what might seem to be very small issues in the larger China context could instead be very big indeed in the so much smaller Pacific Islands contexts.

Overall, the impetus for change in the region was described as being more internally than externally driven. It was certainly not driven by China, but the changes associated with China's increasing role in the region boosted confidence in change on the part of internal actors.

At the end, the Deputy Head of Mission of the Chinese Embassy in Samoa, Yang Liu, responded to many of the points that had been made in discussion, promising, in the case of many of them, that the viewpoints would be carefully reported. He concluded by taking up the suggestion that the Pacific needed to feed the dragon, tame the dragon and ride the dragon:

> Professor Kabutaulaka made a very good metaphor of comparing treating with China as feeding and riding the Dragon, although I would say Dragon as a totem of the Chinese nation is not easy to be tamed. But I want to say that China and the PICs are economically complementary and have great potential for mutually beneficial cooperation ... China is a kind and auspicious Dragon flying in full wings, and you do not have to feed or tame the Dragon to live with it. What you need to do is simply to treat the Dragon as a friend rather than a threat or pet, and then you can easily win its heart.

At this conference Pacific views were certainly heard, and expectations were raised that they would be considered constructively in China in this spirit of 'mutually beneficial cooperation'. And participants from China had the opportunity to respond, which they did, occasionally with an eloquence not uncommon in the Pacific.

Notes

1. Michael Powles, a former ambassador to China and to the United Nations, also served as high commissioner to Fiji, Kiribati, Nauru and Tuvalu and spent much of his childhood in Samoa. He was organiser of this conference on behalf of the New Zealand Contemporary China Research Centre and the partner universities – National University of Samoa, Sun Yat-sen University, Guangzhou, and Victoria University of Wellington.
2. 'Dragon in Paradise: China's Rising Star in Oceania', John Henderson and Benjamin Reilly, *The National Interest* 72 (2003): 94–104
3. *China in Oceania: Reshaping the Pacific?* Edited by Terence Wesley-Smith and Edgar A Porter, Berghahn Books, 2010
4. *The Pacific Islands in China's Grand Strategy: Small States, Big Games*, Jian Yang, Palgrave Macmillan, 2011
5. Our Sea of Islands, in *A New Oceania: Rediscovering Our Sea of Islands*, University of the South Pacific, Suva, 1993

'Ava ceremony of welcome: visiting participants

I.
OFFICIAL OPENING

Prime Minister Hon Tuilaepa Lupesoliai Sailele Malielegaoi delivers the Opening Address

Opening Address

Hon Tuilaepa Lupesoliai Sailele Malielegaoi
Prime Minister of Samoa

There is little doubt of China's present strong and increasing influence in the Pacific. The capacity of China's demonstrated economic power, if not quite yet its growing military might, to further project this influence would seem to warrant your conference's dedicated examination of the implications for the Pacific.

The singling out however of a country and its motives sometimes creates an implicit impression that all is not quite what it seems and there are conspiracies afoot. It is a sentiment that would easily attend discussions of 'what China wants' with its growing strength, the ubiquity of its diaspora and not least the often relentless pursuit by the media of perceptions of China's levels of assertiveness in promoting and securing its interests. It will not be a surprise if the mere holding of your conference has generated these kinds of sentiments already.

Fortunately, I note from the programme the impressive scholarly credentials and practical expertise of the many presenters and the balance they bring to the treatment of the conference's topic. This objectivity is clearly very important to the exchanges and outcomes of your conference to help inform the policy makers not just in Beijing and in the Oceania capitals but in those of all the international actors from outside the region presently active or intending to be so in the Pacific. The extent of knowledge available in your conference should ensure in-depth assessment of China's Pacific expectations and vice versa of the Pacific's expectations of China.

We read and hear of the views of analysts and observers that point to colliding interests and inevitable rivalry between a rising China and the United States – not to mention the other international players – with the worrying prospects of confrontation and even conflict. It would be most interesting to receive the objective scholarly and expert examination that your conference will bring to bear on such gloomy forecasts, particularly in the context of the economic and physical security of the Pacific.

In terms of the conference's stated topic, Samoa's own contact with China dates back to the Chinese labour migrants in the early part of the last century. You will hear later of the experiences and immense contribution that the early migrants and their descendents as well as the more recent migrants from China have made to the life of our country. Presentations on Samoa's very important economic partnership and commercial arrangements with China are also included on the programme.

I wish only to add very briefly in connection with the economic partnership that right from the start, Samoa sought China's support in areas that other traditional donors were not engaged in, but we considered vital to Samoa's development aspirations and nation building. Through effective internal coordination, a very high level of complementarity was achieved between the separate contributions China and other development partners generously made available to assist Samoa's overall development.

The official diplomatic relations between Samoa and China were established 40 years ago in 1975. The relationship started very modestly and I can say that the decision by Samoa's leadership at the time was made without any expectations of what the future might be like. The decision obviously did not feature very much the contrasting existing political ideologies of the time. If anything, the decision probably had more to do with our Chinese migrants originating from Canton and that was the China that Samoa knew!

In any event, although for many years Samoa's relationship with China grew only incrementally, we nevertheless recognised and appreciated very much what to us was clearly a very genuine effort by Beijing in that earlier period to deepen the relationship. The leaps and bounds since are a much more recent phenomenon that paralleled China's own growing economic strength.

Besides the partnership supporting Samoa's development aspirations, the intervening years were marked with high-level visits of China's leadership, which included the early visit of General Secretary Hu Yaobang soon after the start of formal relations, the visit of Vice Premier Zhu Rongji just prior to becoming Premier, Chairman Jia Quinglin and members of the Standing Committee of the Politburo, Mr Changchun Li and Mr Wu Guanzheng. Samoa's leadership including our successive Heads of State and Prime Ministers visited China and met China's leadership in Beijing from the time of Deng Xiaoping's presidency.

In my own visits to China made over several years before and after I became prime minister, I noticed, each time I visited, new additional and large areas of China planted with trees and greenery, even around the road from Beijing's airport to the city. It was evidence to see and reinforced the announced efforts of China to address the global issue of Climate Change close to the hearts of all our Pacific countries. The joint announcement late last year by President Xi Jinping and President Barack Obama on the respective actions post-2030 of their countries on climate change meant a great deal to the Pacific as it would also be globally.

Samoa. from the beginning of official recognition of China. adhered to the One-China Policy, and found comforting that the interactions between the two countries have always been characterised by mutual respect for sovereignty, integrity and close friendship. These principles in my view were again very well reflected in President's Xi Jinping's thematic presentation for the 'establishment of a strategic partnership of mutual respect and common development' made to Pacific leaders attending the Summit meeting in Nadi in November last year.

Finally, whether accepted or protested, the reality is that geographic size, wealth and military might do count. When all three come together in very large amounts for any nation, everyone else sits up and takes notice with a flurry of projections of new opportunities but also assessments of threat level perceptions.

Right now, the omens for global peace and security are not auspicious with persistent warfare in Eastern Europe and the Middle East, the deadly spread of rampaging Islamists rejecting any secular order, and the corrosive effect of festering hot spots of resentment around the world.

The Pacific by comparison, and I would like to think by a 'very long shot', is still an 'Ocean of Tranquility'.

The enduring hope is that for everyone involved and with interests in the Pacific, the catch phrase must not be about rivalries and confrontations. Instead the narrative should be about care for the Pacific, the creation of opportunities, common development and mutual respect. The serious and committed application of wise and like minds to these principles should not just benefit all but simultaneously as well.

I look forward to the discourse and examinations of your conference's vital topic.

In closing I thank the Victoria University of Wellington, the Sun Yat-sen University of Guangzhou, the National University of Samoa and convener Mr Michael Powles for organising this important conference, which with great pleasure I declare officially open.

Ambassador Mme LI Yanduan

Welcome Address

Her Excellency Mme Li Yanduan
Ambassador of the People's Republic of China, Apia

It gives me great pleasure to attend the 'China and the Pacific' Conference and deliver the welcome remarks to all the participants, although I know that the real honor should be given to the organisers and sponsors of this event. Thank you all for making this event possible. I should also thank Prime Minister Hon Tuilaepa for your gracious presence here and enlightening address just now.

I understand this Conference is the first of its kind ever held in a Pacific Island country (PIC), which offers a good platform for academic and policy-wise discussions of China's role in the Pacific Island region, a very important topic which has gained more relevance with the rapid development of relations between China and Pacific Island countries in recent years. Actually we couldn't have chosen a better time to discuss our subject matter since we are now living in a rapidly changing world, most notably with China's political and economic might growing quickly, which many scholars would attribute to be the most defining variables of the political landscape in the Pacific region. Given that, and in light of China's increasingly active diplomacy in the region, it is not surprising to see some heated debate in both the media and academia on China's role and its long-term strategy in the region. That's why this conference is very important and we are delighted to see that the conference has attracted many prominent scholars and policy makers in the region, who will surely shed more light on our subject matter after putting your great minds together. So welcome everyone!

In my view, the study of our subject matter should be conducted in a holistic approach and put in a historical, political and economic context, just as we are going to do later. Undeniably, the current international studies are dominated by Western literature and theories, whereas the Oriental studies or specifically the Asia studies are far from being adequately represented. So I am happy today to see that many Chinese scholars are invited to this conference, who can offer China's side of the story and make valuable input into this conference. And I believe their remarks will be more interesting than mine since they are not bound by diplomatic etiquettes and will feel free to speak. Here I would only try my best to offer some food for thought to our participants.

While these issues of methodology and paradigms should be left to academics for better judgment, I want to emphasise that we are now living in an increasingly diversified world and we should be open to alternative thinking when it comes to one country's diplomacy, just as we have already accepted that the developmental paths of different states are far from being singular and universal as we used to believe. China's unique developmental path featuring reform, opening up and peaceful development in the past decades has eloquently proven that a country could well follow a totally different diplomacy which is exceptional to the conventional wisdom that a country is bound to be aggressive when it gets stronger.

As to China's role to the Pacific and the world, there are currently two totally different theories among some Western academics. One is the older 'China threat' theory, meaning a stronger China may lead to hegemony. The second is the newer 'China crisis' theory, which cites China's slowed-down economy as evidence of China's diminishing international impact and commitment. For a simple answer I would say neither of these two theories is well-founded. Let me brief you on China's recent development to make my point.

In recent years, China has indeed faced downward growth pressure. Starting from 2012, China's GDP has grown lower than 8% after 30 years' rapid growth. However, as Premier Li Keqiang recently pointed out in Davos Forum Meeting, China's economy is still in good shape. We have entered a state of new normal, which means we will turn the size- and speed-oriented growth model to one that values quality and efficiency. Starting from 2013, China has started the endeavour to comprehensively deepen reform under new historical conditions. Under a sluggish world economy, we did not conveniently resort to short-term stimulus; instead we vigorously pursued structural reforms, taking measures like streamlining administration and targeted deregulation, hence further unleashing the innovation and productivity. Thanks to these measures, China's economy has enjoyed stable performance with its growth, inflation and unemployment rate well kept within a proper range.

Under this new normal, we will decisively embark on a path of green and low-carbon sustainable development and further deepen the opening up and win-win strategy with other countries to serve the common benefit of the whole world. With the 7.4% growth rate, the Chinese economy is still growing at the fastest speed in the world, which will continue to present the world with 'China opportunities' for development. It is estimated that in 2014, China's economic growth accounted for 27.8% of the world economic growth and over 50% of growth in Asia.

Last November, the Chinese government held the second Central Conference on Work Relating to Foreign Affairs since the founding of new China, and laid out a comprehensive plan for China's diplomacy under the new historical conditions. It has been made clear that China should develop a distinctive diplomatic approach befitting its role as a major responsible country; that it is important to carry on the independent foreign policy of peace and promote a new type of international relations featuring equity, justice and win-win cooperation; and that China should seek other countries' understanding of the Chinese dream and pursue the well-being of both the Chinese people and the people of all other countries. As per relations with developing countries, we will continue to uphold justice and pursue shared interests, working hard to strengthen unity and cooperation with other developing countries, safeguarding their legitimate rights and interests and promoting the common development of China and other developing countries.

Facts speak for themselves. The fact that China has chosen to and will continue to pursue peaceful development is the inevitable outcome of the historical, institutional and current situation. First, historically speaking, China is a peace-loving nation, which has never pursued an aggressive foreign policy even in its peak of power as a world-leading empire in history. As a benevolent empire in the past, the very occasional wars it resorted to were mostly defensive in nature. Second, ideologically speaking, the new China – as a socialist country which has itself fallen victim to imperialism and colonialism – has always been strongly opposed to hegemony. The so-called new imperialism or colonialism of China is anything but true and nothing but defamation, which China will not tolerate to have anything to do with. Third, realistically speaking, China has pursued peaceful development out of its own realistic interest, which is to make more friends in international community to maintain a favourable international environment for its national development. In short, the peaceful development is a win-win strategy that serves the common interest of both China and the rest of the world.

Ladies and gentlemen, Pacific Island countries are an integral and important part of the developing world, which China, as a developing country itself, always attaches great importance to and feels obliged to align with. Although China and PICs are far apart geographically, both peoples enjoy natural intimacy and time-honoured friendly exchanges, which date back as far as 150 years ago. Since 1975, China has established diplomatic relations with eight Pacific Island countries, and our bilateral relations have since grown strong and steady. China is a sincere friend and cooperative partner of the island countries, who have always respected each other politically, complemented each other economically, and supported each other in international and regional affairs.

China's relations with PICs have gained further momentum and thus entered a fast track of development in recent years. In 2006 and 2013, China held two Ministerial Conferences of China-Pacific Economic Development and Cooperation Forum, giving great impetus to mutual economic cooperation. Since 2006 the average annual growth rate of trade between China and Pacific Island countries has been maintained at 27%, with that of Investment averaging 64%. Since 1975, China has been providing development assistance to various PICs, delivering over 100 projects in industry, agriculture, infrastructure and public utility, and conducted a great number of technical assistance programs in fields of health, education and sports etc. We have also provided to PICs more than 4,000 training opportunities and hundreds of scholarships.

Last year saw a new chapter of China's relations with PICs, with President Xi Jinping visited Fiji in November, the first visit to the Pacific Island region by China's Head of State, and held summit meetings with leaders of the eight PICs including

Samoa to jointly draw a blueprint for the bright future of our mutually beneficial cooperation. In the meeting, President Xi pledged five-point measures intended to strengthen relations with PICs, which include building a strategic partnership featuring mutual respect and common development, enhancing high-level exchanges, deepening practical cooperation, expanding people-to-people and cultural exchanges, and intensifying multilateral coordination. In terms of development cooperation, China pledged more developmental aid to finance infrastructure, agricultural, environmental and new energy projects for sustainable development in PICs. In five years' time, China will offer 2,000 scholarship opportunities and 5,000 study and training places of all kinds to the island countries. China will also continue dispatching medical teams to relevant island countries and encourage more Chinese tourists to travel there. All these measures are warmly welcomed by the PIC leaders, who are willing to work closely with China to further uplift the bilateral relations to a new level.

The year of 2015 will witness the 40th anniversary of diplomatic relations between China and Samoa as well as Fiji, the first two Island countries to establish diplomatic ties with China. China and the two countries will hold a series of celebratory events to mark the deep-rooted friendship and fruitful cooperation between our peoples. Through decades of close cooperation, the eight PICs have become the accountable friends of China in the region, who have firmly supported One-China Policy. We highly appreciate having PICs as our good friends and believe that the further development of the China-PICs friendship and cooperation into a strategic partnership serves the common interests of our peoples. The Chinese government is ready to make the 40th anniversary a pivot for working with the PIC governments and people to enhance mutual understanding and friendship between our countries, expand and deepen mutually beneficial cooperation in all fields, and continue our mutual support and sound cooperation in the international and regional arena.

Ladies and gentlemen, It is our belief that China and PICs enjoy great potential in mutually beneficial cooperation and it is our unswerving long-term strategy to jointly forge a strategic partnership based on mutual respect and common development with PICs. Our policy toward the Pacific Island region is to promote sustained peace and common prosperity in the region, where we do not pursue narrowly defined self-interest or a sphere of influence in any form. Our strategic partnership with PICs holds an open, inclusive and balanced principle and is not targeted at any third party. We are willing to share experiences of development cooperation with other aid-giving countries on the basis of equality and mutual respect. It is my sincere hope that after this conference, we can reach some consensus on our subject matter and hence help the general public have a better understanding of China's role in the region. Finally I wish the conference all the success and our participants all the best. Thank you all.

Keynote Address

Tony Browne
Chair, New Zealand Contemporary China Research Centre

China's growing role in the South Pacific is a logical aspect of its re-emergence as a global and regional power. China has global objectives – to exert political and diplomatic influence commensurate with its size, history and global standing, to advance and protect its economic security and the prosperity of its people, to secure access to resources, to ensure the security of its borders and the stability of the region in which it is located. China has become a global power, in many ways the dominant power in the Asia Pacific.

China's expanded international role, and its role here in the Pacific, is played out at multiple levels – the diplomatic and political, the defence and security, the economic and development assistance, the cultural and educational, and through the Chinese diaspora.

China's role and impact will be a feature of any discussion of the Pacific for the foreseeable future. That is a reality that is here to stay. How and why it came about is less important than where we in the South Pacific fit into an Asia-Pacific region so heavily influenced by China, and where that will lead. The tone of China's engagement with South Pacific countries will be important – as important as the economic or physical legacy its presence and growing involvement may leave.

We meet in the year commemorating the 40th anniversary of the start of China's diplomatic presence in the island nations of the South Pacific. China established diplomatic relations with Fiji in November 1975, and with Samoa the following day. China's initial effort, as it was in New Zealand, was political rather than economic. This focus was compounded by the region's loyalties being divided between Beijing and Taipei. We have chosen not to make this a theme of this conference. In doing so we have perhaps left ourselves open to the charge of ignoring one of the driving forces for China's expanded presence, but since the 2008 unofficial truce with Taipei, this has assumed considerably less importance.

The influence of China in the Pacific is not measured only in terms of the interventions and commitments of the government in Beijing and its representatives in the region. For a hundred or more years the image of China in the region was pre-eminently that offered by resident Chinese communities. Those communities date back to the 1870s. In most cases they became part of the social and economic landscape of the countries where they settled. One need only look along Beach Road here in Apia to see the lasting impact on the economic and social fabric of this country. The Attorney-General will speak of this. But in Vanuatu, or the New Hebrides as it then was in the mid-1960s where I first had dealings with a Pacific Islands Chinese community, it had much more of a frontier type impact. The role of Fung Kwan Shee as the purveyor of 44 gallon metal drums of undrinkable Algerian wine, and cans of Ma Ling chicken bones, left me with scars that have not entirely healed.

Recent Chinese migration raises new issues, new tensions, and in theory new economic opportunities. The last ten years have seen the most rapid expansion of Chinese migration to the region in history. This is not a phenomenon special to the Pacific, but its impact on small communities is every bit as great here as anywhere. These new communities, many from Fujian, are tough, durable, opportunistic, hardworking, and in some areas intensely disliked for their delocalisation of business activity. They have no particular connection with longer-standing families and social circles. These are not legates of the Beijing authorities. But for so many Pacific Islanders they are the vanguard and physical expression of China's growing interest in the region. Graeme Smith raises interesting insights into the way they are viewed in Chinese official circles, prompted by the heightened consular pressures they bring when that unpopularity finds an outlet in communal unrest, as we saw in Honiara and Nuku'alofa in 2006, and PNG in 2009.

The sub-theme of this conference is the 'View from Oceania'. It is not an occasion where we gather with security and strategic experts from that global industry to consider other countries' views, or other ideological perspectives on where the interests of this region would best lie or how they might best be managed. We are here to ensure that views of this region, of its leaders, its scholars and its public, are heard. There are, inevitably, elements of great power rivalry with which Pacific Islands have to grapple. Overhanging our discussion will be the proposition then Secretary of State Hillary Clinton argued three years ago when discussing regional geostrategic competition at a Pacific Forum Leaders meeting in Rarotonga – that the Pacific is 'Big enough for all of us', though that formulation was not without controversy. Is this indeed how Pacific Island states see it? Or does the record point further so as to validate the late Ron Crocombe's 2007 thesis that Asia is replacing the West in the region?

However we answer that question there is little room for argument that China has instituted a level of dialogue between national leaders, and has invested more time and diplomatic energy here than has any other country from outside the Pacific Forum region. The Prime Minister has commented on Samoa's experience. China's rhetoric that all diplomacy should be conducted as exchanges between equals, notwithstanding differences in population, military power, geographic size or economic might, has led to Presidential and Prime Ministerial doors in Beijing being more readily open to Pacific Island leaders than those in any other major capital. I expect that a diplomatic analyst assessing the political impact of such regular contact would find that it is more profound than many outside the region may want to realise.

Wen Jiabao's visit to Nadi in 2006 was an important landmark. The Premier not only floated the prospect of RMB 3 billion in preferential loans but convened what was termed the first China-Pacific Island Countries Economic Development and Cooperation Forum. President Xi Jinping similarly spent time meeting regional leaders in Fiji only three months ago, promising a significant boost in aid, and establishing the Strategic Partnership with the eight countries recognising Beijing. I will not catalogue the full scope of diplomatic activity between these two milestone visits. This needs however to be measured not only in terms of frequency but also in terms of what is said at such meetings, and what is done by way of follow-up. To take one example: Vice Premier Wang Yang's reference, at the 2013 forum in Guangzhou, to climate change being the 'common challenge to all mankind' will resonate with island countries when compared with others who show some ambivalence on the subject.

Yet the question remains, to what extent does China have a 'Pacific policy' as against its engagement in this region being a relatively uncalibrated extension of its global strategies? Has China's engagement with Pacific Island countries been shaped by circumstances in those countries, or has a template for China's universal international practice been placed over its dealings here? How does China manage its relations with Caribbean states for example, with parts of Africa, with countries closer to home in Southeast Asia? Philippa Brant has looked at this, and Terence Wesley-Smith has made comparisons with China's dealings in the Caribbean. There will be a chance here to test the conclusion that emerges from Dr Jian Yang's 2011 book on China and the Pacific that essentially said that China's activities in this region were shaped by considerations and priorities in China itself more than by circumstances of the region.

Coming from New Zealand one is all too aware of the impact that a growing China has on a country's export performance and ongoing prosperity. The prospect of China offering new markets for Pacific Island produce, resources and goods is widely mooted, but the evidence gives only limited cause for enthusiasm. Chinese trade and investment with the region is growing, but it is highly uneven, and heavily concentrated – some 70% on PNG, (which is largely *sui generis* in terms of this discussion). Only in the Ramu nickel mine is there a Chinese investment of the size and impact that characterises so much of China's international investment.

To understand China's economic impact we have to go well beyond aggregated figures. China's export figures have been skewed by construction equipment and construction materials. We need too to understand local impact, the extent of local participation in projects promoted from and by Beijing, the role played by ethnic Chinese as the vehicles, and sometimes the primary beneficiaries of China's economic outreach. That requires substantial pieces of research across many countries if we are to understand fully what we mean by China's economic impact in this region. The annual *Blue Book of Oceania*, edited by Professor Yu Changsen at the Sun Yat-sen University's Center for Oceania Studies, gives a useful annual commentary, (though only in Chinese at this stage), on China's engagement with individual Pacific countries.

Putting PNG to one side, the principal Pacific Island resource opportunities for China lie in fisheries and other marine resources. China played a key role in establishing a regional fisheries management regime, and Premier Wen Jiabao gave an assurance at his Nadi meeting in 2006 that China would support Pacific Islands' 'legitimate interests regarding maritime resources exploration and protection'. It was an important commitment. China's adherence to that regime is something that will be examined tomorrow.

China's aid in the Pacific has undergone an abundance of comment, much of it analysis by anecdote, but that does not and should not pass for scholarship about the extent, content or impact of its development assistance to Pacific Island nations. That aid has been enough to resonate in the region. But it is nowhere near replacing Australia as the region's largest donor, or even matching New Zealand's aid levels. Yet those relativities may change. At President Xi Jinping's meeting with regional leaders in November he upped the level of China's proffered assistance to USD 4 billion in aid funding over the next five years.

China offers new options for Pacific nations to develop costly infrastructure needs, including projects in areas such as hydroelectric power development to reduce dependence on expensive fossil fuel imports. China's criteria for its aid have placed it at variance with more traditional donors, New Zealand included, though as always with aid policy there is room for healthy debate about appropriate priorities. That policy of being willing to support projects, often political, often oriented to the elite, brought some tension to relations between China and other donors – as seen in China's rejection of the Cairns Compact. It is a subject on which Pacific Island views have been quite widely expressed, and will no doubt be heard again here.

Chinese projects have often involved the use of Chinese architects, Chinese engineers, Chinese labour, and have incurred some criticism as being poorly designed for local conditions and requiring expensive maintenance. But China has been willing to tackle infrastructural projects that other donors did not or could not take on. Thirty years ago, when I lived down the road in Moto'otua, near the old hospital, the need for its upgrading or preferably replacement was urgent. The new hospital, opened late last year, is an eloquent rejoinder to China's critics.

So are Chinese attitudes changing? Does the tripartite project for the Cook Islands water scheme herald closer alignment between China and traditional donors? In this conference we will look closely at this project, with Finance Minister Hon Mark Brown, here with us to give the definitive Cook Islands assessment of what this example of coordination and cooperation has produced for his country.

Recently China has put growing emphasis on concessional loans rather than grants or interest free loans – till such loans now make up nearly 60% of China's aid to Pacific Island states. Managing loan repayments has the potential to introduce new levels of complexity into governments' relations with Beijing. In a sense we are entering the second chapter of China's aid involvement in the region, marking the transition from the region often being the beneficiary of a relatively untrammelled flow of largesse to China's assistance being cast as part of a more integrated and complex partnership.

Important too is the number of Pacific Islanders who are gaining their higher level education not in traditional countries of study, but in China. President Xi Jinping's offer of 2,000 scholarships over five years may have a long term impact that turns out to be the most important dimension of all of Chinese assistance.

We have ahead of us two and a half days of debate on fascinating, sometimes controversial, but nonetheless important issues that will help shape the next decades of Pacific Islands diplomacy and development. Let me extend the conference organisers' thanks to all who have travelled to Apia to take part in these deliberations, and to our hosts at the National University of Samoa for their hospitality and for the excellence of their arrangements. On behalf of the three partner universities I look forward to a free-flowing discussion on perhaps the most important long-term shift in this region's dynamics in the last two decades.

2.
CHANGING GEOPOLITICS:
CHINA AND THE PACIFIC

Dame Meg Taylor

China's Growing Impact on the Regional Political Order

Dame Meg Taylor
Secretary General of the Pacific Islands Forum Secretariat, Suva

It is an honour to be given the opportunity to contribute to this important conference, which is, by happy coincidence, part of my first official visit to Samoa.

I have been given the task, as the Secretary General of the Forum, the political grouping of sixteen independent self-governing Pacific states established in 1971, to speak on 'China's growing impact on the regional political order'. I will do this from the perspective of the Pacific Islands Forum Secretariat that I represent, based on the long and close relationship it has enjoyed with the People's Republic of China since 1989 when China became a Post Forum Dialogue Partner. China has had a close working relationship with many of the Forum members, with Samoa and Fiji being the first Pacific countries to establish diplomatic relations with China in 1975 and with China establishing embassies in our region as early as 1976.

In the context of the discussion over the next two and a half days, the Pacific Islands Forum Secretariat as a political institution is aware of the fluid geopolitics and the changing regional economics of the Pacific. China is now the major trading partner for Australia and New Zealand, a key trading partner for larger Forum Island Countries such as Papua New Guinea and a key political partner for a large number of Forum Island Countries. The influence of long term partners, some metropolitan powers and other Pacific powers has shifted as Forum Island Countries reposition themselves to collaborate with partners such as China, Japan, Korea, the European Union and Taiwan.

Some powers, like the USA, have clear strategic interests in the region. Others are driven by a desire to access natural resources. China's interests in the geopolitics of this region are inextricably tied to its economic interests, through development assistance, investment lending and direct investment, that have conditionalities with regard to labour and sourcing of equipment, for example.

Let me first touch on China's presence in the region.

China enjoys diplomatic relations with ten Forum members – Australia, Cook Islands, Federated States of Micronesia, Fiji, New Zealand, Niue, Papua New Guinea, Samoa, Tonga and Vanuatu. Since China first formalised diplomatic relations some 40 years ago with two of our Pacific Island countries in 1975, the friendship and ties between China and the Pacific have seen remarkable expansion and strengthening. This is a demonstration of mutuality and clear willingness between Pacific governments and China to foster greater and shared understanding and beneficial cooperation.

Six other Forum members – Kiribati, Nauru, Republic of the Marshall Islands, Palau, Solomon Islands and Tuvalu – recognise Taiwan. This dichotomy has presented the Forum with unique challenges in the conduct of meetings and the multitude of activities implemented by the Forum Secretariat, while at the same time respecting the sovereignty of members and the integrity of Forum processes mandated by the Forum Leaders.

There are intrinsic complexities involved when negotiating with China that need to be understood. Most of the Pacific countries that have diplomatic relations with China note that where they have a choice between China and other development partners – especially in infrastructure, they prefer to work with China because they have far less conditionality and much less complex and time consuming procedures and they receive the money or aid/loan in much less time than from all other development partners. They also have the hope that the loans will be turned into grants later or they will be forgiven. There are in fact conditionalities associated with China's development assistance. It is just that they are different conditionalities.

Having said that, however, the working relationships have been productive. For example, China respects and participates in all of Samoa's national aid management mechanisms – China attends the government-convened quarterly donor meetings and is now starting to contribute to discussions. In the Cook Islands too, China attends the government-led donor partners roundtable meetings.

China has also made some tentative moves to engage in regional peer reviews of aid effectiveness, under the Forum Compact. In October 2013, for the first time, China observed the Cook Islands Peer Review.

China's South-South Tripartite engagement with the Cook Islands and New Zealand to improve the water supply system on Rarotonga, Cook Islands, was also a positive development.

Turning to trade, China's contribution as a major Dialogue Partner of the Pacific Islands Forum has and continues to contribute substantively to the development of the Pacific Islands through trade and investment, infrastructure development, loans and grants, amongst other crucial support. This is an outcome reflective of China's relentless economic drive and reform that reflects its own development and economic success. But the Pacific remains a very small part of China's global trade.

Between 2000 and 2012 trade between China and its diplomatic partners in the Pacific increased significantly from USD 248 million to USD 1.77 billion. China's total trade with the Pacific (or Oceania), including New Caledonia and countries that recognise Taiwan for the same period, amounted to USD 2.7 billion. While manufactured goods flowed from China, the Pacific region contributed materials from the primary sector to meet China's demand for raw materials, resulting in a trade imbalance in favour of the region. The region's trade with China only represents less than 0.12% of China's worldwide trade.

The Pacific has a range of products and services to offer and Chinese investors have been encouraged to look at the trade and investment opportunities in the Pacific Island countries. But we need to seriously engage with China on broader trade and economic cooperation arrangements.

In support of these trade and investment initiatives, the Pacific Islands Trade and Invest (PT&I) network of Offices are being strengthened for increased private sector engagement. The Pacific Trade and Investment Office in Beijing is at the forefront of developing stronger private sector engagement with Pacific Island countries and Chinese businesses.

In relation to development assistance, up to 2013, it is estimated that China has provided RMB 9.4 billion in development assistance to the region. Between 2005 and 2009 China provided USD 1.42 billion to the region, 4.2% of China's global aid package.

It is reported that during this period Fiji was the region's largest recipient of Chinese development assistance, receiving USD 865 million or 60%, followed by Papua New Guinea with USD 236 million, Tonga USD 133 million, Samoa USD 102 million, Cook Islands USD 47 million, Federated States of Micronesia USD 33 million and Niue USD 1.6 million.

In 2006 the first China–Pacific Island Countries Economic Development and Cooperation Forum was held. Since then the region has witnessed an increased flow of Chinese development assistance to the region. At the last China–Pacific Island Countries Forum in 2013, China announced a USD 1 billion concessional loan for infrastructure and a further USD 1 billion commercial loan for infrastructure projects to support economic and social development.

Additionally China pledged to provide zero tariffs for 95% for our products, 2,000 scholarships over the next four years, expand the region's tourism market in China, provide agricultural assistance and render support on environment protection, disaster prevention and mitigation in the region. By 2013, China's projects in the region amounted to USD 5.12 billion. This has boosted construction and transport infrastructure sectors in Samoa, Papua New Guinea, Tonga, and Fiji.

China's economic impact in the region is increasingly significant. Its Foreign Direct Investment in the region has risen, particularly in the minerals, construction, retail and wholesale sectors. The single largest Chinese investment in mining in the region is the USD 1.8 billion Ramu Nickel mine in Papua New Guinea.

By 2013 more than 150 Chinese companies have invested in the Pacific, with about USD 1 billion in non-financial direct investments.

The impact and effectiveness of Chinese development assistance in the region is not yet fully clear due to difficulties with data collection and lack of harmonisation of Chinese development assistance with other development partners. Chinese development assistance is provided along bilateral lines, which require capacity for effective implementation by the recipient country. Whilst China is generous in its support to Forum Island Countries, the ability of Forum Island Countries to repay the high level of Pacific debt to China has been raised as a concern by the IMF. (Since the conference in Apia, in his address to the United Nations Summit on the Sustainable Development Goals on 19 September 2015, President Xi Jinping included in a list of new aid measures a reference to China writing off some loans to least-developed, small island states. Many in the Pacific will hope that at least some Pacific Island countries are included.)

Infrastructure remains a priority for Forum Island Countries in their development. China has emerged as the key partner supporting important infrastructure developments in several of our Pacific Island Countries, particularly at a time when some multilateral partners have shied away from engaging in large infrastructure projects. For example:

- USD 47.71 million was borrowed by the Government of Tonga from the China Exim Bank in 2010 for road construction and the rebuilding of its burnt out CBD. This has been a major contributor to Tonga's government debt, which now stands at 43% of GDP, and raises concerns about Tonga's high risk of external debt distress.
- In Samoa, part of the post-tsunami reconstruction assistance included loans from the Exim Bank for rehabilitation valued at USD 149 million.
- In recent years Vanuatu has received considerable funds from China, initially as loans and later converted into grants, to build a range of government buildings and other infrastructure, including on outer islands.
- In the Cook Islands, funding from China was used for various construction projects. Perhaps marking a turning point in aid coordination, a large water infrastructure development project was undertaken using Chinese and New Zealand companies.
- With the Federated States of Micronesia approaching the end of the Compact of Free Association agreement, it is now working on shifting its US-centric foreign policy to China, which is now supporting a range of major infrastructure projects in Pohnpei and in the states.

Whilst China is an important partner in development assistance, there remains a question regarding China's strategic interests in the region. These have not been prominent in the past, as compared with the United States and Australia. When comparing levels of military financial support, China's current assistance is only a fraction of that provided by Australia.

However, China provides military assistance to Fiji, Tonga and Papua New Guinea by way of uniforms, training and funds for equipment and the refurbishment of military quarters. In 2011 China agreed to provide Tonga with USD 1.6 million and in 2013 provided USD 2 million military grant aid to the Papua New Guinea Defence Force. In terms of formal recognition in the Pacific Islands, under current arrangements China's military has not participated in regional defence discussions.

Transnational crime and law enforcement is another issue I wish to highlight. For the past several years Regional Law Enforcement Secretariats have reported that

Asian organised crime groups predominantly linked to China and Taiwan have become increasingly entrenched in the region, representing a threat to stability and the rule of law.

Operating in a number of Pacific Island countries such as Fiji, Papua New Guinea and Vanuatu, these crime groups have been reported to camouflage their activities with legitimate business networks and have been linked to various crimes such as drug trafficking, human trafficking, prostitution, extortion, loan sharking and illegal gambling. This is an area of concern that needs deeper cooperation between the Government of China and Forum countries.

The Post Forum Dialogue (PFD) Partners session is a meeting between Forum Leaders and the Forum's development partners held immediately after the Forum Leaders' Retreat. The Forum has 17 PFD partners. Over the past two and a half decades, China has progressively engaged as a major partner to the Pacific region, both through development cooperation in the form of trade, loans and grants, as well as through diplomacy.

Additionally, China friendship with the Pacific has stood the test of time. It has supported and has come to the assistance of many of our Pacific Island countries in addressing climate change or natural disasters, food security, declining energy resources or global financial instability – these are global forces that have severe impacts on many of our island countries and expose the inherent vulnerabilities of island communities.

In conclusion, recent events in the Pacific have highlighted China's desire to make its presence felt in the region. President Xi Jinping's meeting with eight Pacific Leaders in Nadi, Fiji in November 2014 signalled a desire by China to engage in greater dialogue regarding diplomatic and development cooperation ties. The November 2014 talks highlighted issues of critical importance to Pacific Leaders – one being climate change – as a key area for further partnership between China and Pacific countries.

Whilst China engages on regional issues with less intensity, it focuses on bilateral partnerships building strong relationships with recipient countries. However, as China's presence in the region increases through its trade and economic development partnerships, the Forum Secretariat would like to see China as a regional development partner focusing on matters of common interest.

At present, China does not engage actively in helping Pacific Island countries pursue deeper regional integration. Leaders in 2014 gave a very clear signal that this is a high priority for them, when they adopted a new Framework for Pacific Regionalism, which the Secretariat is now in the process of implementing. This is a paradigm shift in the way regional priorities are determined by the region's political leadership, with an expectation that regional partners and donors will act on these priorities.

China's willingness to be an implementing partner for regional initiatives would be a positive development.

The Chinese Pacific:
An Historical Overview

Dr Paul D'Arcy
Associate Professor, School of Culture, History and Language,
Australian National University, Canberra

The People's Republic of China and peoples of Chinese ancestry resident in the Pacific Islands have figured prominently in Pacific Island affairs since 2000 because of their economic influence and perceived and real ties to groups and nations beyond the Pacific Islands. Ethnic Chinese populations in the Pacific Islands generally make up less than one per cent of the total population, but invariably figure prominently in business. The term 'Chinese' covers a diverse assortment of ethnic and political entities. China, Taiwan, members of Chinese minorities from Southeast Asian nations such as Malaysia, and peoples of Chinese ancestry resident in the Pacific Islands, in some cases for generations, have attracted particular attention in the Pacific Islands since 2000. Chinese and Pacific Islanders are used here as convenient umbrella terms that nevertheless mask the diversity of perspectives and lifestyle within each.[1]

The Emerging Academic Consensus on China in the Pacific since 2000
In 2007 the late Professor Ron Crocombe published *Asia in the Pacific Islands: Replacing the West*, in which he asserted that Asia was replacing Western former colonial powers as the primary source of external influences in the Pacific Islands.[2] Crocombe estimated the total Chinese population in the Pacific Islands at around 80,000 as of October 2006. The main concentrations are around 20,000 each in Papua New Guinea and Fiji, 15,000 in the Commonwealth of the Northern Marianas, 14,000 in French Polynesia, and 4,000 in Guam.[3] More have entered the Pacific since then, but accurate figures are hard to ascertain because of gaps and flaws in data collection in many Pacific Island nations. Many members of the long-term Chinese communities express concern about post-1990 Chinese arrivals' lack of sensitivity to local ways, and are just as likely to view them as disruptive competitors than as potential business and marriage partners. These latter arrivals are known as *huayi*, a Mandarin term meaning ethnic Chinese that is particularly applied to ethnic Chinese with passports other than from China. *Huayi* are distinguished from previous migrants by their weak ties to China, and their high degree of mobility in search of opportunities in the global economy that has emerged over the last three decades. While the businesses of more established Chinese are perceived

Dr Paul D'Arcy

as benefiting locals, those of *huayi* tend towards get-rich-quick enterprises such as logging that bring little evident benefit to locals. Tensions also mounted over Chinese and Taiwanese government and business interests attempts to buy support and win favour with local politicians.[4]

Matters came to a head in 2006 with riots against Chinese businesses associated with unpopular governments in Solomon Islands and Tonga.[5,6] The 2006 disturbances in Honiara and Nuku'alofa were also linked by many commentators to rivalry between Taiwan and China for influence among Pacific Island nations, and particularly to how 'cheque-book' diplomacy was destabilising domestic and regional politics. Six Pacific Island nations recognise Taiwan – Kiribati, Marshall Islands, Palau, Solomon Islands, Tuvalu and Nauru. The remaining eight Pacific Islands nations – Cook Islands, Federated States of Micronesia, Fiji, Niue, Papua New Guinea, Samoa, Tonga and Vanuatu all recognise China.[7] Competition for influence in the Pacific Islands escalated in 2006 and 2007, with China, Taiwan, and Japan declaring major increases in their Pacific aid budgets and the United States publically declaring its intention of reversing years of relative neglect of the Pacific.[8] Fortunately, sense prevailed, and a possible sustained and escalating competition for influence in the Pacific through aid has not taken place since 2007. The global economic downturn makes this increasingly unlikely in the immediate future.

Relations between China and Taiwan improved significantly from 2009.[9] Chinese-Taiwanese tensions have been replaced by mounting tensions between Japan and China over the disputed Senkaku/Daioyu Islands and between the United States and China over influence in the Western Pacific in general.[10] As yet, none of these new tensions has disrupted Pacific Island nations' domestic politics or international relations.

By 2007, a clear division was apparent in the outlook of Western commentators on Chinese influence in the Pacific Islands. On the one hand, commentators such as Australian journalist Graeme Dobell and academic Ben Reilly expressed concern about China's and Taiwan's use of aid to secure exclusive recognition from Pacific nations at the expense of the 'other' China. They see this aid as destabilising to Island politics. Others disagree. Scholars such as Terence Wesley-Smith, Greg Fry, and Tarcisius Kabutaulaka contrast China's lack of interference in internal affairs and refusal to comment on domestic policy in the Pacific Islands favourably with the more patronising approach perceived to come from other aid donors such as Australia. It is also seen as providing an alternative to free market philosophies underlying much aid conditionality from Western donors, especially drives to cut government expenditure and replace it with private sector providers.[11] Few of the critical assessments of China in the Pacific have sustained their analysis over lengthy time periods to follow up on the concerns they drew government attention to.[12]

A division of opinion between optimistic and more cautious conclusions was also apparent in 2007 in a second, related debate about the capacity of Pacific Island states to rectify their own problems. Many of those who express serious concerns about Chinese influence in the Pacific also publish gloomy prognoses about the ability of states within the so-called 'Arc of Instability' to Australia's immediate north to make significant economic advances and secure political stability without external assistance. Their concern about Chinese influence in Pacific nations reflects the assumption that some of these nations are failed states.[13] Those who see China as less of a threat also tend to share a more optimistic view of Pacific Island nations capacity to deal with external influences and internal problems.

The first Pacific Island focused book arguing against the threat discourse was published in 2010 by Terence Wesley Smith and Ed Porter. Their edited collection, *China in Oceania*, argued that those critical of Chinese actions in the Pacific underestimate the proactive nature and astute pursuit of self-interest of Pacific Island governments in engaging with China. Wesley-Smith had first advanced this line in 2007. Wesley-Smith and most Pacific Island specialists writing on Pacific Island–China relations argue China has allowed Pacific Islanders a greater degree of freedom of choice over aid donors than at any other time since independence by being the one significant contributor to not push for compliance with free market principles as a requirement of development aid and loans.[14]

New studies since 2010 have tended to support the broad findings of Wesley-Smith and Porter's 2010 study. These new studies have also expanded into new fields. China expert Graeme Smith's study has produced a number of detailed ground-breaking works on the new Chinese in Papua New Guinea.[15] In 2014, the full findings of a large AusAID-funded programme on the Chinese mine at Ramu in Madang Province in 2010 were published as a large edited collection, *Pacific Asian Partnerships in Resource Development*.[16] *China in Oceania* and *Pacific Asian Partnerships in Resource Development* collectively involved over 30 academics. With the exception of Wesley-Smith's contribution to both works, there was no overlap. Yet, both independently reached broadly similar conclusions in viewing China as less of a destabilising force in the Pacific than had hitherto been asserted, and in viewing Pacific Islanders as astute and active players pursuing their own interests in dealings with outsiders.

The first comprehensive analysis of China's motivations in the Pacific Islands was only published in 2011 by Auckland University international relations expert Jian Yang.[17] Having been born and raised in China, Yang argued China did not have a calculated strategy to displace traditional Western players and Japan in the Pacific Islands. Rather, Beijing's strategy is more about maintaining a form of international peace that allows China to focus on developing the domestic economic and technological foundations at the heart of modern national power in the global world.

Historical Perspectives on Future Scenarios

Most of the authors writing since 2000 focus almost exclusively on the last ten years, and also restrict their geographical focus. The embryonic nature of much of this analysis has led to a great deal of uncertainty and speculation. Detailed fieldwork-based case studies of new Chinese communities and activities have only recently begun to be published, and are already casting doubt on much of the assertions of the last decade. Only the Chinese communities in Papua New Guinea and Fiji have been subject to substantial studies, and even then, these studies are more descriptive than analytical. They provide a valuable resource upon which to build other studies of specific aspects of these communities or for comparative studies.

Willmott has conducted brief comparative analysis using his training in sociology to highlight the variation in sex ratios and Chinese sub-culture of origin within different Chinese communities in Pacific nations, differences in their interaction with local communities, and the related aspect of degree of cultural coherence over time. In regard to assimilation and cultural/community coherence, there is much merit in conducting detailed surveys of Chinese communities that inter-married into local Pacific Islander communities in New Caledonia, Kiribati, Samoa, Tahiti, and Cook Islands to contrast the largely ethnically Chinese communities subject to detailed studies in Papua New Guinea and Fiji. Cohabitation between Chinese men and Pacific Island women before World War II in Western Samoa and Tahiti ensured that the children of such unions were raised in two cultures, because the men maintained a Chinese cultural community that influenced their children, who also grew up interacting with their Polynesian extended families and norms. However, the small size of the Chinese communities in in New Caledonia, Kiribati and the Cook Islands made the inculcation of Chinese values and identity less feasible.[18]

One of the few studies to adopt this more wide-ranging, comparative approach is Smith's detailed study of new Chinese in Papua New Guinea. Most come from Fuqing, an impoverished area of southeast China with a long history of out-migration. As relatively recent residents of Papua New Guinea, the Fuqing Chinese have little accumulated capital and tend to set up small retail businesses supplied by predominantly longer-established 'old Chinese' wholesalers originally from Southeast Asia. This situation may change dramatically in the near future as the ever diminishing number of old Chinese creates market gaps as wholesalers for better-off Fuqing Chinese to fill, even though the majority still intend to settle in Fuqing after making their money in Papua New Guinea.[19]

If Papua New Guinea is typical, then the nature, influence and degree of integration of recent Chinese migrants into Pacific Island societies will remain fluid. But it seems likely that for the forseeable future persons of Chinese or part-Chinese ancestry will not disproportionately occupy as many important political and economic roles as did the long-established old Chinese in the first decades of independence. Reflecting on this past era, Crocombe noted how 'Sir Julius Chan was twice prime minister of PNG, Anote Tong is the current president of Kiribati, Gaston Tong Sang is president of French Polynesia, Jim Ah Koy was minister of finance in Fiji and at least two other heads of Pacific Islands' governments do not discuss their Chinese heritage.'[20]

Conclusion

The historical record of old Chinese in the Pacific reveals a fragmented record of diversity within and between communities, but united by successful adaptation to local communities, with or without intermarriage. These studies are largely empirical rather than thematic, with few comparative studies being conducted beyond brief surveys by Bill Willmott and Crocombe's large study.[21] There are a number of local histories and local or national histories of Chinese communities across the Pacific.[22] There are many studies still to be written on these older Chinese Pacific communities, especially for those with Chinese language skills. The lessons of the past suggest the pattern of successful Chinese adaptation after an initial period of adjustment in a myriad of context-specific ways will continue into the future.

Notes

1 The term China is used here for the People's Republic of China, Taiwan for the Republic of China, and Chinese as a collective term for all ethnic Chinese. This article benefitted from comments and feedback from Lewis Mayo, Pei-yi Guo, Yung-Chao Tung, Karen Kan-lan Tu, and Fei Sheng.
2 Ron Crocombe, *Asia in the Pacific Islands: Replacing the West* (Suva 2007), vii.
3 Crocombe, *Asia in the Pacific Islands*, 93–97.
4 Bill Willmott, 'Varieties of Chinese Experience in the Pacific', in Paul D'Arcy (ed.), *Chinese in the Pacific: Where are they now?*, Special Issue of *Chinese Southern Diaspora Studies*, May 2007, 35–42; 'Chinese contract labour in the Pacific Islands during the nineteenth century,' *Journal of Pacific Studies*, 27 (2–2004), 161–176; *A History of the Chinese Communities in Eastern Melanesia: Solomon Islands, Vanuatu, New Caledonia*, Christchuch, Macmillan Brown Centre for Pacific Studies Working Paper 12, University of Canterbury, 2005, Bessie Ng Kumlin Ali, *Chinese in Fiji*, Suva, 2002; and James Chin, 'Contemporary Chinese Community in Papua New Guinea: Old Money versus New Migrants', *Chinese South Diaspora Studies*, Canberra, The Australian National University, 2008, 117–126, available at http://csds.anu.edu.au/volume_2_2008/117ChinCSDS2008Master.pdf.
5 Tarcisius Tara Kabutaulaka, 'Solomon Islands', *The Contemporary Pacific*, 18 (2), Fall 2006, 424; Graeme Dobell, 'China and Taiwan in the South Pacific: Diplomatic Chess versus Pacific Political Rugby', in Paul D'Arcy (ed.), *Chinese in the Pacific: Where are they now?*, Special Issue of *Chinese Southern Diaspora Studies*, May 2007, 10–22, 10, 18–19); Clive Moore, 'No more walkabout long Chinatown: Asian Involvement in the Economic and Political Process', in Sinclair Dinnen and Stewart Firth (eds.), *Politics and State Building in the Solomon Islands*, Canberra, 2008, 64–95; and Ian Campbell, 'Tonga: The Constitution, the Riot, the Election and Reform', *New Zealand International Review*, 33 (5), Sept/Oct 2008, 2–6.
6 *People's Daily Online*, November 17, 2006.
7 Joel Atkinson, 'China-Taiwan Diplomatic Competition and the Pacific Islands,' *Pacific Review*, 23 (4), 2010, 407–427.
8 *Shanghai Daily*, 'Wen pledges to lift Island ties', 6 April 2006; Jim Hwang, 'What really counts', *Taiwan Review*, 30 November 2006, available at http://taiwanreview.nat.gov.tw/ct.asp?xItem=23510&CtNode=128; Ministry of Foreign Affairs of Japan, *The Fourth Japan-Pacific Islands Forum Summit Meeting*, 2006, available at http://www.mofa.go.jp/region/asia-paci/spf/palm2006/index.html; Congressional Research Service, 'The Southwest Pacific: US Interests and China's Growing Influence', US Congress, April 2007, available at http://www.fas.org/sgp/crs/row/RL34086.pdf; Wen Jiaboa, 'Speech at the opening of the first ministerial conference of the China-Pacific Island countries,' Fiji, 5 April 2006, available at http://english.gov.cn/2006-04/05/content_245681.htm; Gerald Chan, 'Taiwan as an emerging foreign aid donor: developments, problems and prospects', *Pacific Affairs*, Spring 1997, available at http://findarticles.com/p/articles/mi_qa3680/is_199704/ai_n8782447/pg_1., 5; S. Tarte, *Japan's Aid Diplomacy and the Pacific Islands*, Canberra, 1998, 83, 96; Karen Nero, 'The Material World Remade', in D. Denoon (ed.), *The Cambridge History of the Pacific Islanders* (Cambridge, 1997), 359–396, 368, 377–378.
9 Ministry of Foreign Affairs, Republic of China, *Progressive Partnerships and Sustainable Development*, Taipei: May 2009, 8; Jemima Garrett, 'Taiwan ends Pacific diplomatic wars with China', *Radio Australia International*, Posted 25 March 2010, available at http://www.radioaustralia.net.au/international/2010-03-25/taiwan-ends-pacific-diplomatic-wars-with-china/197200.
10 Gavan McCormack, 'Small Islands – Big Problem: Senkaku/Diaoyu and the Weight of History and Geography in China-Japan Relations', *The Asia Pacific Journal: Japan Focus*, available at http://japanfocus.org/-Gavan-McCormack/3464; and 'Troubled Seas: Japan's Pacific and East China Sea Domains (and Claims)', *The Asia Pacific Journal: Japan Focus*, available at http://japanfocus.org/-Gavan-McCormack/3821.

11 Terence Wesley-Smith and Edgar A. Porter (eds.), *China in Oceania: reshaping the Pacific?*, New York and Oxford: 2010; and Greg Fry and Tarcisius Tara Kabutaulaka (eds.), *Intervention and State-building in the Pacific: The Legitimacy of 'Cooperative Intervention*(Manchester, 2008). This division is discussed in detail in Paul D'Arcy, 'China in the Pacific: Some Policy Considerations for Australia and New Zealand', State Society and Governance in Melanesia Programme, Discussion Paper 2007/4, October 2007, SSGM, RSPAS, ANU, http://rspas.anu.edu.au/melanesia/dplist.php?searchterm=2007.

12 Fergus Hanson, 'The Dragon in the Pacific: More Opportunity than Threat', *Lowy Institute Policy Brief*, 2008, http://www.lowyinstitute.org/Publication.asp?pid=823, and 'China Stumbling through the Pacific'.

13 Susan Windybank and Mike Manning, 'Papua New Guinea on the Brink', *Issues Analysis*, 30, Centre for Independent Studies, 2003; and Ben Reilly, 'The Africanisation of the South Pacific', *Australian Journal of International Affairs*, 54 (3) (2000), 261-268.

14 Wesley Smith, *China in Oceania*; and Wesley-Smith and Porter, *China in Oceania*.

15 Graeme Smith and Paul D'Arcy (eds.), 'Global Perspectives on Chinese Investment', special issue of *Pacific Affairs*, 86 (2), June 2013; Graeme Smith, 'Chinese Reactions to Anti-Asian Riots in the Pacific', *Journal of Pacific History* 47 (1) (2012), 93–109; Graeme Smith, ' Are Chinese soft loans always a bad thing?' LowyInterpreter, available at http://www.lowyinterpreter.org/post/2012/03/29/Are-Chinese-soft-loans-always-a-bad-thing.aspx, 29 March 2012; Paul D'Arcy, Patrick Matbob and Linda Crowl (eds.) *Pacific Asian Partnerships in Resource Development* (Madang, 2014); Kate Barclay and Graeme smith (eds.), The International Politics of Resources: China, Japan and Korea's Demand for Energy, Minerals and Food, special issue of *Asian Studies Review*, 37 (2), 2013, especially Graeme Smith, 'Nupela Masta? Local and Expatriate Labour in a Chinese-Run Nickel Mine in Papua New Guinea', 178–95, and Kate Barclay and Graeme Smith,'Introduction: The International Politics of Resources', 125–140.

16 Darcy, Matbob and Crowl, *Pacific Asian Partnerships*.

17 Yang, Jian, *The Pacific Islands in China's Grand Strategy: Small States, Big Games*, Basingstoke, England, New York, 2011.

18 Willmott, 2007; and Lynn Pan (ed.), *The Encyclopedia of the Chinese Overseas (Second Edition)*, Singapore, 2006, 292–296, 299–303, 300 and 303.

19 Smith, 'Chinese Reactions to Anti-Asian Riots in the Pacific', 93–95; and Smith, 'Fuqing Dreaming: "New" Chinese Communities in Papua New Guinea', in D'Arcy, Matbob and Crowl, *Pacific Asian Partnerships*, 126–140. See also Chin, 'Contemporary Chinese Community in Papua New Guinea'.

20 Crocombe, *Asia in the Pacific Islands*, 90.

21 Bill Willmott, 'Origins of the Chinese in the South Pacific', in P. Mcgregor (ed.), *Histories of the Chinese in Australasia and the South Pacific*, Melbourne, 1995, 129–140; 'A History of the Chinese Communities in Eastern Melanesia: Solomon Islands, Vanuatu, New Caledonia, Christchurch, Macmillan Brown Centre for Pacific Studies Working Paper 12, 2005; 'Varieties of Chinese Experience in the Pacific', in Paul D'Arcy (ed.), *Chinese in the Pacific: Where are they now?*, CSDCD Occasional Paper 1, May 2007, 35–42; and 'The Overseas Chinese Experience in the Pacific', in Terence Wesley-Smith and Edgar A. Porter(eds.), *China in Oceania: reshaping the Pacific?*, New York and Oxford, 2010, 93–103; Crocombe, 'The Fourth Wave', and *Asia in the Pacific Islands*.

22 As well as Crocombe and Willmott's general surveys, the following are the best nation-specific studies of Chinese communities in the Pacific Islands. Papua New Guinea, Solomon Islands, Vanuatu, New Caledonia, Fiji, Samoa, Tonga, Cook Islands, French Polynesia, Kiribati, FSM, Palau, Marianas, Guam, Hawai'i, for example, Sophie Vognin, 'La population chinoise de Tahiti au XIXe siècle', in *Le Peuplement du Pacifique et de la Nouvelle-Calédonie au XIXe Siècle (1788–1914), Condamnés, Colons, Convicts, Coolies*, Chân Dang & Paul de Deckker (eds.), Paris, Editions l'Harmattan (for l'Université Française du Pacifique), 1994, 236–237.

China's Engagement with the South Pacific: Past, Present, and Future

Professor Liu Shusen
Deputy Dean, School of Foreign Languages and Director, Centre for Oceanian Studies, Peking University, Beijing

The history of the relationship between China and the South Pacific is longer than the history of China's relationship with Europe and America, although it had been scarcely noticed or of less concern until recent decades in the wake of China's rise as a world power. The gradual rise of China since the late 1970s not only results from its political and economic reforms such as the opening-up policy to survive the disastrous consequences of the Cultural Revolution (1966~1976), its subsequent economic development with an average ten per cent annual GDP increase for over three decades, and its continuously expanding relationship and partnership with other countries and regions worldwide, but also makes it necessary to redefine its relationship and partnership with other countries and regions including the South Pacific for the promotion of mutual developments and common benefits in the present age of globalisation.

Historically, both China and the South Pacific have been organic parts of human civilisation for many millennia, but in spite of recent archaeological field studies in such coastal regions as Fujian, Guangdong and Taiwan in southeast China and relevant encouraging findings of genic, cultural and linguistic similarities and association between the Chinese and the Polynesian and of the highly possible migration of the Chinese to some of the South Pacific Islands in the Neolithic Era, few opportunities of substantial and lasting contact and correlation had appeared until the early decades of the 19th century, when large groups of Chinese labourers went to Australia and New Zealand, where they were employed in the booming business of gold mining. As an exception, Zheng He (1371-1433) made seven voyages from 1405 to 1433 as a mariner, explorer, diplomat, and the admiral of the imperial fleet of more than 300 ships, visiting and exploring more than 30 countries largely in Asia and Africa, which possibly included a brief visit to Darwin in Australia. Even though Zheng He's odyssey to Darwin can be confirmed as a historic event, China's governmental relationship and engagement with the South Pacific did not take place in a relatively big and effective way until the early decades of the 20th century. However, the situation has dramatically improved since the 1970s, when China established diplomatic relations with Australia and New Zealand in 1972, with Fiji and Samoa in 1975, and with Papua New Guinea in 1976. Given that China and the United States established diplomatic relations in 1979, the development of China's relationship with the above mentioned South Pacific countries turned out to be of historic and strategic significance for China's reforms at the end of the Cultural Revolution. Then from 1982 to 2007 diplomatic relations were also established between China and Vanuatu, Micronesia, the Cook Islands, Tonga, and Niue, reflecting the ongoing process of China's increasing engagement with ten countries in the South Pacific as an important part of its global vision and partnership.

As a result of the impact of the Cold War and ideological conflicts and confrontations pervasive in the entire world after World War II, China's relationship with the South Pacific countries and regions from the early 1970s to the early 1980s virtually focused on expanding and strengthening diplomatic ties as top priority and promoting trade and economic collaboration at the same time. The climax of China's interest and engagement with the South Pacific during this period was the official visit of Hu Yaobang (1915-1989), Secretary-General of the Communist Party of China, to Australia, New Zealand, Fiji, Papua New Guinea, and Samoa in 1985, as the first of such high level visits of China's national leaders to the South Pacific in history. Consequently, the visits of national leaders between China and the South Pacific countries were reciprocal, accelerating the development of bilateral relations in many aspects such as trade, economy, education, tourism, and so on.

Since the establishment of diplomatic relations with China, the China–Australia Student Exchange Scheme was set up in 1974, and then Australia and New Zealand took the lead in promoting bilateral relations with China by visits of high-level governmental heads and sending students to Chinese universities to study the Chinese language, history, literature and other subjects. Some of the students who studied in Peking University and other Chinese universities in the 1970s became well established and internationally well-known scholars in Chinese studies from the South Pacific perspective, such as Geremie Barmé (1954–) of Australian National University and Paul Clark (1953–) of the University of Auckland. The former not only contributes significantly to Chinese studies by his own research as chair professor of Chinese history, his theory known as 'New Sinology', and his leadership as director of Australian Centre on China in the World at Australian National University, but also helps build up a common vision of transcontinental partnership and mutual dependence between China and the South Pacific because of his academic achievements and their influence. The latter, who has established himself as a professor of Asian studies and an authority in studying Chinese movies, has been playing a leading role in introducing and promoting New Zealand Studies in China by co-teaching the annual course 'New Zealand History and Culture' at Peking University since 2008. As those cases indicate, the foundational function of overseas education for young people in bringing China and the South Pacific to a closer relationship and partnership in many aspects of society would show up in the 1980s.

With regard to the students of Australia, New Zealand and other South Pacific countries studying in China in the 1970s, they are estimated to outnumber their Chinese student counterparts in the same period, most of whom were only a small group of Chinese sophomores known worker-peasant-soldier undergraduates studying at a teachers college in Canberra from 1974 and 1978. However, the situation was soon changed when the Chinese government realised the necessity of consolidating the foundation of its relationship with the South Pacific by sending students to Australia and New Zealand after 1977, as a part of the cultural and educational exchanges and bilateral cooperation. As a follow-up effort to open up to the international community and develop China's higher education – which had broken down during the Cultural Revolution, when Chinese universities and colleges were accordingly closed as a political effort to prevent young students from being affected and corrupted by the value and ideology of bourgeoisie and revisionism in the old system of education – the Chinese government began sending the first group of young and middle-aged Chinese university lecturers of English to Australia as graduate students in the University of Sydney in 1979. In addition, some of the university lecturers of other academic fields, who were also selected through English proficiency tests and political reviews, were also sent to Australia and other English-speaking countries like the UK, Canada, New Zealand and Malta, studying as graduate students[1]. They were expected to come back upon graduation and play a leading role in the nationwide campaign of improving the popularity and quality of English education in Chinese universities.

As a collaborative programme initiated by both Chinese and Australian governments to train selected Chinese university lecturers in some of the Australian universities, the Chinese government sent the first group of Chinese lecturers of English to the Department of English at the University of Sydney and provided them with a living stipend, while their tuition was waived by the Australian government. The group of Chinese students was made up of nine scholars from several Chinese universities, including Hu Zhuanglin (1933–) of Peking University, Hu Wenzhong (1935–) of Beijing International Studies University, Huang Yuanshen (1940–) of East China Normal University, Qian Jiaoru (1940–) of Nanjing University, and Hou Weirui (1943–2001) of Shanghai International Studies University. Since then these scholars have been known as the famous Gang of Nine, who would all become leading scholars in association with Australian studies as well as promoters of China–South Pacific relationships and partnerships due to their pioneering studying experiences in Australia.[2]

With little knowledge of Australia and no experience of international visits, those middle-aged university lecturers of English went to study in the University of Sydney in the spring semester of 1979, only two years after the Cultural Revolution came to an end, and they stayed there as hard-working graduate students for two years. After completing their graduate programmes, all the members of the Gang of Nine returned to their Chinese host universities and became leading scholars in their fields, including Australian literature, linguistics, and English and American literature. Their attainments and contributions also include their pioneering leadership in establishing the earliest centres for Australian studies in quite a few Chinese universities where they worked. As a result of their efforts to promote Australian Studies in China, 42 centres for Australian Studies have been subsequently established in Chinese universities and colleges today, which is more than the total number of all the other centres for Australian Studies in all the other countries in the world, including Australia. As Australia is located in Oceania, their contribution to promoting Australian Studies also lays the earliest foundation for Oceanic studies as a new area study in China.

As a priority of China's relationship with the South Pacific and an important part of its reform strategy in the early 1980s, the Chinese government adjusted its policy for higher education, approving Chinese students to go abroad for further education at their own expense, apart from increasing the number of governmentally funded students to go abroad for postgraduate studies. Such an unconventional and dynamic policy of education has made it possible for thousands of Chinese students to enter other countries for higher education since the 1980s. From then on, the number of such students has been steadily increasing on an annual basis till today, and those Chinese overseas students contribute significantly to strengthening the relationship of China with the international community, including the South Pacific.

As a matter of fact, China's increasing engagement with the South Pacific is correlated with the increase of Chinese students studying as undergraduates and postgraduate students in the region, because higher education remains a crucial but often overlooked cornerstone in the bilateral relations of countries in the world. According to the statistical data provided by the Department of Education of the Australian government, the total number of Chinese students in Australian universities and colleges in 2014 was 152,898 (As a comparative reference, the relevant number of Chinese students studying in Australian universities and colleges was 68,857 in 2004, and 91,551 in 2010, respectively), making up approximately 25% of the population of international students in higher education in the country.[3] The total number of Chinese students in New Zealand higher education in 2013 was 24,682 (As a comparative reference, the relevant number of Chinese students studying in New Zealand higher education was 21,256 in 2010), making up approximately 27.8% of the population of international students in the country.[4] As annually increasing numbers of younger Chinese students are sent abroad for middle and high school education and even primary school education, the total number of Chinese students studying in the South Pacific definitely makes the above statistics bigger and continuously rising.

From the perspective of global comparison, according to the research data provided by the Institute of International Education located in the USA, the total number of international students in the USA in 2013–2014 was 886,052, and Chinese students were 274, 439, making up of 31% of the international students.[5] The research report of the UK Council for International Student Affairs shows that the number of Chinese students in British higher education in 2013–2014 was 87,895, making up 29.3% of the international students (Non EU students).[6] In view of the disparity of the national population and the number of universities and colleges between the USA, UK, Australia, New Zealand and other countries in the South Pacific as a whole, the tripartite proportion of the numbers of Chinese students studying in the USA, UK and the South Pacific respectively indicate what an important role education has been playing as a part of China's engagement with the South Pacific.

The role of higher education in both China and the South Pacific is as reciprocal as other aspects of a society, such as trade. In recent years, when the number of Chinese students in the South Pacific keeps increasing on an annual basis, South Pacific students studying in China have also been increasing significantly. In the light of the statistics of the Ministry of Education of the Chinese government, the number of South Pacific students in China in 2014 was 6,272, making up 1.33% of the international students in China, but it was 32.24% more than the number of South Pacific students in China in 2013, namely 1529.[7] Studying abroad in its essence is the choice and investment of individual students and their families, so the fast and substantial development of bilateral education is mainly developed by people in both China and the South Pacific, and therefore as history has proved, education in both China and the South Pacific will always function as the root and foundation for international relations and other social engagements. In addition, students with experiences of studying in either the South Pacific or China are inclined to identify with the bilateral relationship and play an active role in the process of policy-making of China – South Pacific relations at various levels when they work upon graduation.

From the late 1980s to the late 1990s China's engagement with the South Pacific was characterised by tenacious efforts to maintain and consolidate diplomatic relations with Pacific Island countries and provide them with economic and financial support. Such a policy was also applied in Africa, Latin America, Asia, and other continents of the world during the same era of various ideological or diplomatic confrontations. In the meantime, China's engagement with the South Pacific also experienced some severe and unprecedented challenges, such as diplomatic tension and conflicts, which resulted from both China's own reform and development and the complexity of international relations, which were concerned with the political, military or economical instability of some of the countries and regions in the area or even of the entire world.

The policy change of China's engagement with the South Pacific showed up in 1999, when the Chinese president Jiang Zemin (1926–) paid the inaugural state visit of a Chinese President to Australia and New Zealand, the first of its kind since China's establishment of diplomatic relations with the two countries in 1972; he reached agreement with the Australian Prime Minister John Howard (1939–) that both countries should be committed to improve bilateral relations by promoting economic cooperation of complementary nature, especially in mining industry and technologies, in addition to promoting the cooperation in consular affairs, law enforcement and education. Such a historic visit was soon followed by the state visit of the Chinese President Hu Jintao (1942–) to Australia and New Zealand in 2003 and then to Australia in 2007 once again; the visit of Wu Bangguo (1941–), the Chairman of the Chinese National People's Congress, to Australia and New Zealand in 2005; and the visit of Wen Jiabao (1942–), the Chinese Premier, to Australia, New Zealand and Fiji in 2006, when he attended the ministerial forum in Fiji on the economic cooperation between China and the Pacific Island countries and proposed that China and the Pacific Island countries make joint efforts of building up a new collaborative relationship on the basis of a vision of gradual and long-term mutual developments, reciprocity and common benefits. Mention should be made that those unprecedented high-level visits of China's national leaders at the turn of the 21st century were also interweaved by the frequent visits of the national heads of Australia, New Zealand, Fiji, Samoa and other South Pacific countries to China, indicating the actively ongoing interaction and collaboration between China and the South Pacific.

The economic turn of the bilateral relationship between China and the South Pacific in the first decade of the 21st century also represents the new trend and principles of China's foreign policy in the new era of international relations, which highlights peace, mutual development and harmony of civilisations for a better future for mankind.

Such a policy turn has brought significant changes and improvements in bilateral relations and development, which can be convincingly exhibited by statistical reports respecting the investment, trade, education and other aspects of society between China and the South Pacific. Such a policy turn may also account for the signing of the free trade agreement between China and New Zealand in 2008, as the first of its kind between China and developed countries as its trade partners. Hopefully, China and Australia will get a free trade agreement signed within this year, which will be helpful to build up a stronger tie and more productive cooperation between China and the South Pacific in many respects.

China's recent policy towards the South Pacific has been best communicated by the state visit of the Chinese President Xi Jinping (1953–) to Australia, New Zealand and Fiji in November 2014, after his participation in the 2014 G20 Summit in Brisbane. His visit to Fiji was the first state visit of a Chinese President to a Pacific Island country in history, which shows China's increasing interest and wish to further develop relations with Pacific Island countries. One of the highlights of his visit was his meeting with national heads of eight Pacific Island countries including Fiji, Micronesia, Samoa, Papua New Guinea, Vanuatu, the Cook Islands, Tonga, and Niue, when he expounded the five major principles of further developing relations with the South Pacific Island countries. As the basis of China's policy towards the South Pacific in the new era as well as other countries of the world, President Xi Jinping stressed that China always respects the South Pacific Island countries' own rights to independently choose their social system and development path and supports their equal participation in international and regional affairs and their safeguard of their legitimate rights and interests.

Those principles, which are also related to China's vision of its position and role in the world, include, first of all, the establishment of strategic partnership featuring mutual trust and common development. As he emphatically emphasises, the South Pacific Island countries are important members of the great Asia–Pacific community and welcome to participate in the construction of the 21st Century Maritime Silk Road for Asia-Pacific economic integration. Secondly, mutual visits, exchanges, and cooperation at all levels between China and South Pacific Island countries should be further enhanced, including governmental talks to make strategic plans, party-to-party exchanges for mutually deeper understanding and collaboration, and people-to-people communication as the basis of bilateral relations. Thirdly, both sides should make more efforts to deepen the mutual cooperation in trade, agriculture, fishery industry, infrastructure and energy resources, for which China has granted zero-tariff treatment to 97% of items exported from less-developed countries. Fourthly, more efforts should be made to enhance cross-cultural and educational exchanges and cooperation. China is committed to providing a quota of 2,000 scholarships for South Pacific students to study in China and a quota of 5,000 scholarships for study and training in various fields for the eight South Pacific Island countries in the following five years, extending various kinds of support within the framework of South-South cooperation for the South Pacific Island countries dealing with climate changes and converting maritime and other kinds of resource advantages into development advantages. Fifthly, China and the South Pacific Island countries should enhance the mechanism of multilateral coordination within the framework of South-South cooperation to deal with global governance, energy security, food security, poverty alleviation, disaster reduction, humanitarian aid, and earthquake and tsunami warning systems in support of economic development and stability and prosperity of the South Pacific Island countries.[8]

Such important state visits and announcements of new policies epitomise China's increasing concern and high-profile engagement with not only the eight island countries but also all the other island countries and regions in Oceania. China's engagement with the South Pacific is also a part of the One Belt, One Road initiative promoting economic cooperation and development in the global context. For those purposes, the Chinese government has made a series of continuing efforts recently to improve China's engagement and cooperation with the South Pacific countries, including the Ministry of Education establishing two national research bases for Oceanian Studies in both Peking University and Sun Yat-sen University in 2012. The two research bases are expected to make a comprehensive and in-depth study of Oceania, including history, culture, governmental systems and management, international relations, education, science and technology, natural resources, agriculture and industry, and all other aspects of society, and provide governmental departments and organisations with specific research reports as references for policymaking at all levels.

Although much has been achieved at governmental levels to enhance and develop the constructive and win-win relationship between China and the South Pacific, the future of the bilateral relationship deserves more effort at academic and other non-governmental levels. If an academic forum as a platform of multilateral dialogues between China and the South Pacific is set up, which takes place on a regular basis, for instance, in the structure and function of the Beijing Forum,[9] it will help promote mutual understanding and cooperation between China and the South Pacific and help realise the potential of people-to-people engagement and collaboration for the common future of China and the South Pacific.

Notes

1. According to a statistic report, 860 university faculty members were sent abroad for graduate study programmes in 1978, and the number was increased to 1,750 in 1979. See 'A Survey of Chinese Overseas Students in Australia', a paper Hu Zhuanglin presented at the 12th International Conference of Australian Studies in China, sponsored jointly by East China Normal University and Shanghai University, Oct. 28–30, 2010, Shanghai, China.
2. For more information on the study and life of the Gang of Nine in the University of Sydney, see Hu Zhanglin's reminiscence 'Interpreting the Gang of Nine', collected in Lee C. Owens and Rosita Holenbergh (eds.) *Beyond Thirty: Australia-China Educational Exchange Retrospect and Prospect, Proceedings of the Thirtieth Anniversary International Conference*. 5–6 December, 2002 at the University of Sydney.
3. See 'International Student Enrolment Data 2014', Australian Government Department of Education (https://internationaleducation.gov.au/research/International-Student-Data/Documents/INTERNATIONAL%20STUDENT%20DATA/2014/2014Dec_0712.pdf).
4. For the statistics provided by the New Zealand government, see 'International Students in New Zealand' (http://www.educationcounts.govt.nz/statistics/international-education/international-students-in-new-zealand).
5. For the details of the statistics, see the following source (http://www.iie.org/Research-and-Publications/Open-Doors/Data/International-Students/Leading-Places-of-Origin/2012-14).
6. The data are quoted from the homepage of the UK Council for International Student Affairs (http://www.ukcisa.org.uk/Info-for-universities-colleges--schools/Policy-research--statistics/Research--statistics/International-students-in-UK-HE/#International-(non-UK)-students-in-UK-HE-in-2013-14.).
7. The data are quoted from the homepage of the Ministry of Education of the Chinese government (http://www.moe.edu.cn/publicfiles/business/htmlfiles/moe/s5987/201503/184959.html).
8. For references on those principles, see 'Foreign Minister Wang Yi Talks about President Xi Jinping's Attendance at the G20 Summit and Visits to Three Countries Including Australia' (http://www.fmprc.gov.cn/mfa_eng/topics_665678/xjpzxcxesgjtldrdjcfhdadlyxxlfjjxgsfwbttpyjjdgldrhw/t1214285.shtml)
9. Beijing Forum is an annual international forum established in 2004 and co-sponsored by Peking University, Beijing Municipal Commission of Education and Korea Foundation for Advanced Studies. The general theme of Beijing Forum is 'The Harmony of Civilizations and Prosperity for All', aiming at promoting the study of humanities and social sciences around the world. It is also intended to promote academic development and social progress across the world in order to contribute to the development and prosperity of humankind. For more information on Beijing Forum, see 'Introduction to Beijing Forum' (http://www.beijingforum.org/html/folder/3.htm).

A Regional Perspective

Fekita Utoikamanu
Deputy Director-General, Secretariat of the Pacific Community,
Noumea and Suva

This regional perspective will be provided mainly from that of the Secretariat of the Pacific Community (SPC), but a brief reference to other regional organisations will also give some indication of the importance of the kind of regional support to be provided to Pacific Island member countries and its positive impacts of enhancing dialogue and engagement, trade, and educational, cultural and tourism exchanges with China.

The Secretariat of the Pacific Community (SPC) is one of eight intergovernmental organisations with varying country membership, and with specific regional mandates to support its respective members' sustainable development, peace and security efforts. Other regional agencies include Pacific Islands Forum Secretariat (PIFS); Forum Fisheries Agency (FFA); South Pacific Tourism Organisation (SPTO); Secretariat of the Pacific Regional Environmental Programme (SPREP); Pacific Power Association (PPA); University of the South Pacific (USP); and the

Pacific Islands Development Programme (PIDP).

The engagement of China and the Pacific at a regional level has been strategic and targeted utilising several different modalities launched at official, academic and private sector levels. At the political level, China is a partner to the Pacific Island Leader's annual post-Forum dialogue. China has provided direct grant funding to the Pacific Islands Forum Secretariat to support implementation of the Pacific Plan priorities, and also provides funding for the China-Pacific Island Regional Scholarships Programme for study awards in China, which is in addition to bilateral scholarships to the eight countries that have diplomatic relations with China. However, all Pacific Island members of the PIF are eligible to apply for these scholarships. Support has also been provided for the Shanghai World Expo in 2010, as well as to the PIFs Trade and Invest Office in Beijing.

China's engagement with the technical regional organisations has reflected its own interests as well as the interests of the agency and its membership. China has provided annual financial support to SPREP since 2003, and has an interest in several areas of its work including promoting sustainable development, conservation, bio-diversity, climate change and waste management. This year for the first time SPREP has hosted two students on attachment from the University of Tsinghua University in Beijing.

China was the first member from outside the Pacific region to join SPTO in 2004. SPTO has highlighted that 'Chinese tourists are the future for tourism in the Pacific.' China, through its National Tourism Administration, extends an invitation annually for SPTO members to be included in their main travel show. Multi donor/partner cooperation has been put in place to support marketing of the Pacific region. An example in 2013: SPTO, IFC, China and the Pacific Island Trade Invest Beijing jointly cooperated on a Pacific region marketing venture. It has been reported that since 2013, there has been an 84 per cent growth in Chinese visitors to the Pacific and in 2013 alone 98 million Chinese travelled abroad, spending more than USD 128 billion. Last year, SPTO launched a website for South Pacific tourism training to assist tourism operators to sell South Pacific destinations to Chinese tourists. Several other promotional activities to support national as well as regional tourism were also undertaken. At a bilateral level there has been foreign direct investment in the tourism industry, as well as new visa-free agreements (e.g. Fiji had 23,000 visa-free tourists in 2013), hotel ventures and the first charter of flights from Shanghai to Fiji in February this year.

In 2004, China acceded to the Convention on the Conservation and Management of Highly Migratory Fish Stocks in the Western and Central Pacific Ocean, and has engaged with the Forum Fisheries Agency and the other twelve Pacific members on related fisheries issues.

China's engagement with the University of the South Pacific was formalised in 2011 with the Beijing University of Posts and Telecommunications (BUPT) and the Confucius Institute Headquarters of China/Hanban, and the first regional Confucius

Institute was established at USP in 2012. It offers studies in Chinese language as well as Chinese culture and history. From USP's viewpoint, the Confucius Institute will not only contribute to the internationalisation of the university but will also help the South Pacific Region integrate into the global economy. Teaching points have been opened in Lautoka, Vanuatu Emalus Campus. Plans are in progress for the establishment of Chinese classes in the Cook Islands and here in Samoa.

SPC's 26 member countries include four metropolitan members (United States of America, New Zealand, Australia and France), and full coverage of all 22 Pacific Island countries, trusts and territories. SPC provides technical assistance, policy advice, training and research to its member states, and works across over 22 sectors to achieve three development outcomes: sustainable economic development; sustainable natural resource management and development; and sustainable human and social development. SPC's work is determined and led by its member states' development priorities.

Although there has not been any direct formal engagement with China, SPC has in the past implemented several projects either with development assistance from China, or in support of direct requests from countries to access markets in China. SPC received a portion of the USD 2 million grant funding provided by China directly to the Pacific Islands Forum Secretariat in 2007 to support the implementation of the Pacific Plan priorities in two areas including: (i) Integrated Ports Development (USD 413,000) and the (ii) Pacific Regional Information & Communications System (PacRICs) component of the SPC's ICT Outreach (USD 1.054 million). These programmes were implemented over a four-year period 2009–2012. Since the completion of these two programmes, SPC has not received any further China grant funding.

However, a recent Independent Expert Review of SPC in 2013 recognised China as an emerging donor of East Asia, and recommended that it should be further explored as a potential future development partner as part of its long-term financing strategy to fund programmes and activities provided by SPC to its member countries. SPC's annual budget is around USD 78 million, with over 60% project funding. The European Union and the Australian Government provide the bulk of the funds for project implementation.

On the basis of requests from countries for SPC and other CROP Agencies' direct support, it is apparent that Pacific Island countries are seriously looking at tapping into the China market in several areas including agriculture, fisheries and tourism. A regional approach towards supporting some specific aspects of access to markets is required due to economies of scale, and the limited human and financial resources in many member countries.

The question of how the Pacific region's agriculture and forestry industries can access the expanding Chinese economy and its growing need for food and timber was fully explored by SPC with the support of a European Union funded Facilitating Agricultural Commodity Trade (FACT). It was recognised that whilst there were opportunities for high-value niche markets, there were also a number of challenges including transport logistics, trade protocols, strong competition from Southeast Asia and the need for effective marketing. The potential for lucrative and evolving markets for various organic products was also recognised and is now well over USD 1 billion.

SPC's Biosecurity and Trade Support Team (BATS) supported a certified organic Noni company in the Cook Islands to secure organic certification to the Chinese market, and has commenced exporting to China in January 2015.

SPC's Increasing Agricultural Commodity Trade (IACT) program, funded by the European Union, aims to strengthen the export capacity of the Pacific countries in the primary industries of agriculture, forestry and aquaculture. IACT has supported an agricultural business in Fiji to export papayas to Hong Kong.

With the official development assistance of China directed to only eight Pacific Island countries, with occasional support provided to regional CROP agencies under various agreements and operational arrangements, there is a lot of room for consideration of China's engagement to be more inclusive. This could include the full consideration of the following possible modalities:

(1) Enhanced support to programmes offered at regional level, including the option, where relevant, of implementation of bilateral funded programmes if required by member countries. There are several good examples of bilateral funded programmes implemented by SPC at the request of the member country concerned due to absorptive capacity and limited technical abilities for implementation;
(2) More active partnership at a regional level where required; and
(3) More regular dialogue through established mechanisms as well as other fora.

Conclusion

Compared to its bilateral engagement including ongoing grants, interest-free loans administered through state finances and concessional loans administered through China Exim bank with the eight Pacific Island countries that have established diplomatic relations with China, the cooperation at regional level has been strategic and targeted. There is therefore a lot of scope and potential for further increased engagement at regional level. In addition, in view of the increasing demand by member countries to access the large China market in the tourism, agriculture and fisheries sector, there is also further scope for coordinated support to provide the required services to support relevant member countries.

References

'China joins SPTO', *China Economic Net*, 3 March 2004.

'China and Taiwan join SCP Fisheries Commission', FFA press release, 2 December 2004.

'Review of the China Fund for the Pacific Islands Forum Secretariat', The Ambdji Group Pty Ltd, October 2012.

'Accessing China's market for good and timber', SPC Press release, 21 May 2012.

'SPC Trade project looks at challenges and opportunities', SPC Press release, 21 May 2012.

'Confucius Institute opens at regional University', USP Press release, 8 September 2012.

'Pacific finds innovative ways to strengthen position in China Out Bound Market', *Tonga Daily*, 3 December 2013.

'SPTO rolls out 2014 trade and road shows', *Tonga Daily*, 16 Jan 2014.

'SPTO: Chinese tourists the future for Pacific', *China Daily news*, 10 August 2014.

'Infrastructure Projects, Agricultural and Fisheries Trade and Tourism to Benefit from China Meeting', Prime Minister's Office Press Release, PNG, 24 November 2014.

'Government of China contributes to regional environmental action', SPREP website, 17 December 2014.

'SPREP strengthens ties with Government of China', SPREP website, 10 February 2015.

China's New Leadership and Its Perceptions of the Asia Pacific Region

Professor Bo Zhiyue
Director, New Zealand Contemporary China Research Centre, Victoria University of Wellington

With its phenomenal economic rise in the past three decades, China has extended its reach in the global marketplace. A powerhouse in the Asia Pacific region in general, China has become a major player in the economic development of the Pacific Island nations since at least 2006.

This paper will provide a brief outline of generational changes in China's political leadership, highlight its perceptions of the Asia Pacific region in general and discuss its priorities under the current leadership.

China's New Leadership under Xi Jinping
In its entire history of 94 years, the Chinese Communist Party (CCP) has had eleven top leaders under various titles. In the past two decades, scholars of China studies

have generally accepted a new category of political generations proposed by Deng Xiaoping. According to Deng, the paramount leader of China from 1978 to 1994 without ever being number one Party leader, the CCP leadership between 1935 and 1989 could be classified into three generations.[1] The first generation leadership had Mao Zedong at the core, the second generation leadership Deng, and the third generation leadership would have Jiang Zemin (China's president from 1993 to 2003) at the core.

When Hu Jintao was elected general secretary of the CCP in November 2002, he was not described as the core leader of the fourth generation leadership in the Chinese official media. But Hu and his colleagues in the Politburo Standing Committee have been generally considered in the literature as the fourth generation leadership. Again, when Xi Jinping was made CCP general secretary in November 2012, he was not described as the core leader of the fifth generation in the Chinese official media. But scholars of China studies refer to Xi's leadership as the fifth generation leadership.[2] China's 'new leadership' in this paper refers to the fifth generation leadership under Xi Jinping.

Compared to his predecessors, especially Jiang Zemin and Hu Jintao, Xi Jinping is much more powerful in his first two years. He has consolidated power very quickly and has managed to change the decision-making structure from one of the 'collective leadership' to one of 'one-man dominance.' Under the current decision-making structure, it is critical to understand Xi Jinping's policy preferences for a good understanding of China's policies in general.

China's New Foreign Policy

In a nutshell, the Chinese new foreign policy under President Xi Jinping is 'one insistence, two buts' ('*yige jianchi, liangge danshi*' in Chinese). The 'one insistence' refers to the statement that the new leadership under Xi Jinping would continue the peaceful development strategy of the previous administration under Hu Jintao. However, at the Politburo meeting on January 28, 2013, Xi Jinping introduced the first 'but:' *but* China would never sacrifice its rightful rights or its core interests.[3] One and a half years later, after having suffered some serious setbacks in international affairs, Xi, at the meeting marking the 60th anniversary of the initiation of the five principles of peaceful coexistence on June 28, 2014, introduced another 'but': *but* China is willing to develop its relations with the rest of the world on the basis of the five principles of peaceful coexistence.

Evidently, Xi Jinping is more nationalistic than his immediate predecessor. This statement can be illustrated by the frequencies of the 'core interests' ('*hexin liyi*' in Chinese) mentioned in *People's Daily*, the mouthpiece of the CCP. As displayed in the chart, the term started to appear in the Chinese official media in 2003 but became frequently used in 2008. The usage of the term peaked in 2010 after President Hu Jintao had managed to 'legitimise' the term in the joint statement with his counterpart, President Barack Obama, on November 17, 2009.[4]

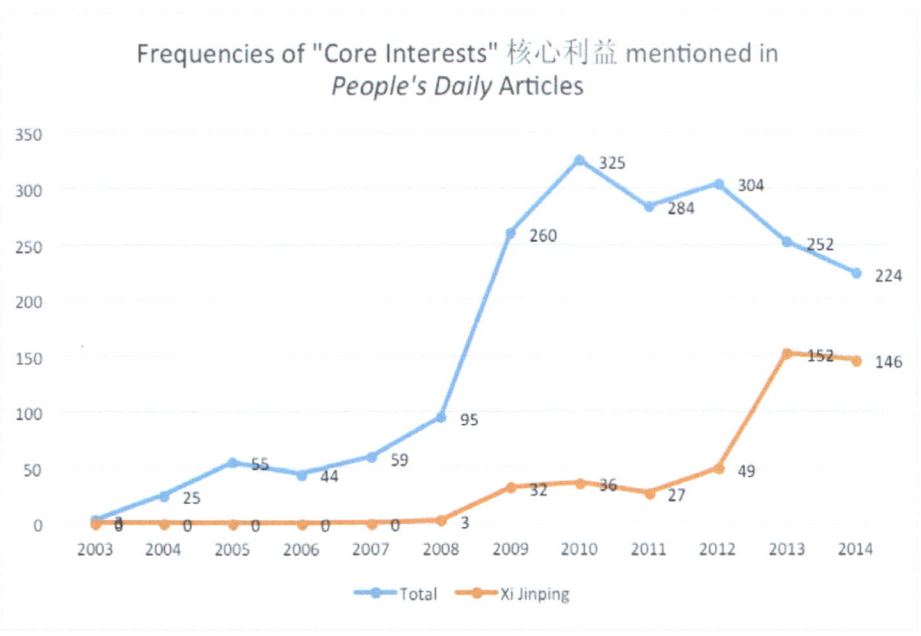

Frequencies of "Core Interests" 核心利益 mentioned in *People's Daily* Articles

Source: *Renmin Ribao (People's Daily)*, January 1, 2003 to September 22, 2014.

What is fascinating about the chart is that there is a clear divergence between the total frequencies and the frequencies related to Xi Jinping since 2008. From 2003 to 2007, Xi Jinping was not associated with the mentioning of the term 'core interests.' After his entry in the Politburo Standing Committee, he maintained a low profile over China's foreign policy while the nationalistic sentiment was rising. In his first year as China's president in 2013, however, when the nationalistic sentiment witnessed a relative decline in general, he became a champion of China's core interests. The total number of times the term 'core interest' was mentioned declined from 304 in 2012 to 252 in 2013, but the number of times it was associated with the name of 'Xi Jinping' increased from 49 in 2012 to 152 in 2013.

A clear indication of Xi's nationalistic foreign policy is his introduction of an air defence identification zone over East China Sea in November 2013. Without warning and prior consultation with concerned parties, the Ministry of National Defence of China declared an East China Sea Air Defense Identification Zone on November 23, 2013. The zone covers most of the East China Sea, including the Japanese controlled Senkaku Islands (or Diaoyu Islands in Chinese). The initiative was controversial not only because it overlaps with similar zones of Japan, South Korea, and Taiwan but also because it was announced unilaterally.

Partly as a result of this nationalistic foreign policy, the United States was driven closer to Japan. Successive administrations of the United States tried to engage China in the aftermath of the Tiananmen Incident by being intentionally 'ambiguous' over certain issues, including the extent to which the US-Japan Security Treaty (formally, 'Treaty of Mutual Cooperation and Security between the United States and Japan'[5]) would be applied to the controversial Senkaku Islands. However, during his visit to Japan in April 2014, President Obama made it clear that the treaty does cover the islands.[6]

China's new leadership under Xi Jinping began to backpedal its foreign policy in June 2014. At the meeting marking the 60th anniversary of the initiation of the five principles of peaceful coexistence on June 28, 2014, President Xi Jinping reaffirmed that China would implement its policy of peaceful development. China's peaceful development strategy, as he stated, is 'in the interest of China, in the interest of Asia, and in the interest of the world.'[7] China would develop friendly relations with other countries of the world and continue mutually beneficial and win-win cooperation with them.

Clearly, over the course of less than two years, the new leadership experimented with different foreign policy options. It started with a more assertive and nationalistic foreign policy but changed back to a more cooperative policy not so different from the harmonious foreign policy of its immediate predecessor.

China's Perceptions of the Asia Pacific Region

In terms of the perception of the Asia Pacific region, China's new leadership has priorities. The United States is always the most important actor in the region. President Xi Jinping has proposed to build a new type of great power relationship with the sole superpower in the world.

Japan is also very important for China's policy in the region because it is a major rival in security terms. Since Xi Jinping became the top leader of China, the relationship between the two countries has significantly deteriorated. China and Japan have maintained their economic relations, but their political and security relations have witnessed their worst times since 1972. According to a BBC World Service Poll released in June 2014, 3% of Japanese people view China's influence positively, with 73% expressing a negative view, the second most negative perception of China in the world (after German people with 76% expressing a negative view). In the meantime, 5% of Chinese people view Japanese influence positively, with 90% expressing a negative view, the second most negative perception of Japan in the world (after the people of North Korea with 91% expressing a negative view and only 1% being positive).[8]

Thirdly, China takes ASEAN nations very seriously. The 10 members of the ASEAN have interesting relations with China. On the one hand, all of them want to develop their economic relations with China. China is the second largest economy in the world and is number one trading partner with many of them. On the other hand, several countries in the region have overlapping claims with those of China over territories in the South China Sea. They often work with China over economic cooperation but take sides with the United States over security issues.

Finally, China is also keen to develop its presence in the South Pacific, but Pacific Island nations receive the lowest priority in China's foreign policy agenda in the Asia Pacific region.

China's Perceptions of the Pacific Island Nations

China's perceptions of the Pacific Island nations can be traced to 1971. On October 25, 1971, the UN adopted Resolution 2578 to admit the People's Republic of China (PRC) into the UN General Assembly and Security Council with 76 voting in favour, 35 against and 17 abstentions. Less than 12 hours later, on the evening of October 26, Chairman Mao Zedong held a meeting of concerned officials in his residence. Mao proposed a new policy towards those three different groups of countries. For supporters, China should unite with them. For abstainers, China should deal with them correctly. For countries who opposed the PRC, China should learn to work with them because they do not form a monolithic block.[9]

One year after China was made a member of the UN, two countries of the region, Australia and New Zealand, formalised their recognition. Australia established diplomatic relations with China on December 21, 1972 and New Zealand on the 22nd. Then in 1975, Fiji[10] and Samoa established diplomatic relations with the PRC, on November 5th and 6th, respectively.

Hu Yaobang, General Secretary of the Chinese Communist Party (CCP) from September 1982 to January 1987, was the first top leader of China to visit countries in the south Pacific. He visited five Oceanian countries in April 1985: Australia, New Zealand, Samoa,[11] Fiji and Papua New Guinea.

In the early years of the 21st century, the Pacific Island nations became targets of China-Taiwan rivalry. President Chen Shuibian, a leader of the independence-oriented Democratic Progressive Party (DDP), launched a diplomatic charm offensive in the region, trying to convert these nations to the recognition of the Republic of China (ROC) instead of the PRC. He visited Palau and the Solomon Islands in January 2005[12] and the Marshall Islands, Kiribati and Tuvalu in May 2005.[13] He visited the Marshall Islands again and attended the Second Taiwan-Pacific Allies Summit in October 2007.[14]

In response, the PRC also began to pay closer attention to the Pacific Island nations. In April 2006, Premier Wen Jiabao visited three Oceanian countries: Australia, New Zealand and Fiji. He was the first premier to visit Pacific Island nations. He attended the First Ministerial Conference of the 'China-Pacific Island Countries Economic Development and Cooperation Forum' and proposed to establish a new type of mutually beneficial and cooperative economic and trade relations with the Pacific Island countries.[15]

Most recently, President Xi Jinping also visited the same three Oceanian countries of Australia, New Zealand, and Fiji. It was also in Fiji where Xi proposed to establish 'strategic partnership relations of mutual respect and common development' with the Pacific Island countries and extended his invitation to these countries to join

China's initiative of the 'Maritime Silk Road of the 21st century.'[16]

In conclusion, China's new leadership – i.e., the fifth generation leadership – under Xi Jinping has experimented with different foreign policy options and eventually decided to implement the peaceful development strategy of its immediate predecessor. In terms of its priorities in the Asia Pacific region, China ranks its relations with the United States as the most important, followed by its rivalry with Japan. China has to deal with ASEAN nations on two fronts and has expanded its presence in Oceania. Most significantly, during his visit in November 2014, President Xi Jinping not only visited Australia and New Zealand but also proposed to establish 'strategic partnership relations' with Pacific Island nations.

Notes

1   Deng Xiaoping, 'We must form a promising collective leadership that will carry out reform', 31 May 1989, in Deng Xiaoping, *Selected Works of Deng Xiaoping* Volume 3, Beijing: Renmin Chubanshe, 1993, pp. 296–301.
2   For a detailed study of the fifth generation leadership, see Bo Zhiyue, 'China's Fifth Generation Leaders: characteristics of the new elite and pathways to leadership,' in Robert S. Ross and Jo Inge Bekkevold, eds., *China in the Era of Xi Jinping*, Washington, DC: Georgetown University Press, forthcoming.
3   For a report on the meeting, see http://news.xinhuanet.com/politics/2013-01/29/c_114538253.htm.
4   For the joint statement in English, see https://www.whitehouse.gov/the-press-office/us-china-joint-statement.
5   For a reference, see http://en.wikipedia.org/wiki/Treaty_of_Mutual_Cooperation_and_Security_between_the_United_States_and_Japan.
6   Ankit Panda, 'Obama: Senkakus Covered Under US-Japan Security Treaty,' *The Diplomat*, April 24, 2014, http://thediplomat.com/2014/04/obama-senkakus-covered-under-us-japan-security-treaty/.
7   For a Chinese text of his speech, see http://news.xinhuanet.com/politics/2014-06/28/c_1111364206.htm.
8   For details, see http://www.globescan.com/images/images/pressreleases/bbc2014_country_ratings/2014_country_rating_poll_bbc_globescan.pdf.
9   Huang Hua, *Huang Hua Memoirs*, Beijing: Foreign Language Press, 2008, p. 253.
10 Fiji was the only country from this region that cast an abstaining vote on the resolution to admit China to the United Nations.
11 He was the first top Chinese leader to visit Samoa.
12 For details, see http://www.taipeitimes.com/News/taiwan/archives/2005/01/27/2003221119.
13 For details, see http://taiwaninfo.nat.gov.tw/ct.asp?xItem=21285&CtNode=103&htx_TRCategory=&mp=4.
14 For details, see http://english.president.gov.tw/Default.aspx?tabid=553.
15 For details, see http://news.sohu.com/20060405/n242643312.shtml.
16 For details, see http://news.xinhuanet.com/politics/2014-11/22/c_1113361879.htm.

Reflections on the Experiences of the Chinese Community in Samoa

Tuatagaloa Aumua Ming Leung Wai
Attorney-General of Samoa

The experience of the Chinese community in Samoa has not only been challenging but also very rewarding, particularly for those who have stayed in Samoa and for their descendants. Chinese have been migrating to Samoa for 150 years. This paper explores the challenges faced by Chinese in Samoa and will discuss the Chinese community's contribution to the development of Samoa.

My Background
My great-grandfather Leung Wai (a.k.a. Ah Wai or Avai) was from Guangdong province. He was born in 1886. Aged 24, and one week after he got married, he travelled to Samoa. He worked as an assistant to Dr Oskar Thieme.[1] He became a successful businessman in Samoa and managed to avoid repatriation.[2] His eldest son Ming (my grandfather after whom I was named) was born in 1918 and sent to China at the tender age of 8 for education. He stayed with my great-grandfather's first wife who raised him as her own. Ming later married a Chinese woman named Hung (Hana) Lock (my grandmother), also from Guangdong.

The four eldest children of Ming and Hana died as a result of the hardships of the Second Sino-Japanese War (1937–945). The only child of Ming and Hana born in China who survived was my father, Bee Leung Wai. Ming, Hana and Bee managed to leave China in 1950 to come to Samoa, their passages having been paid for by my great-grandfather Leung Wai.

Bee Leung Wai married my mother Taituuga Kuinivia Aumua from Sapunaoa and Poutasi, Falealili. I am married to Fiti Fuimaono L. Vito and we have four sons.

Four Waves of Chinese Migration
I have decided to divide the Chinese migration to Samoa into four time periods:
- First wave (1840s to 1890s) – Chinese free settlers;
- Second wave (1900s to 1930s) – Chinese contract labourers (indentured labourers);
- Third wave (1950s to 1990s) – Full-blooded Chinese who are related to Chinese residing in Samoa; and
- Fourth wave (2000 to present day) – Full-blooded Chinese who have relatives in Samoa and full-blooded Chinese who have no blood connection to Samoa.

Samoa's Bureau of Statistics does not have any records relating to the number of Chinese residing in Samoa (present and past) so I have had to rely on the few books that I came across during my research, my own experience and conversations with Chinese living in Samoa (both full-blooded Chinese and part Chinese). I did not come across any records or evidence of Chinese migrating to Samoa during World War II so that period (1940s) is not included in my 'four waves' of Chinese migration to Samoa. The records I did manage to obtain in relation to the number of Chinese immigrants in the third and fourth waves of migration were inadequate so I have kept my paper brief in relation to those two waves and my observations are based mostly on what I have experienced, witnessed and heard.

First Wave of Chinese Migration 1840s–1890s

The few Chinese settlers who migrated to Samoa in the first wave were apparently successful with the business ventures that they pursued in Samoa. This is no surprise given the industrious nature and hard work ethic shared by many Chinese. These early Chinese settlers thrived economically. I will mention just a few:

- Ah Sue was a cook, box maker and shop owner. His son later became the publisher and editor of the *Samoanische Zeitung* newspaper, which was Apia's bilingual German and English weekly paper at the time.[3]
- Ah Ching came from the Fujian Province in China.[4] After ten years at sea, Ah Ching decided to settle in Samoa. He married the daughter of a chief from Manono and had ten children. Eventually he became a successful proprietor and businessman and even went on to form a Traders' Association with other European traders.[5] His success enabled him to send his children to China for education; three returned to Samoa and their families were successful in both business and the professions.
- Ah Mu[6] came in about 1875, having first been 'adopted' by British sailors at a very young age and spending several years at sea. He was the first Chinese to be a Mormon in Samoa and also became a successful businessman. Ah Mu was instrumental in bringing the Church of Jesus Christ of Latter Day Saints to Samoa and in providing it with the necessary land and resources.[7]
- One of Ah Mu's grandsons (M. Ah Mu) fought in World War I.[8] Some descendants of Ah Mu have used the surname 'Rivers'. There is a prestigious private primary school called 'Ah Mu Academy' located at Pesega named after this famous early Chinese settler. Constance Tafua-Rivers, one of the senior lawyers in my office is a descendant of Ah Mu. One of Ah Mu's well-known descendants is Hon. Hans Joe Keil, who was a former cabinet minister and is a successful businessman.

In 1880, following pressure from the European consuls and businessmen in Apia, the then King of Samoa, Susuga Malietoa Laupepa issued a declaration banning further Chinese from settling in Samoa.[9] Despite the declaration, Malietoa Laupepa's government did not stop subsequent Chinese from settling in Samoa. The

Attorney-General Tuatagaloa Aumua Ming Leung Wai

Chief Justice of Samoa His Honour Patu Tiava'asu'e Falefatu Sapolu and Hon Luamanuvao Winnie Laban, Assistant Vice-Chancellor, Victoria University of Wellington, listening to Attorney-General Ming Leung Wai

Chinese free settlers that came after 1880 during the first wave of Chinese migration included Ah Siu, Ah Fook, Ah Soon, Ah Kiau, Ah Yen, Ah You, Ah Chong, Ah Gee and Ah Man.[10] These settlers successfully petitioned Governor Solf of the German Administration in 1904 to be treated as free settlers so they could continue to live in Samoa and operate their businesses.[11]

The Chinese settlers who came in the first wave of migration became successful businessmen in their own right. For example, Ah Soon married Katherine the daughter of another early Chinese settler Ah Kuoi.[12] Ah Soon had served on a German naval ship, spoke German, and after settling in Samoa was very successful in business. Several of his descendants were prominent in government and in community service.

Second Wave of Chinese Migration 1900s–1930s

Samoan people did not wish to work in the commercial plantations owned by the Europeans.[13] It was said at the time that it was 'impossible for the Samoan to fit into the role of a steady plantation workman because he has no conception of western industrial life'. Initially labour was brought from the Solomon Islands, but labourers were brought from China in 1903. Planters in Samoa found these Chinese labourers to be hard working and reliable and wanted more labourers from China. As a result, more Chinese labourers were brought to Samoa and from 1903 to 1913, a total of 3,868 Chinese labourers came to Samoa.

The Chinese labourers' working conditions were atrocious and did not improve even when the editor of *Samoanische Zeitung* newspaper urged planters to treat the Chinese labourers properly. Flogging was allowed for: 'hiding, laziness, running away, disobedience, insulting behaviour, breaking the curfew and even for not bowing low enough in respect of their masters.'

The harsh working conditions and ill treatment of the Chinese labourers was brought to the attention of the Chinese Government, which decided not to allow the recruitment of more Chinese labourers until the German Administration improved their working conditions. The German Administration acquiesced and agreed to improve matters. Wages were raised, medical care was provided and flogging was abolished. It also agreed to allow China to send over a Consul (Lin Jun Chao) in 1909 to look after the interests of the Chinese labourers.[14] The German Administration also established the position of Chinese Commissioner to look after the welfare of the Chinese labourers.[15]

The recruitment of Chinese labourers continued and by 1913 a total of 3,868 labourers were brought to Samoa. Some were repatriated and in 1914 there were 2,184 Chinese indentured labourers working in Samoa.

In 1914, New Zealand's Expeditionary force landed in Samoa and replaced the German Administration. This new military administration tried to improve working conditions for the Chinese labourers and also commenced wholesale repatriation of the Chinese labourers. Between 1914 and 1918, three major repatriations took place which reduced the Chinese labour force in Samoa to about 832.[16] The labour shortage had an adverse effect on the planting industry and therefore greatly angered the planters who were facing bankruptcy. Matters were made worse by the canker disease on the cocoa plantations and devastation caused by the rhinoceros beetle on the coconut plantations. As a result, the planters called for the return of Chinese labourers. The demand for the return of Chinese labourers initially fell on deaf ears because British policy at the time had just abolished Chinese indentured labour in the Transvaal and Malaysia. However, the unique situation in Samoa led to a compromise. Wholesale repatriations were stopped and some of the Chinese labourers already in Samoa were re-hired for the duration of World War I.[17] Just before New Zealand replaced the military administration of Samoa with a civilian administration, new Chinese labourers were brought to Samoa in 1920 and many more Chinese labourers followed over the next 15 years.

The Chinese indentured labour system in Samoa was criticised by the opposition Labour party in New Zealand. This led the New Zealand Administration to change the indentured labour system to one of 'free labour' in 1923. The change to a 'free labour' system resulted in higher wages and allowed the Chinese labourers to change employers upon the satisfaction of the Chinese Commissioner. Any surplus of Chinese labourers was absorbed by the New Zealand Administration. However, the free labour system did not make allowances for sickness and bad weather and a percentage of the wages was still deducted to cover medical care.[18]

Forceful Repatriation

Repatriation at the end of the contract period was clearly spelled out in the Chinese labourers' employment contracts. The cost of repatriation was to be borne by the employer. The Samoa Immigration Order 1930 also required immigrants to be repatriated unless granted special dispensation. This Order was later amended in 1947, which allowed the Administrator to remove the immigration status for those Chinese deserving to stay in Samoa.

Whilst some welcomed returning home to China, others wanted to remain in Samoa, especially those who had married Samoans and had children. However, forceful repatriation of the Chinese still took place, probably driven by the fear that the Chinese would dominate the many businesses in Samoa due to their 'industry and determination to succeed economically'.[19]

The German Administration had not actively enforced the repatriation of the Chinese labourers. Its repatriation rate had been about 44%. However, New Zealand's rule under its military administration after 1914 was more forceful in its repatriation policy. Its repatriation rate was around 57%. There were 2,184 Chinese labourers in Samoa in 1914 but by 1919, about 1,254 of these labourers were sent back to China.

The New Zealand civilian administration that replaced the military was not as strict on the wholesale repatriation of Chinese labourers. The civilian administration had allowed a minority of labourers with good records to be re-engaged.[20] Some were even given restricted free settler status. However, such relaxation of the repatriation policy changed in 1936 when the Labour party won the elections in New Zealand. About 168 Chinese labourers who were employed as 'domestic servants, artisans, and labourers on plantations other than cocoa plantations' were sent back to China in December 1937.[21] After 1937, only 326 Chinese labourers remained in Samoa.[22]

Of the 200 Chinese labourers that were in Samoa by 1948, 104 were repatriated in mid-1948 when they left on the vessel *S.S. Yunnan*, thus leaving around 90 Chinese labourers who then became lawful permanent residents and, later on, full citizens of Samoa, alongside those Chinese who had already been granted free settler status.

It was recorded on 27 April 1951 that 160 Chinese were eligible to vote for the European seats in Parliament.[23] By 1985, only 32 Chinese indentured labourers remained in Samoa.[24]

Those who were successful in being re-engaged as labourers managed to avoid repatriation. Others who had Samoan wives or partners could apply to be exempted from being repatriated but most of the requests were denied.[25] Some Chinese labourers took their sons with them to China. This caused great sadness to their Samoan wives who were not allowed to accompany them since their union was considered illegal at the time.[26]

The forceful repatriation of Chinese labourers was a sad chapter in Samoa's history. Some Chinese labourers had either married or were in *de facto* relationships with Samoan women. Most also had children. In 1916, about 100 Chinese labourers were married to or in *de facto* relationships with Samoan women and at that time had about 108 Chinese-Samoan children.[27] The number of Samoans with Chinese ancestry rose to around 1,000–1,500 in 1930.[28] Despite such strong connections to Samoa, this did not discourage the New Zealand Administration from its policy of returning the Chinese labourers to China.

The repatriation of Chinese labourers resulted in many Chinese-Samoan children growing up without their fathers. In addition, most Samoan-Chinese were not able to locate or trace their Chinese families. I recall the many descendants of Chinese labourers who came to see my Chinese grandmother about tracing their Chinese ancestors' origins. Generally, only the surnames of Chinese labourers were used when they were converted into English e.g. Ah Fook, Ah Chong. Converting them back to Chinese was therefore a problem if the first name was not known. No proper records relating to their identification could be found. It also did not help when the labourers were usually referred to at the time by numbers instead of their names, e.g. Yue Yiek was known as 'Coolie No. 398'.[29] Employment contracts and letters exchanged between Government officials and employers mostly referred to the Chinese labourers by their Coolie numbers.[30]

Recent discussions with officials of the Chinese Embassy revealed that Samoans descended from Chinese labourers still frequent the Embassy for any information that would help them trace their Chinese ancestors. The officials of the Chinese Embassy, whilst sympathetic, were also not able to help given the paucity of information and associated problems of not knowing their full Chinese names.[31]

My great-grandfather Leung Wai was not repatriated. He had sought the help of one of the Tama Aiga, Afioga Mata'afa Faumuina Mulinu'u I and the Chinese Commissioner had nominated Leung Wai, and a few other Chinese, to be granted restricted free settler status. This was granted in 1923 by the Administrator, General George Richardson.[32] It meant that Leung Wai was able to freely operate his businesses in Samoa and to own properties. (I visited my great-grandfather's family and grandmother Hana's family in Taishan, Guangdong, in 1988 with my cousin Michael Leitutolu Rasmussen and members of my grandmother's family.)

Racism

As well as forceful repatriation, the Chinese labourers experienced racism. Some of the Europeans looked down on them and considered them less than human.[33] It was not prestigious to be part-Chinese, especially when the Europeans had the political and social power.[34] Under German rule, laws were passed to restrict the movement of Chinese labourers and to keep Samoan women off the plantations.[35] Matters did not improve when New Zealand took over the administration of Samoa. Indeed, initially laws were passed to make 'laziness' an offence with the maximum fine being 30 shillings.[36] Subsequent laws were passed by the New Zealand Administration aimed to stop relationships between Chinese and Samoan women. For example, Proclamation 42 issued on 30 January 1917 prohibited Chinese indentured labourers from entering a Samoan house. It was also an offence for a Samoan to allow a Chinese labourer to enter his house. Any person who breached such laws was liable to a maximum fine of 5 pounds or maximum imprisonment with labour for six weeks. Another proclamation stopped Samoan women from visiting the labour quarters of the Chinese labourers.[37]

New Zealand went further by passing a law in 1921 that was described by a historian as 'one of the most shameful pieces of legislation ever to be passed into New Zealand law'.[38] This law is found in section 300 of the Constitution Order and prohibited Chinese immigrants who were indentured labourers from marrying Samoan women. The penalty for breaching such law was a fine of 20 pounds or six months' imprisonment. The *Pacific Islands Monthly* (15 July 1939) reported that 34 Chinese labourers and their Samoan wives were imprisoned for breaching such a law. The men were sent to three months in jail whilst the women three days.[39]

These discriminatory laws reflected the racist attitude of some of the influential Europeans at the time towards Chinese. Such racism was usually described as being for the purpose of keeping the Samoan race pure.[40] There were fears that the Chinese would contaminate the Samoan race. However, it was claimed that unions between Samoans and Europeans were accepted because the children from these unions were 'fair skinned and of Aryan stock on both sides [sic]'.[41]

Sadly, some Samoans also showed anti-Chinese sentiments.[42] A decree was issued by the Samoan central native administration for Samoan women to leave their Chinese husbands and return to their Samoan relatives. This was followed by Samoan villages passing regulations to ban cohabitation between Chinese labourers and Samoan women.[43] It appeared that pressure was put by the New Zealand Administration at the time on the villages to issue such regulations.[44]

This was no surprise given the statements made by the first head of the New Zealand military administration in Samoa, that the Chinese were 'inferior' and were a threat to the racial purity of Samoa.[45] In addition, he added that Samoans disliked the Chinese. However, his successor Tate disputed this. Tate stated that 'The Samoan women recognise the Chinese as better husbands than the Samoan men.'[46] In fact, before the arrival of the Europeans, mixed marriages were accepted, and at times, valued by Samoan culture.[47]

When the issue of the repatriation of the last remaining 200 Chinese labourers was discussed by the Fono Faipule, one Faipule commented:

> The acceptance of the Chinese in Samoa is no doubt due to the small number of the Chinese community as compared with over 70,000 Samoans and to the fact that this community is honest, industrious, and above all, of assimilable stock.[48]

The law that prohibited Chinese from marrying Samoans was only removed from the law books in 1961 by the passing of the Marriage Ordinance 1961, which legalised marriages solemnised before 1961 and gave legitimacy to children from such marriages.

Third Wave of Chinese Migration (1950s–1990s)

The third wave of Chinese migration relates mainly to the Chinese immigrants who had blood connections to the Chinese already residing in Samoa. The first of this wave would include my grandfather returning to Samoa with my grandmother and father in 1950.

I did not come across any records of others that came immediately after them. But I am aware of other Chinese who came many years after my grandparents who were related to Chinese already residing in Samoa, e.g. Wong Kees, Chan Mows, Lee Hangs, Chen Paos, Rongs, Locks, Cais, and more.

Most of these Chinese migrated here to find better lives and to help the businesses of their Chinese relatives already living in Samoa. Others came from Hong Kong in the 1980s because of concerns about when China again resumed control of Hong Kong. Some of the Chinese that came in this wave chose to make Samoa their home and most married Samoans. Others chose to either return to Hong Kong or migrate to other countries such as New Zealand.

The ones that stayed were easily assimilated into Samoan society, especially the ones who married Samoan women. Most of them became Christians and their applications for Samoan citizenship were always supported by pastors from the churches they attended. Others attended church in order to learn more about the Samoan people. One claimed that he went to church to learn English even though he was not a Christian.

The majority were determined to learn the culture and Samoan way of life. They showed respect for the laws of Samoa and became part of Samoan society. They claim that they did not experience any racism from the Samoans and found assimilation easy. They love living in Samoa and would only return now and then to China to visit family.

One of the most successful of this third wave of Chinese migration is Frankie Cai from Guangzhou. He came in 1992 to help his uncle's business. He is married to a Samoan by the name of Mayday and they have two children. They own and operate Frankies which comprises a mall and supermarkets around Samoa.

Fourth Wave of Chinese Migration (2000 to present date)

The fourth wave of Chinese migration includes the migration of full-blooded Chinese who do not have relatives in Samoa. Whilst full-blooded Chinese with relatives in Samoa continue to migrate to Samoa in this fourth wave, the number of Chinese immigrants without relatives in Samoa has increased in recent years. Some of them go into the wholesale business, whilst others establish and work for construction companies, e.g. Zheng Construction and Qing Dao Construction. Some of these immigrants came via Tonga or American Samoa. The Chinese immigrants who have relatives in Samoa normally end up working for their relatives. There are also those who came to work on construction projects (e.g. the National Hospital) funded by the Chinese Government. These construction workers normally return to China upon the completion of the projects.

In the last four years, 1,573 Chinese citizens were granted permits to enter Samoa[49] for various purposes, e.g. work in projects funded by the Chinese Government (723), employment (442), business investment (50), and visiting family and friends or dependants (75).

It is observed that the majority of Chinese immigrants who migrated to Samoa in this fourth wave are not married to Samoans. Only time will tell whether this situation will change.

There have been criticisms directed by earlier Chinese migrants against those who came in this fourth wave of migration. One criticism is that some of these 'new' Chinese are giving the Chinese in Samoa a bad name because they do not respect or appreciate Samoan culture and way of life. They are also said to be opportunistic and aggressive with their business tactics, sometimes testing the limits of Samoa's laws. It is no surprise that some of these 'new' Chinese have attracted bad publicity due to breaches of the law, resulting in some deportations and, in the case of involvement in businesses reserved for Samoan citizens, the issuing of official warnings.[50]

Another Chinese who came here in the 1990s said he no longer feels comfortable going to the food market in town because of the taunts and teasing he receives there from the Samoans. He believes that the 'new' Chinese do not appreciate Samoan culture and therefore appear rude to the Samoans. In turn, the Samoans do not respect them. He says that if he does have to go to the market, the taunting stops if he speaks in Samoan to the Samoans involved – and they would usually end up apologising to him.

Currently, the Foreign Investment Act 2000 prohibits foreigners from owning or operating certain businesses such as retailing, transport (taxi, buses and rental cars) and traditional garment printing. This law has prevented most Chinese in the fourth wave of migration from owning or operating such businesses.

Success of Chinese in Samoa

Chinese migrants faced serious hardships, but their hard work ethic, respect for Samoa's law and culture, and perseverance enabled them to be successfully assimilated into Samoan society.

Full-blooded Chinese such as Chan Mow, Fong and Leung Wai were successful business people and came to be accepted by Samoans as their own. This was helped also by the fact that they married Samoans and had children who identified themselves as Samoans with Chinese blood. The Chinese indentured labourers that managed to stay in Samoa contributed to the development of Samoa's economy. Others went into business whilst others continued to work in plantations, either for others or on their own.

In the mid-1930s, the Chinese living in Samoa got together to form the Chinese Club. About 500 Chinese were members of this club at one time.[51] The president of the club was my great-grandfather Leung Wai and its secretary was Ah Kuoi. Concerns with World War II prompted the Chinese Club to collect from each of their members 3 pounds per annum to be sent to the Government in China during the war.[52]

The Chinese Club was later registered as an incorporated society in November 1963 as the 'Chinese Association of Western Samoa'. Those that signed the society's Constitution and Rules included, amongst others, Chan Mow, Ming Leung Wai (my grandfather), Li Hang (father of Papalii Niko Lee Hang, Member of Parliament and former Minister of Finance), Chan Chui, Chan Kau, Chiu Lik, Chan Boon, Ah Fook, Chan Tung, Chan Chui, JM Ah Chong, JT Soon and H Ah Kuoi.

The Chinese Association of Western Samoa still exists to this day and continues to own properties in the town of Apia (currently leased to Bluebird Hardware & Lumber Ltd, which houses about one quarter of this company's large hardware store), Moamoa (fenced but vacant) and Talimatau (over nine acres of land donated by the King of England in 1921 to be used as a cemetery for Chinese and settlement for disabled Chinese[53] but the legal conveyance of such land was effected in 1968 by the Samoan Government[54]).

The descendants of Chinese that managed to stay in Samoa enjoyed more success in Samoa than their forebears. In terms of business, the families descended from

Chinese that have done well include the Ah Likis, Chan Mows and Ah Mus to name a few. The Ah Likis own a commercial bank, construction companies, chain of supermarkets, hardware stores and alcohol and beverage factory, to name a few. The Chan Mows, owners of key properties in town, malls and rental buildings, also operate one of the biggest supermarkets and wholesales in Samoa. Hon Hans Joe Keil is descended from Ah Mu and was a former Cabinet Minister who owns a television station (TV3) and many other businesses which included McDonald's Restaurant before he recently sold it.

As for sports, there is Brian Lima who had played in five consecutive Rugby World Cups for Samoa and is the first Samoan to be inducted into the Rugby Hall of Fame. His father is veteran accountant Tuliaupupu Pala Lima, who is a son of a Chinese immigrant. Pat Lam was a former captain of Manu Samoa. One of the fastest Samoans is Louis Chan Tung. As a teenager he ran the 100 metre dash in 10.6 seconds in the 1970s and was taken by a sprint coach to the United States of America for further training. A famous All Black captain, Tana Umaga, was a Samoan who was also part Chinese. The only Samoan to have won gold medals in the sport of weightlifting for Samoa at the South Pacific Games for three consecutive decades was my father Bee Leung Wai who competed in the bantam weight division. Chinese who came in the third wave of migration also represented Samoa in the international arena of sports, e.g. Frankie Cai for badminton and table tennis, Kenny Cai for table tennis, and Joe Zhou and Ming Han Chan for weightlifting. Joe Zhou was in the Chinese national weightlifting team before migrating to Samoa.

In the political arena, about 20% of the current Members of Parliament of Samoa have Chinese ancestry. In fact, two of the current Cabinet Ministers are part-Chinese. Samoans with Chinese ancestry have held seats in every Parliamentary term since Samoa's independence in 1962.[55]

As for the legal profession, many lawyers and one Supreme Court judge are descendants of Chinese immigrants.[56] The same can be said of doctors, accountants and engineers. Several CEOs of Government Ministries and Corporations also have Chinese ancestry.[57]

Since Chinese cuisine is popular around the world, it is no surprise that some Samoan dishes have Chinese origins. For example, we have *sapa sui* that we never fail to eat on Sundays (which is really the Chinese dish of 'chop suey'). Other food with Chinese origins that is popular amongst the Samoans includes keke puaʻa ('cha siu bao'), keke saina and masi saina (Chinese pastries), alaisa (rice) and falai fuamoa ('egg foo yong').

Conclusion

Samoan society is a very inclusive society and inter-marriage with other races is generally accepted. Consequently, Chinese who migrated to Samoa were able to assimilate with ease into Samoan society, an assimilation facilitated by the natural beauty of Samoan women. The children from these Chinese-Samoan unions are also striking. The children from these mixed marriages are considered to be Samoan and are accepted by Samoans as their own. This is helped by the fact that most of the early Chinese immigrants respect and learn Samoan culture and also marry Samoans.

I recall a story told by my Samoan grandfather about the descendants of one of our relatives who had married a foreigner centuries ago. The children from this foreign union were quite often harassed by their Samoan cousins. The high chief of our family at the time told off his children and warned them not to harass their cousins because 'ua namu Samoa tamaiti'. This literally means that these kids 'smelled Samoan' or in other words, 'were Samoan', and should therefore not be discriminated against.

I am fortunate that I am a Samoan who has Chinese, German and Fijian ancestry. Our Honourable Prime Minister remarked in Parliament on Friday 20th February 2015 that the majority of those in Parliament, including himself, were descendants from different races. He emphasised that this is a good thing and showed the tolerance that Samoan culture has for other cultures. As such, Samoans should have zero tolerance towards racism.[58] He has a good point as we do not want to see in Samoa a repeat of what happened with the riots in 2006 in the Solomon Islands where shops belonging to Chinese were targeted for destruction or, in Tonga in the same year, when businesses owned by Chinese were badly damaged by fires in Nuku'alofa.

In the early 1900s, Samoa's economy depended a lot on its plantations. Had it not been for the Chinese indentured labourers, these plantations would have failed. The full-blooded Chinese who came to Samoa during the fourth wave of migration need to understand and respect Samoan law and culture to ensure their full acceptance by Samoans.

The Chinese who have married Samoans and their descendants are considered to be Samoans and have experienced success in all facets of life in Samoa. The security and safety they enjoy in Samoa is due largely to the inclusive nature of the Samoan culture. Such an enabling environment, coupled with their Chinese work ethic and determination to succeed, has enabled them to thrive and contribute to the development of Samoa.

Soifua and God bless.

Notes

1 Leung Wai Family Reunion Magazine, Samoa (July 1999) at p. 4.
2 Crocombe, Ron, *Asia in the Pacific Islands Replacing the West*, IPS Publications, University of the South Pacific, Suva, Fiji (2007) at p. 32.
3 Tom, Nancy Y.W., *The Chinese in Western Sāmoa 1875-1985 The Dragon Came From Afar*, Western Sāmoa Historical & Cultural Trust, Commercial Printers Ltd, Apia, Sāmoa (1986) at p. 38.
4 Ibid at p. 40.
5 Tom, *The Chinese in Western Sāmoa*, at p. 40.
6 Tom, *The Chinese in Western Sāmoa*, at p. 42.

7 Conversations with Muagututagata Joe Ah Ching.
8 Tom, *The Chinese in Western Sāmoa*, at p. 42.
9 Meleisea, Malama, *The Making of Modern Sāmoa*, Institute of Pacific Studies, University of the South Pacific, Suva, Fiji (1987) at p. 168.
10 Tom, *The Chinese in Western Sāmoa*, at p. 43.
11 Ibid.
12 Ibid at p. 42.
13 Campbell, Persia Crawford, *Chinese Coolie Emigration to Countries Within the British Empire*, P S King & Sons Ltd, Orchard House, Westminster, London (1923) at p. 88.
14 Ibid at pp. 4, 5 & 82.
15 Tom, *The Chinese in Western Sāmoa*, at pp. 4 & 73.
16 Decker, *Labour Problems in the Pacific Mandates*, at p. 92.
17 Ibid at p. 93.
18 Ibid at p. 107.
19 Meleisea, *The Making of Modern Samoa*, at p. 171.
20 Decker, *Labour Problems in the Pacific Mandates*, at p. 114.
21 Decker, *Labour Problems in the Pacific Mandates*, at p. 115.
22 Ibid.
23 Ibid at p 63.
24 Ibid at p. 71.
25 Ibid at p. 70.
26 Ibid.
27 Field, *Mau Sāmoa's Struggle for Freedom*, at p. 31.
28 N. A. Rowe of the New Zealand Administration cited by Meleisea, *The Making of Modern Samoa*, at p. 172.
29 Tom, *The Chinese in Western Sāmoa*, at pp. 18–20.
30 See exhibits in Ibid at pp. 75–81.
31 Conversations with officials of the Chinese Embassy in Samoa.
32 Tom, *The Chinese in Western Sāmoa*, at p. 44.
33 Field, *Mau Sāmoa's Struggle for Freedom*, at p. 55.
34 Crocombe, *Asia in the Pacific Islands*, at p. 32.
35 Keesing, pp. 370, 453 as cited by Decker, *Labour Problems in the Pacific Mandates*, p. 120.
36 Proclamation No. 17, 13 May 1915 as cited by Field, *Mau Sāmoa's Struggle for Freedom*, at p. 31.
37 Proclamation No. 42, January 30, 1917; and Proclamation No. 56, May 1, 1918, NZ Parliament cited by Decker, *Labour Problems in the Pacific Mandates*, at p. 120.
38 Field, *Mau Sāmoa's Struggle for Freedom*, at p. 57.
39 Tom, *The Chinese in Western Sāmoa*, at p. 97.
40 Hiery, Hermann Joseph *The Neglected War – The German South Pacific and the Influence of World War I*, University of Hawaii Press, Honolulu, Hawaii at p. 169 and Meleisea, *The Making of Modern Samoa*, at p. 173.
41 N. A. Rowe of the New Zealand Administration cited by Meleisea, *The Making of Modern Samoa*, at p. 172.
42 Hiery, *The Neglected War*, at pp. 167–168.
43 Hiery, *The Neglected War*, at p. 168.
44 Field, *Mau Sāmoa's Struggle for Freedom*, at p. 32 and Hiery, *The Neglected War*, at p. 168.
45 Meleisea, *The Making of Modern Samoa*, at p. 171.
46 Field, *Mau Sāmoa's Struggle for Freedom*, at p. 55.
47 Meleisea, *The Making of Modern Samoa*, at p. 157.
48 Tom, *The Chinese in Western Sāmoa*, at p. 85.
49 Records of the Immigration Division, Ministry of Prime Minister & Cabinet.

50 Records of the Office of the Attorney-General of Samoa.
51 Tom, *The Chinese in Western Sāmoa*, at p. 100.
52 Ibid.
53 Tom, *The Chinese in Western Sāmoa*, at p. 100.
54 Deed of Conveyance between the Independent State of Samoa and the Chinese Association of Western Samoa Inc. dated 31 May 1968 as recorded in the records of the Ministry of Natural Resources & Environment.
55 Records of the Legislative Assembly of Samoa.
56 There are only 3 local Supreme Court judges in Samoa.
57 They include Alosamoa Erna Vaai-Aiono (Samoa International Finance Authority), Sa'u Justina Sa'u (Unit Trust Organisation of Samoa), Faumuina Esther Lameko-Poutoa (National Provident Fund), Leiataua Alden Godinet (Samoa Life Assurance Corporation), Tuaimalo Ah Sam (Ministry of Communications & Information Technology) and Toomata Ah Kī (Agriculture Store of Sāmoa).
58 See also the Honourable Prime Minister's Ministerial Statement, which touched on this same issue he delivered in Parliament on Monday 26 January 2015 and his earlier comments on 21 January 2015 in *Hansard*.

3. REGIONAL SECURITY

Professor Yu Changsen

The Pacific Islands in China's Geo-Strategic Thinking

Associate Professor Yu Changsen
Executive Director, National Centre for Oceania Studies,
Sun Yat-sen University, Guangzhou

Chinese people's knowledge of Oceania pales in comparison with that of their counterparts living in surrounding areas, and even Europeans. Since the end of the 1970s, when China began to implement its opening and reform policies, universities started to provide a course on Oceania studies and several textbooks were published. However, Chinese scholars' understanding of the Pacific Islands is very basic. For example, in a textbook extensively used in universities, the territory comprising Oceania was described as 'scattered in the vast expanse of the South Pacific waters, constituting the island world'.[1] Many people in China prefer to believe that the Oceania countries are located on 'the edge of the world'.[2]

Geographically speaking, China is indeed very far away from the countries of Oceania, the distance ranging from 4,000 to 10,000 kilometers. Further, the South Pacific region is beyond the historical Chinese 'marine silk road'. Shipping and air contact have not been easy. Even today, there are still no direct flights between mainland China and the Pacific Islands. Most Chinese scholars who are interested in Asia-Pacific issues focus on the US alliance system, of which a key part is Australia, considered a 'south anchor' in the US Asia-Pacific strategic system during the Cold War. Few Chinese scholars devoted to the study of international relations regard Oceania as a top priority. Moreover, Pacific Island countries are indeed small and micro states, which gained independence not long ago. They play only a marginal role in China's strategic thinking.

Of course, this does not mean that the Pacific Islands are not important to China. As one scholar has put it, the Chinese government:

> according to its consistent policy, has given fervent sympathy and active support to national liberation and independence movements in the South Pacific region, and has conducted appropriate exchanges with them.[3]

The Chinese government's good will towards Pacific Island countries was rewarded by their formal diplomatic recognition of China from the middle of the 1970s. However, the major concern of the Chinese government in regarding its Pacific Islands counterparts has related to the political and diplomatic struggle with the Taiwanese authorities for official diplomatic recognition. Oceania's strategic importance to China has been limited given that peripheral countries and great powers (the US and former Soviet Union in particular) merit much more attention from the Chinese government. That said, this trend has changed substantially since the second decade of the 21st century. The rapid increase in economic exchanges and trade between China and the South Pacific countries, has encouraged the Chinese leadership to rethink its strategic approach to South Pacific countries. This trend will grow if China's rise continues, raising the economic and geostrategic importance attached to the Pacific Islands by Beijing. Recent evidence of this is the agreement between China and the Pacific Islands to build a *strategic* relationship.[4]

This paper explores the role Pacific Island countries play in China's geo-geographic thinking now and in the future. Four important roles are, in order:
- first, the important location of various island countries in the context of China's safe maritime transport through the South Pacific sea lanes;
- second, the island countries play a significant role in China's offshore defence strategy in the Pacific along with the further development of blue water navy;
- third, Pacific Island countries remain a major priority of China's leadership in the struggle with Taiwanese authorities for diplomatic recognition, which is closely linked to China's peaceful unification strategy;
- and last, the Pacific Islands can serve as a litmus test regarding China's promise to be a responsible great power commensurate with its rising strength.

The Pacific Islands and China's Maritime Navigation Security

There are more than 20,000 islands in the Pacific Ocean, mostly located near or south of the equator. Apart from Australia and New Zealand, the islands can be divided into three archipelagos – Melanesian, Micronesian, and Polynesian. These island regions are of economic and strategic importance for Chinese maritime security and navigation activities in the South Pacific. As one commentator has concluded:

> Those Oceania developing countries are located in between Asia, Australia, North and South America, and linked with the Pacific Ocean and Indian Ocean. Many international submarine cables are going through that region, both maritime and air transportation lanes also meet there.[5]

As China's domestic economic and external trade grows, so will its reliance on the shipment of goods and dependence on maritime security and freedom of navigation. Statistics show that about 90% of China's total import and export of goods and 40% of petrol and oil depend on marine transportation. By 2020, China's annual maritime trade will reach one trillion US dollars, and these products will be transported mainly by Chinese commercial shipping.[6] It is not surprising therefore that the Chinese government is attaching increased importance to the maritime security and stability of Pacific sea lines of communication. As one analyst clearly described it:

The Pacific Islands in China's Geo-Strategic Thinking

China's petrol, oil and other important raw materials are supplied mainly by maritime transportation, and the delivery of the huge quantity of its finished products to overseas market also chiefly depends on shipping. So the maintenance of security of the sea lines of communication is critical to Chinese maritime security, and even more broadly to its national security.[7]

Simply put, there are three major sea lanes in the Pacific Ocean: a north line, a middle line and a south line. Among them, the South Pacific line stretches from East Asia to South America, Australia and New Zealand, and the total length of the lines is about 10,000 nautical miles. The Pacific Islands are located in the intersection area, and there are many natural harbours in those countries.

Lack of infrastructure has led to bottleneck problems in these countries. China can help them to develop modern shipping industries through the port construction and upgrades. At present, China is vigorously promoting the strategy of the 21st Century Maritime Silk Road, and is treating 'connectivity' as crucial. The Oceania region is regarded as the south part of the new Silk Road and great importance is accorded it by the Chinese government.

Meanwhile, Pacific Islands are also important transfer and supply stations for Chinese scientific expeditions to Antarctica. China has undertaken a series of Antarctic scientific expeditions since 1984, studying the potential for the peaceful utilisation of Antarctica. In so doing, China has successfully built four scientific expedition stations including th*e Great Wall, Zhongshan, Taishan, KunLun.* Currently, Chinese Antarctic scientific expedition ships often sail through sea lanes in the Pacific Islands region. With the possible development of Antarctic tourism lines, South Pacific Islands can also serve as halfway stations. Clearly it is desirable for China to promote cooperation with Pacific Island countries in this regard. As one Chinese scholar suggested:

> As long as China and South Pacific Island countries have established good relationships, it will bring about mutual benefits to both parties. If China can build some observation bases or transform stations, not only can it significantly reduce the field of aerospace, marine, oil and gas exploration costs, but this will also enhance space technology development.[8]

In short, the Pacific Island countries are important strategic pivots for the future development of China maritime transportation and navigation.

The Pacific Islands and China's Maritime Defence Strategy

Along with the expansion of China's overseas interests due to its deeper engagement with the international economy, China has sought to boost its maritime power in order to safeguard its interests if necessary. In so doing, China has paid special attention to its Pacific maritime defence strategy. China's maritime strategic priorities now and in the future can be summarized as: safeguarding national sovereignty, protecting marine rights and interests, maintaining the security of sea lanes, and establishing a stable relationship of great powers supporting marine order. For these purposes, China is dedicated to building a powerful blue water navy.

For geographic and strategic reasons as a big country on the Pacific Rim, China has developed its strategic orientation towards the Pacific Ocean. Its dedication towards becoming a strong maritime power is logical even though it has focused historically on and across its land borders.[9] However, China's strategic interest in the Pacific Ocean has been stymied by invisible hands from the alliance of the United States, Japan and Australia. Since early in the Cold War, the US has constructed three 'C' type of Pacific Island chain networks against the Soviet Union and China. Among them, the second island chain is also called the Southwest Pacific Network, of which Guam serves as the center of the Micronesia group, extending from the Guam to Micronesia, New Zealand and Australia. As a result, an arc has been created where the Tasman Sea, the Coral Sea, the Arafura Sea and other important waters are under the tight control of the US-led alliance. This plays a crucial role in enabling the US to contain and deter the Soviet Union and China. Although the Soviet Union has been sidelined by history, this 'C' type of defensive network remains active because China is still a potential threat.

China's maritime strategic thinking relies first on its 'coastal defense' in the first island chain and the surrounding areas including the Yellow Sea, East China Sea and South China Sea. However, China's naval modernisation and its policy of building a real blue water navy for 'offshore active defense' requires breaking through and undermining the US-led defensive network in the second island chain.[10] China's maritime great power dream will not be realised if the second island chain remains intact.

Some of the Pacific Island countries are located in the second and third chains, and thus are important to China strategically. One Chinese analyst noted:

> In the Pacific Ocean, this area (Pacific Island countries) stretch-crosses two strategic channels – from east to north, from south to north – it has therefore always been a strategic location where the fierce competition of various marine powers loomed.[11]

While China's strategic orientation towards the Pacific Ocean is clear-cut, the US government continues to strengthen its presence in this region and has reemphasised that America is a 'Pacific power'.[12] This kind of statement has important implications during a period of escalating maritime disputes in the South China Sea and East China Sea. The US will not turn a blind eye to China's recent assertiveness, and is developing ways of constraining China's rising influence in the region.[13] The US is further strengthening its military presence in the Pacific region, where the Pacific Island region has been regarded as the strategic backyard of America. To prevent infiltration by external forces, America has implemented a 'denial' strategy in the region.[14] However, some Western scholars speculate that China will eventually replace the US as the protector of these small island countries. It seems inevitable that Sino–US competition is ultimately unavoidable in this region.[15]

However, strategic competition between China and the US, if indeed it does emerge in the future, may not necessarily turn into a zero-sum game. If so, Pacific Island countries may not have to choose between China and America. Some even argue that it is counterproductive to suggest great power rivalry is likely in this region.[16] After all, China's policy increasingly favours 'defensive realism' rather than the relentless pursuit of power implied in its opposite of offensive realism.[17] In pursuing its national interests, China can also pay attention to the benefits resulting from strategic cooperation with the US and/or Pacific Island countries. That is why analysts suggest 'soft' rather than 'hard' power behaviour is emerging in the South Pacific.[18]

The Pacific Islands Countries and China's Peaceful Reunification

The peaceful reunification of China is clearly an indispensable part of the Chinese dream as promoted by the top Chinese leadership.[19] The Taiwan issue has been China's biggest internal and foreign challenge. For a long time, both China and Taiwan competed vigorously with each other for international diplomatic recognition, costing them both considerable resources and energy. From the perspectives of geopolitics and China's national reputation, the Taiwanese issue has become a real obstacle to China's rejuvenation.

Since most of the Pacific Island countries were small, under-developed and recently independent, the way was open for the Taiwanese authorities to conduct chequebook diplomacy: the provision of economic aid in exchange for diplomatic recognition. Within the current 22 'diplomatic allies' of Taiwan globally, six of them are from Pacific Island countries, they are Solomon islands, Nauru, Kiribati, Marshall Islands, Palau and Tuvalu. The Taiwanese authorities have given high priority to Pacific Island countries in their diplomacy. As one local Taiwan scholar concluded:

> Although Taiwan is far away from those countries in the South Pacific, they are very important to the Taiwanese authorities at three levels: the achievement of diplomatic relations with Taiwan; bolstering America's strategic dominance in the Asia Pacific; as well as improving Taiwan's strategic posture in East Asia. Therefore, we (Taiwan) cannot underestimate the importance of those countries in the south Pacific.[20]

In order to secure 'diplomatic relations' with Pacific Island countries, Taiwanese authorities have continued to strengthen their influence in these countries through the investment of political, economic and cultural resources. The investment of political resources involved 'visit diplomacy', 'summit diplomacy', 'transit diplomacy' and so on. Meanwhile, the Taiwanese government increased economic aid to Pacific countries in an attempt to win the support of top-ranking officials in the Pacific. Culturally, the Taiwanese authorities have touted the cultural similarity between the aboriginal peoples of Taiwan and Pacific Islanders. More importantly, the Taiwanese authorities have worked with the US in order to retard the rising stature of China in this region.

The diplomatic tug of war in the South Pacific between China and the Taiwanese authorities continued for some time. According to Yang Jian, 'the reality is that for many years until recently to compete with Taiwan diplomatically was perhaps the most important factor for China's growing involvement in the South Pacific.'[21] During the late 1980s and early 1990s in particular, when China experienced serious domestic political turmoil, the Taiwan regime tried to take advantage of the opportunity to sabotage the normal relationships between China and some of the Pacific Island countries.[22] China's diplomatic relations with the Pacific Island countries suffered somewhat as a result.

As time went on, China's remarkable economic growth and its return to a stable political situation paved the way for China to consolidate and develop friendly relations with Pacific Island countries strictly in accordance with the One-China policy. At present, there are eight Pacific Island countries that have formal diplomatic relations with mainland China, slightly more than the number supporting Taiwan. China's economic relations with the Pacific Island countries have grown recently and the total volume of trade between mainland China and the Pacific Island countries has greatly exceeded Taiwan/Pacific Island trade. On foreign aid, China has become the third largest donor to Pacific Island countries, behind only Australia and New Zealand.[23] Moreover, China is a full dialogue partner of the Pacific Islands Forum, the leading regional organisation. It seems that China now has the upper hand.

In 2008 the Kuomintang candidate Ma Ying-Jeou was elected president of Taiwan and a 'diplomatic truce' emerged. The long-standing diplomatic rivalry in the region was temporarily suspended. However, this truce might be reversed while the goal of peaceful unification remains a challenge. Taiwan will presumably continue to utilise its diplomatic leverages in the region and seek to expand its 'international space', for example by striving for formal membership of the United Nations and other international organisations. Taiwan's 'chequebook diplomacy' and 'democratic values diplomacy' remain attractive in the South Pacific region. The sophisticated diplomacy used by Taiwan in the Pacific Islands region may therefore continue to pose a strategic challenge to mainland China's foreign policy in the region.

The Pacific Islands and China's Soft Balancing Strategy

Among the 14 Pacific Islands sovereign countries, 12 of them are UN member states. In addition, there are about a dozen territories subject to American or French jurisdiction or influence. In the future, if some of these territories can achieve independence and join in the UN as formal members, the influence of the Pacific Islands will nominally increase. There is a considerable Chinese diaspora scattered in those islands, with a total of approximately 80,000, amounting to about 1% of the total population.[24] Though many of these Chinese have intermarried with the local people, and have deeply integrated into local society, their Chinese heritage and links to both Chinese and local culture, are assets in the promotion of friendly relations between China and Pacific Island countries.

Recently, China has invested aid in various infrastructure projects in Pacific Island countries. According to the 'China's Foreign Affairs' white paper, from 2000 to 2012, the Chinese government has offered about 30 major projects to six Pacific Island countries – Papua New Guinea, Fiji, Federated States of Micronesia, Samoa, Tonga and Vanuatu. These include the construction of official government buildings, e-government networks, and infrastructure such as highways, bridges, and hydropower and sea embankments. The Chinese government also offered considerable free aid and grants for human resources training, cultural communication, medical and health care and fields such as emergency assistance.[25] More importantly, Chinese aid is generally free of political conditions. As a result, both political elites and the general public can enjoy the benefits of Chinese aid, and it lays a strong foundation for mutually beneficial relations between China and Pacific Island countries.

In the future, through the sophisticated use of economic tools and a thorough understanding of needs, and with the cooperation of the local people, China may be able to ensure the sustainable development of island countries. This is evident from the concept of 'green innovation and win-win cooperation' proposed at the second China–Pacific Island Countries Economic Development and Cooperation Forum held in November 2013 in Guangzhou, China. China is working hard together with the international community to tackle poverty and solve development problems in the Pacific Islands region.

Meanwhile, China can use its increasing soft power (through Confucius Institutes and the other tools of public diplomacy) to cultivate local elites and public opinion, and promote a good image of China in this region. As one scholar observed:

> [China's public diplomacy can] shape the (favourable) image of China as a peaceful and responsible country which honours the equality of sovereignty whether countries are big or small, and this may enhance mutual understanding and trust in the South Pacific.[26]

Indeed, China's economic aid and public diplomacy have produced positive returns. Many Pacific Island countries have publicly started to 'look north'[27] and to look forward to the 'dragon's hug'.[28] More important, they have expressed their willingness to further strengthen their relations with China as a key component of their diplomatic strategies and national policies. Many Island leaders have made Beijing their first official overseas destination. These positive trends were underlined in 2014 when Chinese President Xi Jinping visited Fiji and held meetings with Pacific leaders. On this visit, President Xi Jinping announced new economic cooperation initiatives including zero tariff treatment of 97% of goods imported from least-developed countries, offered 1,000 training scholarships, and promised support on climate change issues.[29]

Conclusion

China is in the early stage of formulating its grand strategy for the new century. Traditionally, great powers, peripheral countries and developing countries have dominated China's grand strategic thinking. In contrast, the Pacific Island countries play only a marginal role. Yet, due to China's rise and the recent expansion of its global interest, Beijing now pays considerable attention to Oceania, and gives priority to strategic relations with Pacific Islands. China's maritime security and freedom of navigation in the Pacific, its defence strategy, maritime development and diplomatic rivalry with Taiwan have all been factors. In short, a review of the place of Pacific Island countries in China's strategic blueprint is in order.

Notes

1. Wang Jian Tang, *The Contemporary Oceania (Dang dai da yang zhou)*, Guangdong Education Press, Guangzhou, 1991, p.138.
2. Yi Wen and Yang Zi eds, *The Oceania Countries—the Edge of the World (Da Yang Zhou Zhu Guo – Shi Jie Bian Yuan Zhi Guo)*, Military Literature Press, Beijing, 1995.
3. Wang Tai Ping, ed., *Fifty Years of PRC Diplomacy (Xin Zhong Guo Wai Jiao Wu Shi Nian)*, Beijing Press, Beijing 1999,P.1532.
4. Xinhua News Agency, 'China, Pacific Island Countries Announce Strategic Relationship', http://news.xinhuanet.com/english/china/2014-11/22/c_133807415.htm.
5. Wang Jian Tang, *The Contemporary Oceania (Dang dai da yang zhou)*, Guangdong Education Press, Guangzhou, 1991, p.182.
6. Xi Qi, 'The Development of Chinese maritime geo-strategy and China Navy in the early twenty-first Century (Er Shi Yi Shi Ji Chu Zhong Guo Hai Shang Di Yuan Zhan Lue Yu Zhong Guo Hai Jun De Fa Zhan)', in *Chinese Military Science (Zhong Guo Jun Shi Ke Xue)* no. 4, 2004, p.80.
7. Gabriel Collins, 'China's Dependent on Global Sea Public Goods', in Erickson, A.S., Goldstein, L J. and Li, Ni eds, *China the United States, and 21st Century Sea Power: Defining a Maritime Security Partnership,* translated by Xu Sheng etc., Ocean Press, Beijing, 2014, p.26.
8. Xie Xiao Jun, 'Prime Minister Wen's trip to South Pacific', Wen Zong Li De Nan Tai Ping Yang Zhi Xing, the Aged (Lao Nian Ren), no. 5, 2005, pp.8–9.
9. John K. Fairbank, 'China's Foreign Policy in Historical Perspective', *Foreign Affairs*, 47, no. 3,, April 1969, 449–63.
10. David Bennett, 'China's Offshore Active Defense and the People's Liberation Army Navy', *Global Security Studies* 1, no. 1, 2010, 126–41.
11. Xie Xiao Jun, 'Prime Minister Wen's trip to South Pacific', Wen Zong Li De Nan Tai Ping Yang Zhi Xing, the Aged (Lao Nian Ren), no. 5, 2005, p.8.
12. 'US defence Secretary: "We are a Pacific Power, We Aren't Going Anywhere"', *The Guardian*, 11 August 2011, at http://www.theguardian.com/world/2014/aug/11/us-defence-secretary-we-are-a-pacific-power-we-arent-going-anywhere; Hillary Clinton, 'America's Pacific Century,' *Foreign Policy*, November 2011, at http://www.foreignpolicy.com/articles/2011/10/11/americas_pacific_century.
13. Robert Ross, 'Chinese Nationalism and Its Discontents', *The National Interest*, no. 116, November/December 2011; Hugh White, 'The Obama Doctrine', *The Wall Street Journal*, November 25, 2011.
14. Statements of Derek Mitchell, Principle of Deputy Assistant Secretary of Defense, Asian and Pacific Security Affairs, Submitted to the House of Foreign Affairs Committee, Subcommittee on Asia, the Pacific and Global Environment, September 29, 2010.

15 Betel Vintner, 'The South Pacific, China's New Frontier', in Anne-Marie Brady, ed., *Looking North, Looking South, China, Taiwan and the South Pacific*, World Scientific publishing Co., 2010, . 30.
16 Jenny Hayward-Jones, *Big Enough for All of Us: Geo-strategic Competition in the Pacific Islands*, NSW: Lowy Institute, 2014.
17 Tang Shiping, 'From Offensive to Defensive Realism', in Robert S. Ross and Zhu Feng eds, *China's Ascent: Power, Security, and Future of International Politics*, Ithaca and London: Cornell University Press, 141–162.
18 Marc Lanteigne, 'Water Dragon? China, Power Shifts and Soft Balancing in the South Pacific', *Political Science* 64, no. 21, 2012, 21–38.
19 David Gosset, 'China Dream Over the Taiwan Strait', *The Huffington Post*, 17 February 2014, at http://www.huffingtonpost.com/david-gosset/china-dream-over-the-taiwan-strait_b_4771628.html.
20 I-Chung Lai, 'Taiwan's South Pacific Strategy', *Taiwan international Studies Quarterly (Taiwan Guo Ji Yan Jiu Ji Kan)*, vol.3, no.3, Autumn 2007, p.147.
21 Jian Yang, *The Pacific Islands in China's Grand Strategy: Small States, Big Games*, Palgrave Macmillan, New York, 2011, p.51.
22 Xi Ming Yuan, *My diplomatic Mission in the South Pacific (Yi Ren San Shi Feng Yu Ji)*, Xin Hua Press, Beijing, 2009, p.38.
23 Yu Chang Sen, 'Chinese Economic Diplomacy toward the Oceania Island States in the first Decade of 21st Century', *Blue Book of Oceania 2013–2014*, Social Science Academic Press, Beijing, 2014.
24 Ron Crocombe, *Asian in the Pacific Islands, Replacing the West*, Suva, 2007, p.93–7.
25 Yu Chang Sen, 'Chinese Economic Diplomacy toward the Oceania Island States in the first Decade of 21st Century', *Blue Book of Oceania 2013–2014*, Social Science Academic Press, Beijing 2014, pp.20–25.
26 Li De Fang, 'The Public Diplomacy Practice of China in the South Pacific Island Countries (Zhong Guo Kai Zhan Tai Ping Yang Dao Guo Gong Gong Wai Jiao De Dong Yin Ji Xian Zhuang Ping Xi), *Pacific Journal*, no. 11, 2014, p.33.
27 Ron Crocombe, 'The Software of China–Pacific Relations', in Anne-Marie Brady, ed., *Looking North, Looking South, China, Taiwan and the South Pacific*, World Scientific publishing Co., Singapore, 2010. pp.35–38.
28 Dragon's hug, *Fiji Times*, 23 November 2014, p.1.
29 *Xi Jing Ping Meet with the Leaders of Pacific Island Countries*: http://news.xinhuanet.com/world/2014-11/22/c_1113361879.htm.

Reordering Oceania: China's Rise, Geopolitics, and Security in the Pacific Islands

Terence Wesley-Smith
Director, Center for Pacific Island Studies, University of Hawai`i at Manoa

Paper prepared for presentation at *'China and the Pacific: The View from Oceania,'* National University of Samoa, 25–27 February 2015 (Revised 10 May 2015).

The debate about China's rise in the Pacific Islands region, or Oceania, tends to focus on implications for the strategic dominance of the United States and its regional partners, particularly Australia. Although this aspect is important, it serves to obscure the possibility that rapidly expanding bilateral relations with China are influenced as much by island leaders and national self-interest as by Beijing, and that those leaders are helping shape the changing regional order in new and significant ways.

This paper explores the implications of China's rise for the strategic, political, and economic interests of the small number of external powers, including the United States, which have exercised considerable influence in the Pacific Islands since the colonial era and, more importantly, for the goals and aspirations of the developing states of the region. It argues that China's rising profile has caused concern among more established external actors but left them with little option but to accommodate the new situation. The paper notes that China's rise has been generally welcomed by island leaders, offering them economic and political opportunities not readily available heretofore. The emergence of the China alternative has disrupted long-standing networks of power and influence in the region, and given island states a degree of control over their own futures perhaps unprecedented in the post-colonial era.

China's Rise in Oceania
In 2006, with the value of trade fast approaching USD 1 billion, Beijing substantially raised the level of its engagement with the region. At the first China-Pacific Island Countries Economic Development and Cooperation Forum in Fiji, then Chinese Premier Wen Jiabao pledged to make available preferential loans worth USD 376 million over three years, establish a fund to encourage Chinese companies to invest in the region, cancel or extend debts maturing in 2005, and remove tariffs on imports from the least developed island nations.[1] At a follow-up meeting in Guangzhou in November 2013, Vice Premier Wang Yang announced, among other

things, an additional USD 1 billion in concessional finance over four years, and a further USD 1 billion in non-concessional loans to be made available through China Development Bank.[2] Even if President Xi Jinping had 'very little new to announce' to Pacific leaders during his visit to Fiji in November 2014, the occasion carried symbolic importance.[3]

Beijing now has formal relations with eight of the 14 independent or self-governing Pacific Island states, and is increasingly active in key regional organisations, including the Pacific Islands Forum. According to China's Vice Premier Wang Yang, bilateral trade has grown at an annual rate of 27% since 2006, and is now valued at USD 4.5 billion.[4] Led by China Metallurgical Corporation's USD 1.4 billion Ramu Nickel mining venture in Papua New Guinea, Chinese commercial investment in the region has also increased rapidly, and construction contracts to Chinese firms now total in excess of USD 5 billion. Aid flows are more difficult to calculate, largely because of disagreement about which transfers to count. Although in 2013 Vice Premier Yang cited a cumulative USD 9.4 billion for 'all kinds of assistance,' Australian researcher Philippa Brant estimates that China distributed a much more modest total of USD 1.5 billion in development assistance to the island states since 2006.[5] In any case, the growth of Beijing's support to the Pacific Islands is impressive, and China now joins Australia, the United States, New Zealand, the European Union, and Japan as a major aid donor to the region.

Scholar Yongjin Zhang argues convincingly that China's new approach to Oceania is best understood as 'an integral part of its new diplomacy toward the global South.'[6] Certainly its pattern of behaviour in the Pacific shares many of the hallmarks of recent engagement with other parts of the developing world, including an emphasis on multilateral relations. The April 2006 summit in Fiji was a first for the region, but it reflects the form and substance of similar events elsewhere, including the Forum on China-Africa Cooperation (FOCAC) series launched in 2000, and the China-Caribbean Economic and Trade Cooperation Forum held for the first time in Jamaica in February 2005. Also, as Hong Kong-based scholar Simon Chen points out, China's activities overseas, including in Oceania, are increasingly characterised by an apparent desire to be perceived as a responsible stakeholder in the international system.[7]

Although China's political and economic profile in Oceania has increased dramatically in recent times, it remains modest relative to its investment in other regions of the world – and to Australia's level of engagement in the Pacific. Two other factors – the search for natural resources, and efforts to expand its political influence – help to define the specific characteristics of China's relations with the island nations of the Pacific. Oceania is important to China as a source of key natural resource inputs for its burgeoning economy. China already imports significant quantities of timber and fish from Pacific Island countries, including the Solomon Islands and Papua New Guinea, and has a particular interest in Papua New Guinea's vast energy and mineral resources.

Although China's quest for reliable access to natural resources helps drive its relations with particular island states – most notably Papua New Guinea – efforts to build political influence are region-wide. Indeed, political motives probably best explain the relatively large number of Chinese diplomats posted to the region, the 'visit diplomacy' that brings many island leaders on goodwill trips to Beijing every year, as well as some of the high-profile aid projects producing sports complexes and other public facilities in island countries. Along with similar efforts in the Caribbean and smaller countries in Africa, China hopes to mute international criticism of its record on human rights, advance its economic goals in institutions like the World Trade Organization (WTO), and block Japan's aspirations to play a more active international role. Until recently China's efforts to isolate Taiwan were of key importance in structuring its activities in the region.

The competition between China and Taiwan for influence in Oceania dates back to the 1970s, after US President Richard Nixon's visit to Beijing and loss of UN membership pushed Taiwan to seek diplomatic recognition wherever it could. Although Taiwan has lost eight of its 30 diplomatic allies since 2003, it remains relatively successful in Oceania, where nearly one fourth of its remaining allies are located. Today, six Pacific Island states (Kiribati, Solomon Islands, Palau, the Marshall Islands, Tuvalu and Nauru) recognise Taiwan, while a further eight (Papua New Guinea, Samoa, Tonga, the Cook Islands, Fiji, Vanuatu, the Federated States of Micronesia and Niue) have formal relations with China.[8]

The rivalry with Taiwan for recognition has been among the most controversial aspects of China's growing relationship with Oceania, and was considered by some to be a key factor influencing China's activities in the region.[9] The 'diplomatic truce' between Beijing and Taipei in recent years provides an opportunity to evaluate these claims.[10] The 2008 elections in Taiwan saw the Kuomintang (KMT) party return to power, and incoming President Ma Ying-jeou brought with him a much more conciliatory approach to cross-Strait issues than his predecessor. The Chinese government responded positively to Ma's overtures, and, in September 2010, China's Premier Wen commented that political relations between the two sides had reached 'the most promising point in decades.'[11] In the general elections of January 2012, President Ma was re-elected by a comfortable margin and relations with Beijing have continued to improve. These developments support Chinese foreign policy expert Robert Sutter's claim that the balance of power in cross-Strait relations has tilted significantly towards China.[12]

In the Pacific, most of the apparent changes have been on the Taiwan side of the equation. Taipei's 2009 White Paper on Foreign Aid Policy signaled a move away from 'chequebook diplomacy,'[13] and during a visit to the Solomon Islands in March 2010, President Ma declared that Taiwan and China had 'stopped trying to win over each other's diplomatic allies.'[14] Although the 'diplomatic truce' has frozen attempts to reduce the number of states that recognise Taiwan, it has not precipitated other significant changes in Beijing's policy towards Oceania. Indeed, the November 2013 meeting with regional leaders in Guangzhou and a year later in Fiji suggests that China's interest in the region continues on an upward trajectory.

It is too soon to properly assess the impact of improved China–Taiwan relations on Beijing's attitude towards the Pacific. For one thing, the truce itself could well be compromised by any number of developments, including a resurgence of support for independence among the Taiwanese electorate, or a hardening stance in the US Congress towards arms sales to Taipei. Furthermore, as Simon Shen argues, the whole focus on the 'diplomatic truce' may itself be misguided. Instead, Shen suggests, Beijing's tolerance of the status quo reflects a new foreign policy emphasis designed to demonstrate that China is a responsible power in the international system. Shen argues that the larger strategic design is no longer to win over the remaining states that recognise Taipei, but to 'pave the way for future Chinese reunification and the 'Chinese Dream' by engaging all kinds of possible state and non-state actors.' He suggests further that this approach may well persist even if President Ma and the KMT fall from power in the next elections.[15] In any event, it is clear that, although competition with Taiwan has been an important component of Beijing's foreign policy in Oceania, it is not the only factor driving Beijing's activities in the region.

Strategic Balancing

Despite some claims to the contrary,[16] Beijing's activities in the Pacific Islands provide little evidence of a grand strategy driven by hegemonic aspirations. Certainly, the notion of 'hard balancing' with military power seems far-fetched, at least as it might implicate the Pacific Islands region. Like their global counterparts, regional threat scenarios usually reference China's growing military expenditure and expanding naval capacity. However, it is clear that China will not have the military capacity to challenge the global dominance of the United States any time soon.[17] It is also important to note that creating such global capabilities has not been a priority for Beijing. Instead, military planners have focused consistently on a narrowly defined set of strategic objectives in the East and South China Seas.

The dramatic increase in the capabilities of the People's Liberation Army Navy to operate in the Near Seas (i.e. inside the 'first island chain') has significant implications for the interests of the US and its allies in the Asia-Pacific region, especially coupled with Beijing's new assertiveness in pursuing its objectives there. Indeed, the declaration of an air defense identification zone (ADIZ) in the East China Sea, moves to regulate foreign fishing in the South China Sea, and the ongoing dispute with Japan over the Senkaku/Diaoyu islands leads scholar Denny Roy to conclude that there is intent on the part of China 'to establish a maritime sphere of influence, with exclusive rights to resources.'[18] Whether that is the case or not, it is clear that the long-standing ability of the US Navy to operate 'whenever and wherever it wants' in the Western Pacific is now compromised, and that this represents a potentially serious axis of friction between the two powers, as well as between China and regional neighbours like Japan, Vietnam, South Korea, and the

Philippines.[19]

The implications of all of this for the island countries of Oceania are less clear. Most of the Pacific Island states do not lie close to the strategic sea lanes that service China's burgeoning trade in raw materials and energy, or to marine chokepoints, such as the Straits of Malacca. Few would appear to offer strategic assets in the event of conflict with Taiwan, and those that might, like Guam and the Commonwealth of the Northern Marianas, are already firmly under US strategic control and, in the case of Guam, heavily militarised. And none are directly implicated in the ongoing disputes associated with China's contested Near Seas periphery. Some commentators have suggested that China is actively seeking port facilities in the region for its naval vessels, citing Chinese-funded wharf and port development projects in Tonga, Papua New Guinea and elsewhere.[20] However, there is no evidence that these projects have been instigated for anything other than commercial purposes – and no apparent reason why China's military planners would prioritise such initiatives under present circumstances.

The evidence for some forms of 'soft balancing' in Oceania is more solid. Tokyo's unease with recent developments is clear, and Japanese scholar Kobayashi Isumi states bluntly that the substantial increase in aid to the Pacific Islands announced in May 2006 was intended to counter Beijing's growing sway in the region.[21] Furthermore, the United States, which has maintained a relatively low profile in the region since the end of the Cold War, is now attempting to 'renew its focus and commitment' to the island nations through enhanced diplomatic efforts and increased financial assistance.[22] Although perhaps not the only factor driving this change in posture, the rise of China in Oceania is clearly an important part of Washington's new strategic equation.

However, it is notable that neither of these balancing initiatives have lived up to initial expectations, at least as they impact the Pacific Islands region. There have been no more dramatic increases in Japanese aid in recent years. The reopening of a USAID office in the islands region in October 2011, this time in Port Moresby, demonstrated a symbolic return to an earlier profile for the United States, as has a steep rise in the number of visits by American officials to island capitals and regional meetings. However, at least to date, this new commitment appears to lack both coherence and substance. US Secretary of State Hillary Clinton arrived at the 2012 meeting of the Pacific Islands Forum in the Cook Islands to great fanfare, but her pledge of an additional USD 32 million in US aid was modest by any standards. The Obama administration's pivot to Asia-Pacific, it seems, is much more about Asia and much less about the insular Pacific.

When it comes to increased interest in the region, the main actor is clearly Australia. Researcher Jonathan Pryke identifies a boom in aid to the Pacific Islands region from OECD sources (i.e. excluding China) in recent decades, with Australia accounting for the lion's share (65%) of the total increase since 2002.[23] However, the trigger for this surge in aid is not directly related to the rise of China. Rather it is fueled by the emergence of a new conventional wisdom that makes connections between security threats and 'failed' and 'failing' states.[24] A large portion of Australia's aid in recent years has gone to support an interventionist state building effort in the Solomon Islands, which experienced significant domestic conflict in the early years of the century, and to regional programs also heavily focused on good governance and state capacity-building initiatives.[25] China does not subscribe to this reform agenda and is therefore seen by decision makers in Canberra as placing such initiatives in jeopardy.

Conflict and Cooperation

The ultimate objective of Australian aid and diplomacy in the region remains the strengthening of the neo-liberal state in island places. The urgency of the task has increased with a heightened awareness of 'non-traditional' transnational security threats such as pandemics, drug and people smuggling, and terrorism – the latter especially after the events of 9/11, as well as the 2002 Bali terrorist bombing that killed a large number of Australian citizens. The main focus is on preventing state failure or, as in the case of the Solomon Islands, rebuilding dysfunctional state institutions. The means to achieve these ends have become more aggressive, with Australia prepared to intervene more directly in the domestic affairs of island states.[26] Multilateral efforts are also an essential part of this threat-reduction strategy. In particular, the Secretariat of the Pacific Islands Forum, the premier regional organisation, has been seen as a key conduit for promoting reform efforts, guided until recently by the Pacific Plan, a 'master strategy' for regional integration heavily influenced by neo-liberal ideas.[27]

The major concern for Australia and other established powers active in the region is that the rise of China will disrupt the extensive structures of regional influence carefully constructed over many years to preempt non-traditional security risks. At issue is, first of all, Beijing's long-standing practice of providing support to its aid partners without political conditions, except adherence to the One-China Policy. This provides Pacific leaders at least the possibility of avoiding some of the unwanted pressure associated with the aid-leveraged, Western-led reform agenda.

However, it is worth noting that Beijing's bilateral agreements do not require island states to modify or relinquish their ties with Western powers, and recent multilateral initiatives appear specifically designed not to replace the existing architecture of regional cooperation. Indeed, Beijing has been careful to avoid any direct challenges to existing patterns of leadership. Perhaps in part to assuage Australian fears that a rising China would derail ongoing attempts to enhance regional cooperation and encourage good governance, Beijing pledged support for the Pacific Plan, then a major blueprint for such efforts. In February 2008, it also signed the Kavieng Declaration on Aid Effectiveness, a local version of the Paris Declaration on Aid Effectiveness, which provides guidelines for donor countries involved in Papua New Guinea.[28] However, in September 2011 China indicated that there were limits to its willingness to conform when it made it clear that it would not be bound by the Cairns Compact, a 2009 agreement of the Pacific Islands Forum, which identifies strict criteria for regulating regional development efforts.

Critics also cite a range of other China-related actions that they regard as disruptive to regional order, including the unpredictability of aid flows from year-to-year; the lack of provision for the long-term maintenance of infrastructure projects; a lack of transparency in dealings with Chinese government officials; and the lack of local flow-on benefits from construction projects where everything, including labour, is imported from China.[29] These are familiar complaints from other parts of the global South, where some observers have argued that these shortcomings reflect the inadequacies of China's aid bureaucracy, or the ineptitude or inexperience of Chinese companies, and raise the possibility that at least some of these points of friction will improve over time.[30] Scholar Graeme Smith researched labour practices during the construction phase of the massive Chinese-operated Ramu Nickel mine in Papua New Guinea and discovered a disturbing array of health, safety and pay issues. Smith attributes these issues to a number of factors, including the inexperience of the Chinese company involved, working conditions back home and efforts to keep costs down. But he also found evidence of a learning curve, as new investors learn from their mistakes and find better ways of 'getting things done' as a matter of corporate self-interest.[31]

Especially since Beijing's 'Going Out' strategy was implemented in the mid-1990s, Chinese companies have significant incentives to invest abroad, and seem to be exercising an increasing degree of independence from state control. The Pacific Islands region has not been immune to these developments, and Chinese companies are increasingly involved in a whole range of projects, including large-scale resource extraction, industrial initiatives, infrastructure development, as well as smaller-scale retail and wholesale activities. Although the 'Going Out' policy was predicated on close collaboration between the state and Chinese corporations, often it is the corporations rather than the state that takes the lead in overseas commercial ventures. Work by Philippa Brant analysing Chinese-led resource development projects in Fiji and Papua New Guinea finds that it is common for the companies to negotiate access with local actors before 'bringing the state with them' to provide grants, and interest-free or concessionary loans to move the project forward.[32] Increasingly the logic associated with the expanding Chinese presence in the region has more to do with commercial factors than foreign policy directives emanating from Beijing.[33]

An emerging focus of concern for critics of China's activities in the region is the amount of debt assumed by island governments in Chinese-funded infrastructure projects. They point out that Samoa, Cook Islands, and Tonga have already taken on levels of debt from China's Exim Bank that are unsustainable in these small economies, even at concessional rates of interest. And they worry that the assistance package announced at the 2013 Guangzhou forum provides for a further USD 2 billion in concessional and non-concessional loans over the next four years.[34] These are legitimate concerns because, if past patterns are any guide, the most important actors facilitating access to these loans will be Chinese corporations with little interest in the longer-term ramifications for government debt loads or default.

Pacific Island Agency

Some analysts have argued that China has exploited particular regional vulnerabilities to establish itself in Oceania and, in the process, encouraged corruption and instability in island states. Not only do these allegations remain unsubstantiated, but they serve to obscure the possibility that bilateral relations with China are influenced as much by island leaders and national self-interest as by Beijing.[35] A 2010 collection of country-level studies of relations between Pacific Island states and China and Taiwan belies any sense of external domination or manipulation.[36] What we see instead are Pacific Island leaders making rational decisions about what they see as their best interests in the face of changing opportunities in the external environment. Although there may be concern about large and relatively unfamiliar powers acquiring significant stakes in Pacific futures, there is also clear appreciation of what those powers can bring to the table. Officials acknowledge the fact that China pledges not to interfere in domestic policy, comment on governance or other development issues, or attach conditions to transfers of aid and other resources. Pacific leaders also respond positively to the egalitarian qualities of contemporary Chinese diplomacy, noting that they are treated with respect regardless of their nation's size, resource endowment or system of government.

Perhaps the most important element associated with China's heightened presence is the opening up of new options. For the first time in generations, Pacific leaders can make new choices regarding aid, trade and investment opportunities, as well as contemplate alternatives to dominant development paradigms often presented as necessary, universal and non-negotiable. In 2012 President Anote Tong of Kiribati noted the new level of engagement in the region by outside powers, and indicated that he found 'these initiatives most welcome indeed . . . It is nice to be relevant.'[37]

It is clear, for example, that the nature of China's evolving relationship with Fiji has been determined as much by decision-makers in Suva as by their counterparts in Beijing. Fiji's 'Look North' policy emerged in the aftermath of the civilian coup of 2000 as an effort to diversify diplomatic and economic relations away from traditional partners pressuring Fiji to restore democratic institutions. This coincided with China's interest in raising its regional profile and the relationship between the two countries has grown significantly, especially since the 2006 military coup further deepened the divide with Western countries.[38] However, it is important to note that, while former military commander and current Prime Minister Frank Bainimarama has repeatedly emphasised the significance of these ties, China has not always reciprocated with pointed statements of its own. Indeed, Beijing has been at pains not to over-exploit this opportunity for regional influence so as to avoid any direct confrontation with Fiji's traditional partners, particularly Australia. Before

Fiji's return to elected government in 2014, Hanson and Hayward-Jones accused China of 'bankrolling a pariah military dictatorship.'[39] But Beijing's decision to continue its relationship with Fiji when others decided to impose sanctions is entirely consistent with its pledge not to interfere in the domestic affairs of partner states. Furthermore, it seems that much of the increase in Chinese economic activity in Fiji in recent years has nothing to do with any special favours from Beijing. Rather, in typical fashion, most of these resource and infrastructure development projects have been initiated by Chinese companies, with funding either from the pool of concessional financing made available to the region and announced by **Premier Wen Jiabao** in 2006, or on commercial terms from the China Development Bank.[40]

Reordering Oceania

In an influential assessment of the potential for geo-strategic competition in Oceania resulting from the rise of China, Australia's Lowy Institute analyst Jenny Hayward-Jones concludes that the region is 'big enough for all of us.'[41] This echoes comments made by US Secretary of State Hillary Clinton at the 2012 meeting of the Pacific Islands Forum, and is based on two main arguments. The first is that, to date, China has not demonstrated an explicit desire to compete for leadership in the region. The second is that, even if that did become a priority sometime in the future, China's ability to 'challenge a well-established order dominated by a number of key external powers with whom the countries of the region have long-standing and deep ties' remains in doubt.[42]

Hayward-Jones' reassuring analysis reflects an emerging consensus in the Western countries most active in the region, particularly Australia and New Zealand. Despite ongoing concerns about the longer-term implications of China's rise in Oceania, and keenly aware of their own growing economic entanglements with China, decision-makers in Canberra and Wellington have responded pragmatically to the new situation. In 2012, then Australian Parliamentary Secretary for Pacific Island Affairs Richard Marles indicated that China's increased presence in the region was 'fundamentally welcomed' by Australia, and, in April 2013, Australia signed the Australia-China Development Cooperation Memorandum of Understanding, which allows for cooperation on aid initiatives involving health issues and water resource management.[43] Former New Zealand diplomat Chris Elder and scholar Robert Ayson note that New Zealand needs 'to adjust to the reality of China's growing South Pacific influence,'[44] and in 2012, New Zealand and China agreed to collaborate on a project to improve water quality in the Cook Islands.[45]

The Hayward-Jones analysis begs some questions about the effectiveness of the Western-dominated order, however large and well-established, especially if that means an ability to ensure conformity and progress towards identified goals. It is not clear if the Canberra-based reform agenda has actually helped strengthen state institutions across the region, enhance 'good governance,' or foster rapid economic growth. Indeed, the most recent survey of progress towards the Millennium Development

Goals shows decidedly mixed results in Pacific Island countries, even in those island states, like the Solomon Islands and Papua New Guinea, where Australian involvement is most intense.[46] Perhaps the most telling test of effectiveness is in the Solomon Islands, where in 2013 the Australian-led Regional Assistance Mission to the Solomon Islands (RAMSI) intervention celebrated its tenth anniversary and is in the process of transferring its functions to more conventional aid mechanisms. Most commentators agree that the RAMSI initiative has made progress on all three pillars of its stated mission, i.e. restoration of law and order, improving the machinery of government, and promoting economic growth. However, most also express concern about the sustainability of these pillars after the well-resourced expatriate officials who have occupied key positions in the bureaucracy depart for home.[47]

Perhaps most important, the Hayward-Jones paper underestimates the significance of Pacific Islander agency in influencing the nature and direction of change in the region. She goes so far as to claim that 'most of the Island states . . . (with the possible exception of Fiji) are not seeking to change the regional order, even if they could . . . .'[48] This ignores growing evidence of dissatisfaction with the status quo. In October 2012, for example, President of Kiribati Anote Tong, expressed his disappointment at the lack of international action on important global issues, particularly climate change, and went on to call for 'a new paradigm shift where the Pacific needs to chart its own course and lead global thinking in crucial areas such as climate change, ocean governance and sustainable development.'[49] Other indications of this desire to chart a more independent course include mounting regional resistance to PACER Plus and other free trade initiatives actively promoted by external powers, the demise of the Pacific Plan in the face of the blistering critique of island leaders, and the successful 2013 effort to get French Polynesia re-inscribed on the UN list of non-self-governing territories, despite strong opposition from France, and without the endorsement of traditional partners like the United Kingdom, Australia and New Zealand. In a recent article, Sandra Tarte argues that some significant changes in Pacific Islands regionalism, including declining support for the Pacific Islands Forum (which includes Australia and New Zealand as members), the increasing prominence of the Melanesian Spearhead Group, and the 2013 establishment of the Pacific Islands Development Forum, are 'driven by the discontent of a growing number of island states with the established regional order and by a desire to assert greater control over their own future.'[50] Despite the full restoration of relations with Australia after the 2014 elections, Fiji, which Hayward-Jones identified as the 'possible exception' to her rule about satisfaction with the status quo, continues to assert that it will not return to the Pacific Islands Forum unless Australia and New Zealand withdraw their membership.

China's increased presence in Oceania has not created the new assertiveness of island leaders, but it has facilitated a number of significant changes in long-established patterns of power and influence in this vast sea of islands. It has opened up alternatives to long-standing political and economic relationships, and, in the process, exposed some weaknesses in a regional order largely designed and managed by the Western powers active in the region. At the very least, it provides Pacific Island leaders the opportunity to push back against an unpopular aid-leveraged regional reform agenda, and puts them in a strong position to influence the shape of a changing regional order. China's profile in the region – especially its corporate dimensions – will likely continue to expand. But whether 'the China model' proves to be a genuine alternative to more established development paradigms and relationships remains to be seen.

Notes

1. Wen Jiabao, 'Win-win Cooperation for Common Development,' (speech, China-Pacific Island Countries Economic Development and Cooperation Forum, Nadi, Fiji, April 5, 2006), reproduced in Terence Wesley-Smith and Edgar Porter (eds.), *China in Oceania: Reshaping the Pacific?*, (New York and Oxford: Berghahn Books, 2010), 198–201.
2. Yang, *Ibid.*; Jenny Hayward-Jones and Philippa Brant, 'China Ups the Aid Stakes in the Pacific,' *The Interpreter*, November 18, 2013, accessed July 22, 2014, http://www.lowyinterpreter.org/post/2013/11/18/China-ups-the-aid-stakes-in-the-Pacific-Islands.aspx.
3. Jenny HaywardJones and Philippa Brandt, 'Fiji Grabs the Limelight as Leaders of China and India Visit,' I, 24th November 2015.
4. Wang Yang, 'Address at the 2nd China-Pacific Island Countries Economic Development and Cooperation Forum,' (speech, Guangzhou, November 8, 2013), Ministry of Commerce, People's Republic of China, http://english.mofcom.gov.cn/article/newsrelease/significantnews/201311/20131100386982.shtml.
5. Philippa Brant, 'The Geopolitics of Chinese Aid: Mapping Beijing's Funding the Pacific,' *Foreign Affairs*, 4 March 2015; Brant 'Chinese Aid in the South Pacific: Linked to Resources?', *Asian Studies Review* 37(2013), 158–177).
6. Yongjin Zhang, 'A Regional Power by Default,' in Wesley-Smith and Porter, *Ibid.*, 49–66.
7. Simon Shen, 'From Zero-Sum Game to Positive-Sum Game: Why Beijing Tolerates Pacific Islands States,' *Journal of Contemporary China*, forthcoming.
8. Joel Atkinson, 'China-Taiwan Diplomatic Competition and the Pacific Islands,' *Pacific Review* 23(2010), 407-427.
9. Graeme Dobelle, 'China and Taiwan in the South Pacific: Diplomatic Chess versus Political Rugby,' in Paul D'Arcy (ed.), *Chinese in the Pacific: Where to Now?*, (CSCSD Occasional Paper, No. 1., Canberra: Centre for the Study of the Chinese Southern Diaspora, Research School of Pacific and Asian Studies, Australian National University, 2007).
10. Atkinson, *op. cit.*, 420–422.
11. 'China May Remove Taiwan Missiles,' United Kingdom Press Association, September 23, 2010, accessed October 10, 2013, http://www.google.com/hostednews/ukpress/article/ALeqM5juK5M5jZnqFbKzKFn-q7_ZAUS1ow.
12. Andrew Jacobs, 'President of Taiwan is Reelected, a Result that is Likely to Please China,' *New York Times*, January 14, 2011, accessed July 20, 2014, http://www.nytimes.com/2012/01/15/world/asia/taiwan-presidential-election.html; Robert Sutter, *Taiwan's Future: Narrowing Straits*, (Seattle: National Bureau of Asian Research, NBR Analysis, April 2011).
13. Taiwan, *Progressive Partnerships and Sustainable Development*, White Paper on Foreign Policy (Summary) (Tapei: Ministry of Foreign Affairs, Republic of China, 2009).
14. Jemima Garrett, 'Taiwan Ends Pacific Diplomatic Wars With China,' *Australian Network News*, March 25, 2010, accessed September 10, 2010 http://australianetworknews.com/stories/201003/2856166.htm?desktop.

15 Simon Shen, 'From Zero-Sum Game to Positive-Sum Game: Why Beijing Tolerates Pacific Island States' Recognition of Taipei,' *Journal of Contemporary China*, forthcoming 2014, 20.
16 See e.g. John Henderson and Benjamin Reilly, 'Dragon in Paradise: China's Rising Star in Oceania,' *The National Interest* 72(2003), 94–104; Susan Windybank, 'The China Syndrome,' *Policy* 21(2005), 28–33.
17 See e.g. Andrew Erickson and Adam Liff, 'China's Military Development, Beyond the Numbers,' *The Diplomat*, March 12, 2013, accessed February 20, 2014, http://thediplomat.com/2013/03/chinas-military-development-beyond-the-numbers/; Marc Lanteigne, 'Water Dragon? China, Power Shifts and Soft Balancing in the South Pacific,' *Political Science* 64(2012), 21–38.
18 Denny Roy, 'US-China Relations and the Western Pacific,' *The Diplomat*, January 16, 2014, accessed February 20, 2014, http://thediplomat.com/2014/01/us-china-relations-and-the-western-pacific/.
19 Robert Kaplan, 'The Geography of Chinese Power: How Far Can Beijing Reach on Land and at Sea?', *Foreign Affairs*, May/June 2010, 34.
20 See e.g. Makiko Yanada, 'Concerns over China's Pacific Ventures,' accessed February 21, 2013, http://www.stuff.co.nz/world/south-pacific/9131965/Concerns-over-Chinas-Pacific-ventures.
21 Kobayashi Isumi, 'China's Advance in Oceania and Japan's Response,' in Wesley-Smith and Porter, *Ibid.*, 85-92.
22 Kurt Campbell, 'US Policy in the Pacific Islands,' (testimony before the House Foreign Affairs Subcommittee on Asia, the Pacific, and the Global Environment, Washington DC, September 29, 2010), US Department of State, http://www.state.gov/p/eap/rls/rm/2010/09/148318.htm.
23 Jonathan Pryke, 'The Pacific's Aid Boom,' *Devpolicyblog*, 2013, Development Policy Centre, Australian National University, accessed February 16, 2014, http://devpolicy.org/the-pacifics-aid-boom-02092013/.
24 Terence Wesley-Smith, 'Altered States: The Politics of State Failure and Regional Intervention,"in Greg Fry and Tarcisius Kabutaulaka (eds.), *Intervention and State-Building in the Pacific: The Legitimacy of 'Cooperative Intervention*, (Manchester and New York: Manchester University Press, 2008), 37–53.
25 Shahar Hameiri, 'Risk Management, Neo-liberalism and the Securitisation of the Australian Aid Program,' *Australian Journal of International Affairs* 62(2008), 357-371.
26 Fry and Tarcisius Kabutaulaka, *Ibid.*
27 Shahar Hameiri, 'The Region Within: RAMSI, the Pacific Plan and New Modes of Governance in the Southwest Pacific,' *Australian Journal of International Affairs* 63(2009), 348–360; Pacific Plan Review, Report to Pacific Leaders (Suva, Fiji: Pacific Islands Forum Secretariat, 2013).
28 Kavieng Declaration on Aid Effectiveness: A Joint Commitment of Principles and Actions Between the Government of Papua New Guinea and Development Partners, February 15, 2008.
29 Fergus Hanson, *China: Stumbling Through the Pacific*, Policy Brief, July, (Sydney: Lowy Institute for International Policy, 2009).
30 See e.g. Deborah Brautigam, *The Dragon's Gift: The Real Story of China in Africa*, (Oxford: Oxford University Press, 2009).
31 Graeme Smith, 'Beijing's Orphans? New Chinese Investors in Papua New Guinea,' *Pacific Affairs* 86(2013), 327–49; Graeme Smith, 'Nupela Masta? Local and Expatriate Labour in a Chinese-Run Nickel Mine in Papua New Guinea,' *Asian Studies Review* 37(2013), 178–195.
32 Brant, *op. cit.*, 2014, 158–177.
33 See also Philippa Brant, 'Charity Begins at Home: Why China's Foreign Aid Won't Replace the West's,' *Foreign Affairs*, October 13, 2013, accessed July 20, 2014, http://www.foreignaffairs.com/articles/140152/philippa-brant/charity-begins-at-home.
34 See, for example, Pacific Institute of Public Policy, *Unsure Refuge: Rash, Unsound Borrowing and Predatory Lending Practices are Leading some Pacific Island Countries Toward Insolvency*, Pacific Institute of Public Policy, Discussion Starter 25, October 2013.

35 See e.g. Henderson and Reilly, *Ibid.*; Windybank, *Ibid.*; Dobelle, *Ibid.*
36 Wesley-Smith and Porter, *Ibid.*
37 Anote Tong, 'Keynote Address at the launch of the Pacific International Relations Forum of the School of Government, Development and International Affairs,' (speech, University of the South Pacific, Suva, Fiji, October 9, 2012), accessed February 12, 2014, http://pidp.eastwestcenter.org/pireport/2012/October/10-11-sp.htm
38 Sandra Tarte, 'Fiji's 'Look North' Strategy and the Role of China,' in Wesley-Smith and Porter, *Ibid.*, 118–132.
39 Fergus Hanson and Jenny Hayward-Jones, 'China's Help May Harm Fiji,' *The Australian*, April 23, 2009, accessed February 12, 2014, http://lowyinstitute.org/files/pubfiles/Hanson_Hayward_Jones%2C_China%27s_help.pdf
40 Brant, *op. cit.*, 2013, 158–177.
41 Jenny Hayward-Jones, *Big Enough for All of Us: Geo-Strategic Competition in the Pacific Islands*, (Lowy Institute Analyses. Sydney: Lowy Institute for International Policy, 2013).
42 Hayward-Jones, *Ibid.*, 7.
43 Richard Marles, Interview with Girish Sawani on Pacific Beat, Radio Australia, May 29, 2012, accessed February 12, 2014, http://ministers.dfat.gov.au/marles/transcripts/2012/rm_tr_120529.html; Sam Byfield, 'Enhancing Aid Cooperation: the Australian-China Development Cooperation Memorandum of Understanding,' *Devpolicyblog*, Development Policy Centre, Australian National University, 2013, accessed February 22, 2014, http://devpolicy.org/enhancing-aid-cooperation-the-australia-china-development-cooperation-memorandum-of-understanding-20130422/.
44 Chris Elder and Robert Ayson, *China's Rise and New Zealand's Interests: A Policy Primer for 2030*, (Wellington: Centre for Strategic Studies, Victoria University of Wellington, Dicussion Paper #11, 2012)
45 New Zealand Aid Programme, 'New Zealand and China Collaborate on World First in Development,' Media Release, September 2012, accessed February 21, 2014, https://www.aid.govt.nz/media-and-publications/development-stories/september-2012/new-zealand-and-china-collaborate-world-fi.
46 Pacific Islands Forum Secretariat, *2013 Pacific Region MDGs Tracking Report*, (Suva: Pacific Islands Forum Secretariat, 2013), accessed February 21, 2014, http://www.forumsec.org/resources/uploads/attachments/documents/2013_Pac_Regional_MDGs_Tracking_Report_FINAL.pdf.
47 See, e.g. Matthew Allen and Sinclair Dinnen, 'RAMSI: Solomon Islands in transition,' *Devpolicyblog*, Development Policy Centre, Australian National University, accessed February 19, 2014, http://devpolicy.org/ramsi-solomon-islands-in-transition-20130801/.
48 Hayward-Jones, *Ibid.*, 13.
49 Anote Tong, *Ibid.*
50 Sandra Tarte, 'Regionalism and Changing Regional Order in the Pacific Islands,' *Asia and the Pacific Policy Studies*, May 2014, 3.

Dr Jim Rolfe

Professor Terence Wesley-Smith

Regional Security and the Role of External Actors

Dr Jim Rolfe
Director, Centre for Strategic Studies: New Zealand,
Victoria University of Wellington

Introduction
External actors have been an historical factor and are a continuing factor in Oceania's security and development. External powers, Spain, France, Portugal, the UK and the Netherlands, became interested in the region as a by-product of the age of exploration from the 16th century. Later, the UK, Germany, the US and France colonised the region and Australia and New Zealand were active as British proxies and in their own right. Chinese business entrepreneurs and labourers were present in the region from an early date.

These outsiders came as explorers and traders, as imperialists (with civil and military officials, and with force) and missionaries, as settlers and beachcombers. Their arrival was inevitable and their effects were equally so. External actors helped make the region what it is today to a large extent, both for good and for bad. That is, external actors improved security (through the provision of health care or education, for example, and the development of communications infrastructures) and they harmed security by introducing foreign diseases, cultural practices with no local foundation and by expropriating and alienating land and, often more importantly, the *mana* of traditional leaders. A mixed outcome.

If the external actors in the two or three centuries to the end of the colonial period were an inevitable result of the ability and desire of European states to explore and derive benefit from the exploration, then so too will the presence of external actors today be inevitable. The motivations might be different, the presence might be more in the control of local authorities and the effects might be different in detail, but overall external actors will provide both security and insecurity to the region. If the presence is inevitable, the aim for the region must be to maximise the benefits and minimise the costs.

The Big Picture
When we consider external actors at a macro level there are some useful indicators that place the region in relation to other similar regions. Development assistance itself, through OECD Official Development Assistance mechanisms, comes primarily from five metropolitan states: Australia (about USD 1041m in 2013), New Zealand (USD 225m), the US (USD 217m), Japan (USD 122m) ,France (USD 125m) and from European Union institutions (USD 94m) from a total of some

USD 2147m coming into the region.[1] These six sources thus provide nearly 85% of OECD development assistance to the region. On top of this, China was estimated to provide around USD 400m in financial assistance in 2011 which, if correct, would make it the second-largest aid provider.[2] A more longitudinal view of development assistance between 2006 and 2013 looks like this:[3]
1 Australia $6.831bn
2 United States $1.770bn
3 Japan $1.225bn
4 New Zealand $1.096bn
5 China $1.057bn

Aid as a percentage of GNI in 2009–2010 ranged from 2.6% in the case of Fiji to 48.6% for the Republic of the Marshall Islands, with an average of around 25% of GNI.[4] This is a significant level of external support to the region and points to economic security issues as the source and levels of the income are substantially outside regional control.

Most of the region is dependent on primary commodity exports and is thus particularly susceptible to externally derived price shocks. The region has been identified by the UNDP as being particularly vulnerable in this respect.[5] Cross-border trade is primarily external to the region. Of the total $310bn in cross border trade in 2102, only about 6% was intra-regional with most of the rest (74%) going to Asian markets, a relatively high percentage for a single region and another source of potential vulnerability.[6]

Migration and tourism, both inwards and external, are important to the region as it develops links with external actors and develops its own cultural communities in other countries. Visitor numbers to the region in 2011, for the countries for which data are available, were about 110% of the population. Clearly, there is much interaction with the wider world.[7] In terms of migration, the region is a net loser of population with up to 18 people per thousand being lost from Tonga in 2012.[8] This has a clear demographic security consequence for the affected states, but these emigrants are an important source of remittances to the region and these two factors with aid and the bureaucracy necessary to deal with it form the concept of 'MIRAB' as being central to the socio-economic system.[9] For the MIRAB states the effects of external factors are magnified, as migration, remittances, aid and the bureaucracy combine to form a significant component of household and national income with consequent effects on national resilience and regional security.

As migrants arrive in the region they are either assimilated effectively or remain slightly outside their host society. In the former case there are few security consequences, and those there are probably positive. In the latter case these 'foreign' communities may act as a focus for national discontent in difficult political, economic or social times. Events at different times in Fiji, the Solomon Islands, Tonga and Papua New Guinea against ethnic minority 'migrants' demonstrate that point.

These kinds of datasets give only a snapshot and the numbers can and do alter dramatically from year to year. But as a snapshot they demonstrate that the region deals with the external world in a number of ways and that its dealings are a source of both strength and vulnerability.

State Actors and their Interactions

Metropolitan states, the United States, Australia and New Zealand, were the colonial power for most of the region's states and political, economic and social links are still very close. Although their relationships and interactions within the sub-regions are different from one to the other, the countries are all 'first and automatic responders' in the case of regional natural disaster, provide financial and other material support through their aid programmes, act as the ultimate guarantors for military security and act as home for most of the region's emigrants. As well, Australian and New Zealand are members of the Pacific Islands Forum and play a significant role in the working of the Forum. France is still a colonial power, and as such a significant regional actor, but its territories are not members of the Forum.

It is a matter of perspective as to whether on balance the role played by these states has been constructive or destructive. It is safe to argue though, that without them the region would be quite different today from the way it is and probably that the region would be materially poorer.

In discussion of extra-regional states and their activities, much of the narrative is about 'geo-strategic competition'; the ways the major external actors compete with each other for influence, access to resources, or status, in the region.[10] Competition is in reality limited and the situation may better be described as a mixture of 'tension and accommodation, cooperation and competition'.[11] This activity may affect the region positively or negatively. What can be said is that it is generally done without significant consideration of the region's own needs.

Individual states have specific relationships with the region.

Australia

Australia is an original member of the Pacific Islands' Forum (then the South Pacific Forum), is the dominant aid provider to the region, primarily to Melanesia and especially Papua New Guinea, and sees itself as the source, in military terms, of much of the region's security needs, although again primarily within Melanesia. Australia works closely with Papua New Guinea especially to improve the functioning of government agencies through partnering and mentoring arrangements between Australian institutions and their PNG counterparts.[12] These activities, which began in the early 2000s as the 'Enhanced Cooperation Programme' might well be seen as a model for the development of robust and effective national government, which is a necessary component of any security system, but there are many difficulties involved in the practical arrangements and the results are mixed.[13] Indeed, the initial Australian Federal Police mentoring mission lasted only eight months following a Papua New Guinea high court ruling in May 2005 that the status of the Australian police officers was unconstitutional. The police were immediately withdrawn, but returned to PNG in 2013, although now acting purely in an advisory role without police executive powers.[14]

Australia has been described as doing the 'heavy lifting' in the Pacific region; certainly for Melanesia and perhaps Polynesia, and as such makes a significant contribution to regional security.[15] Australia was the lead state for the regional intervention in the Solomon Islands (albeit after some years of rejecting Solomon Islands requests for assistance) and will most likely continue to lead (*de facto* if not *de jure*) any future military interventions in Melanesia if they were to be necessary, if only because the preponderance of resources for any intervention will come from Australia.

As well as its development assistance programme, Australia (and New Zealand, France and the US) has an active military assistance programme with the region. Australia's programme, the Defence Cooperation Programme (about A$31m in 2012–13),[16] focuses on training, capability development and, importantly, the Pacific Patrol Boat programme, which provides patrol boats to island states for fisheries protection purposes.

The major criticism of Australia and its relationship with the region is that it tends to see issues primarily from an Australian perspective and attempts to impose Australian preferred solutions to issues rather than allowing solutions to arrive by consensus: slower, less effective in the short term, but the 'Pacific Way'. This point is made in the title of a 2005 paper: 'the Pacific Way or Howard's Way?'[17] In part consequently: 'Around the region, people are questioning where the Pacific fits into Australia's priorities'.[18] No matter where its priorities lie, however, Australia must be counted as a net contributor to regional security.

New Zealand
Like Australia, New Zealand is an original member of the Forum and is a significant provider of development assistance to the region. New Zealand's attention is primarily focused on Polynesia, although unlike Australia, New Zealand spreads its aid more or less evenly throughout the region, in part because the Polynesian states are not able to absorb very large amounts aid. Also unlike Australia and its relationships with the Melanesian states, New Zealand has close cultural and social links with Polynesia.[19]

New Zealand does not see itself as a provider of significant military security; indeed does not see threats to Polynesia as requiring a military response (with the exception of providing regular maritime surveillance patrols by the RNZAF and RNZN throughout the island EEZs).[20] One minor exception to this was in 2006 when a small contingent of New Zealand troops and police (with Australian colleagues) was sent to Tonga, at the request of the Tongan government, to assist in restoring order following riots that had broken out following pro-democracy demonstrations. The troops left within several weeks. New Zealand has sent troops, with Australia, to Melanesian states the Solomon Islands and Papua New Guinea to assist in restoring security in those countries.

Perhaps because of both New Zealand's Maori population and the circumstances of New Zealand's colonisation and subsequent history (which has forced a national discussion about identity) and the significant Pacific community, New Zealand is often seen as more attuned to the 'Pacific way' than is Australia.[21] The reputation may be undeserved, but there is no doubt that it has allowed New Zealand to work with the region in ways Australia has found difficult. The most obvious example of this was during the truce monitoring process on Bougainville between Bougainville separatists and the PNG government in 1997. New Zealand was able to lead the initial truce support intervention because it was trusted by the protagonists in a way that Australia was not, although Australia subsequently took the lead role in the peace monitoring group from mid-1998.

United States
The United States, like Australia and New Zealand in 'their' sub-regions, focuses much of its attention on one part of the region: Micronesia. The Micronesian states all have 'Free Association' status with the United States through what is known as a 'Compact of Free Association'. Compact status gives the citizens of these states access to many US domestic programmes and their countries receive significant financial aid as a matter of law rather than policy. For its part the US has more or less free access for its armed forces and the armed forces of other states are precluded from access without US permission. The US has formal responsibility for the military security of these states and for administering their international defence relationships. This is all significant because of the compact states' location in the western Pacific.

There is concern in some quarters that the compact states themselves and the US also do not adhere to either the spirit or the letter of the compact treaties and thus by their respective actions are diminishing rather than enhancing security as the compact states fail to achieve the compact purposes and goals of economic advancement, budgetary self-sufficiency and political autonomy.[22] Another perspective on the relationship between the US and the compact states is that of 'patron and client' in which the client gives away elements of autonomy, even sovereignty, in return for being able to pressure the patron for benefits that would otherwise not be obtainable.[23] Perceptions of security here depend to some extent on which factors are privileged in the analysis.

China
China is the extra-regional state most often agonised over. Its specific foreign policy objectives generally conform to those of other large states in the desire for stability and proper relationships.[24] As such, its aims could be held by any state in almost any environment. Perhaps the practice is more problematic than the aims themselves?

China provides significant, although unquantified, amounts of 'untied' aid to the region in ways that western states often see as counterproductive. The fear (normally not expressed publicly by Western officials but a continuing subtext of private conversation) is that China will replace Australia, New Zealand and the US as the significant regional power and will somehow subvert the region to conform to a Chinese world view. These worries are probably over-stressed. China's relationship with the region is seen by some as being different in kind from that of the western metropolitan power in that it is in part an expression of 'South-South solidarity', ensuring, according to China, that the region does not have to continue to suffer from the west's colonial instincts. China as a victim of colonialism itself is different in kind according to its own world view.[25]

Generally, China's activities are conducted in terms of the soft power activities of diplomacy (both political and defence), economics and aid rather than through a formal hard power military presence. China's aid programme has been most scrutinised and the general conclusion often is that the aid is intended to have a public relations impact, but that it is often not delivered either effectively or efficiently. That conclusion cannot be carried completely across the region however, as different recipients have different experiences and in Samoa, for example, development assistance has met expectations.

In summary, China has few if any direct strategic interests in the region, no hard power levers and little soft power influence. What influence it does have is based on its aid and economic relationships, which are of variable quality even if locally appreciated because of the autonomy they give the recipient state.[26]

Japan

Japan's main relationships with the region are economic, in the form of aid, and the search for political influence. The search for influence is probably a higher priority than assisting in economic development. In 2014 the draft of a new ODA Charter discusses aid in terms of 'national interest', 'security' and 'defence', and is seen by some analysts as a strategic move to curb 'China's rising influence.[27]

Japan hosts an annual leaders' summit, the Pacific Islands Leaders Meeting, which has been held three-yearly since 1997. These meetings focus on issues important to the region: fisheries; the environment; climate change; and sustainable development, but are not central to regional security in either the traditional or non-traditional sense. The best that can be said for the meetings is that they do no harm and may do some good.

France

France has a continuing relationship with the region through its territories and dependencies, which is where its aid budget is mostly directed. France cooperates with Australia, New Zealand and the United States in the delivery of regional aid to ensure that projects do not overlap. France's main contribution to wider regional security will be shown through the way it handles the different demands for independence and autonomy in New Caledonia, French Polynesia and Wallis and Futuna.

Indonesia
Indonesia's role as an external actor is primarily through its incorporation of Papua (previously Irian Jaya) as an Indonesian province. The Free Papua Movement (OPM) argues that the province should gain full autonomy as an independent state, probably within a Pacific context, but OPM has not been able to gather full support within the province let alone make headway with the Jakarta government. This is a border security issue for Papua New Guinea and for those within Oceania who believe the region should support the independence movement. There is little evidence that the regional political groupings, Pacific Islands Forum or the Melanesian Spearhead Group, are prepared to support Papuan independence.[28]

Conclusion: External Actors and Possible Security Solutions
Many of the region's security issues are home-grown and relate to human security, economic security, good governance and similar issues. To an extent these are a consequence of globalisation and relations with the wider world and as such cannot be wished away. Because of the region's lack of resources, external actors will be a large part of the solution. But external actors cannot be the whole solution. The region itself has to decide how it wants to develop and what needs to be done to achieve its development goals. Only when this has been determined will outside states be in a sensible position to help the region help itself.

External states can provide assistance to the region to allow the region to help itself. That assistance needs to be: relevant; proportionate; sustainable; and based around capacity building. External states should however do no more than provide assistance. They should not do the operational work themselves unless the activities are clearly beyond the region's capacity, such as in the provision of long-range maritime surveillance operations. Other examples of effective assistance models might include Australian, New Zealand and US support to the Pacific Transnational Crime Network, established through the long-standing Pacific Chiefs of Police Conference, or Australia's Enhanced Cooperation Programme with Papua New Guinea.

The development of effective regional institutions, provision of resources (of people, material and financial), and a regional culture that allows the institutions to be effective will be a very long-term project. It is a project that is necessary, and the question of how to manage external actors most effectively is one that should occupy the minds of regional leaders, both political and official. Part of the solution will be organisational and part cultural. All of the solution should be led by the region itself.

Notes

1. Derived from OECD data tables 'Aid disbursements to countries and regions', stats.oecd.org accessed 10 February 2015. The Fiji figure could be distorted because of the effect of sanctions against the then military government.
2. Jenny Hayward-Jones, 'Australia-the indispensable power in a congested sea', Presentation delivered to the Royal United Services Institute's 2nd International Defence and Security Dialogue, National Maritime Museum, Sydney, 26 February 2013., p. 3. http://www.lowyinstitute.org/files/hayward_jones_australia_the_indispensable_power.pdf, accessed 10 February 2015.
3. Philippa Brant, 'Chinese Aid in the Pacific', *Regional Snapshot*, Sydney: Lowy Institute for Public Policy, February 2015. http://www.lowyinstitute.org/files/chinese_aid_in_the_pacific_regional_snapshot_0.pdf, accessed 2 March 2015.
4. Secretariat of the Pacific Community, 'National Minimum Development Indicators', http://www.spc.int/nmdi/mdg8, accessed 2 February 2015.
5. UNDP, *op. cit.*, p. 7
6. McKinsey and Company, *Mckinsey on Payments*, 'Insights into the dynamics of new trade flows', May 2014. http://www.mckinsey.com/insights, accessed 4 February 2015.
7. Derived from population and visitor data in Secretariat of the Pacific Community, *Pocket Statistical Summary*, SPC: New Caledonia, 2013.
8. Index Mundi, http://www.indexmundi.com/map/?v=27&r=oc&l=en, accessed 5 February 2015.
9. Richard P. C. Brown et al, 'Migrants' Remittances, Poverty and Social Protection in the South Pacific: Fiji and Tonga', *Population, Space and Place*, 20 (5) July 2014, pp. 434–454,
10. See for example, Jenny Hayward-Jones, 'Big Enough for all of us: Geo-Strategic Competition in the Pacific Islands', *Analysis*, Sydney: Lowy Institute for International Policy, May 2013; Steven Ratuva, 'A New Regional Cold War? American and Chinese Posturing in the Pacific', *Asia and the Pacific Policy Studies*, 1 (2), 409–422, 2014.
11. Ratuva, *op. cit.*, p. 409.
12. Rowan Callick, 'Australian scheme to boost governance in Papua New Guinea', *The Australian*, 12 February 2015.
13. Allan Patience, 'Discussion Paper 2005/4', *State, Society and Governance in Melanesia*, Canberra: ANU, Research School of Pacific and Asian Studies, 2005; Penelope Murphy, 'PNG Australia Economic and Public Sector Governance Twinning Initiative Phase 1', *Independent Completion Report*, AidWorks Initiative Number ING860 and INI785, Canberra, May 2010.
14. Vandra Harris, 'Building on sand? Australian police involvement in international police capacity building', *Policing and Society*, 20 (1), March 2010, pp. 79–98.
15. Stephen Hoadley, 'Pacific Island Security by New Zealand and Australia: Towards a New Paradigm', *Working Paper 20/05*, Wellington: Centre for Strategic Studies, 2005, p. 14.
16. Australian Government, Department of Defence, 'Table W3.2: South Pacific Region Expenditure', *Annual Report 2012-2013*, Canberra: Department of Defence, 2013.
17. Gregor Allan, 'South Pacific security & the emerging doctrine of 'cooperative intervention': the Pacific way or Howard's way?', *Rhizome*, 1, 2005, pp. 125–144. Howard was of course the Australian Prime Minister from 1996–2007. It should also be noted that the 'Pacific Way' is ignored by Pacific leaders when it suits them.
18. Nic Maclellan, 'Look out Australia, the Pacific mood is shifting', *The Interpreter*, Lowy Institute, 4 February 2015. www.lowyinterpreter.org/post/2015/02/04/australia-pacific-mood-shifting.aspx?COLLCC=1507189444&, accessed 13 February 2015.
19. Some 7.4% of the New Zealand population in 2013 identified as 'Pacific peoples'. Of these, nearly 66% lived in Auckland, and the growth for the Pacific population from 2006–2013 was more than 11%. Source: Statistics New Zealand, 'Pacific people's ethnic group', http://www.stats.govt.nz/Census/2013-census/profile-and-summary-reports/quickstats-culture-identity/pacific-peoples.aspx, accessed 12 February 2015.

20 Australia also conducts regional surveillance patrols and Australia and New Zealand coordinate their activities in this field.
21 As early as 1900 New Zealand was seen as more closely linked to the Pacific Islands than to the 'ogre' Australia as seen in a cartoon of the time showing a maidenly New Zealand rejecting the Australian ogre in favour of a Pacific Island youth: http://www.teara.govt.nz/en/cartoon/33125/different-race-relations.
22 See for example, Compact Review Committee, Federated States of Micronesia, *Five Year Review of the Amended Compact of Free Association*, Pohnpei: Federated States of Micronesia, June 2011; P.R. Sauer, 'No Nation Is an Island: Navigating the Troubled Waters Between Indigenous Values and Donor Desire in the Republic of the Marshall Islands', *Globalization, International Education Policy and Local Policy Formation: Policy Implications of Research in Education*, Volume 5, 2015, pp 131–142; and Keola K. Diaz, 'The Compact of Free Association (COFA): A History of Failures', unpublished MA paper, University of Hawaii, Manoa, 2012. http://scholarspace.manoa.hawaii.edu/bitstream/handle/10125/24265/Diaz_2012_r.pdf?sequence=1, accessed 16 February 2015.
23 Wouter P. Veenendaal, 'Analyzing the Foreign Policy of Microstates: The Relevance of the International Patron-Client Model', *Foreign Policy Analysis*, 2014, pp. 1–17.
24 Evan S. Medeiros, 'China's International Behavior: Activism, Opportunism and Diversification', *Joint Force Quarterly*, 47 (4), 2007, 36–37; and Ministry of Foreign Affairs of the PRC, 'Xi Jinping Holds Group Meeting with Leaders of Pacific Island Countries and Delivers a Keynote Speech . . . ', 22 November 2014. http://www.fmprc.gov.cn/mfa_eng/topics_665678/xjpzxcxesgjtldrdjcfhdadlyxxlfjjxgsfwbttpyjjdgldrhw/t1214281.shtml, accessed 9 February 2015.
25 Marc Lanteigne, 'China, the West and 'Soft Balancing' in the South Pacific', *The China Story*, Australian Centre on China in the World, 16 March 2013. www.thechinastory.org/2013/china-the-west-and-soft-blaancing-in-the-south-pacific/. Accessed 28 January 2015.
26 Jian Yang, 'China in the South Pacific: A Strategic Threat?', *Asia:NZ Foundation*, http://asianz.org.nz/sites/asianz.org.nz/files/China%20in%20the%20SthPacific_DrJianYang.pdf. Accessed 9 February 2015.
27 Purendra Jain, 'The Politics of Japan's New Aid Charter', *East Asia Forum*, 15 December 2014. http://www.eastasiaforum.org/2014/12/15/japans-new-aid-charter-shifts-into-domestic-and-regional-political-arena/, accessed 28 January 2015.
28 Radio New Zealand International, 'Mixed reaction to MSG's response to West Papua group', *Dateline Pacific*, 7 July 2014. http://www.radionz.co.nz/international/programmes/datelinepacific/audio/2602236/mixed-reaction-to-msg's-response-to-west-papua-group, accessed 2 March 2015.

4. CHINESE IN THE PACIFIC

Dr Damon Salesa

Chinese–Samoan Interactions – Influences Both Ways: Entangled and Intimate Histories

Associate Professor Toeolesulusulu Damon Salesa
Head of Pacific Studies, University of Auckland

Found at the bottom of Samoa's shallow waters, the 'bêche de mer', sea slug or lōli had always been a humble creature, not much in demand amongst Samoans. But in the early 1800s this modest creature underwent a boom in value. Traders came from across the world to collect what became perhaps the first commercial-level commodities extracted from Samoa. These lōli were collected in Samoan waters largely for sale in Chinese markets, but not by Chinese ships or workers, rather by Europeans and North Americans. Like sandalwood and whale oil, 'bêche de mer' (or 'trepang' as it was sometimes called) was a commodity driving a new kind of Samoan (and Pacific) economy from the late 1700s. (Bêche de mer was collected on the largest scale in Fiji).[1] Through these developing commercial relationships the draw of the Asian economy – largely meaning the Chinese economy – was experienced in Samoa very quickly, and was to have a lasting and critical effect on Samoa.

The lōli was symbolic of a deep Samoan engagement with Asia that was not dependent on engaging directly with Asian peoples. This had been the case since the arrival of the first non-Polynesian ships to arrive off the coast of Samoa in 1722. These were ships captained by Jacob Roggeveen who was, revealingly, in the service of the Dutch East India Company. From the very beginning then, a key driver behind the European engagement with Samoa was intrinsically tied to Asia. (Which was true, also, of the Spanish presence in the Pacific, which had long been deeply connected to this Asian economy). Samoa – and the Pacific more generally – had a deep structural engagement with Asia before it had an obvious human or social engagement. Before many Samoans and Asians had even met, their markets had.

The distant connections that materialised in sandalwood, whale oil and bêche de mer were indicative of global shifts in trade and geopolitics, new markets and connections. In these shifts the Pacific Islands, including Samoa, were small but indispensable elements. The larger parts of these networks have been well studied, which allows us to see the development of global trade, and recently the centrality of Asia in these developments has been far better appreciated. We could do with such re-examinations of Pacific developments in trade and economy in this period, but the contours of these relationships are clear. Comparatively low volume, specialty items like bêche de mer, were only one part of Samoa's connections with Asia, although they were the most direct. Also shaping these engagements with Asia was Samoa's role in the Pacific energy boom (in the form of whaling and whale oil), and the Pacific's role as a key pathway for global trade – making it a hotbed of militarisation and security. The powerful magnetism of East Asia sat behind so many American and European endeavours, from the Manila Galleons to the US trade with Asia.

I am now in the second year of a project funded by the Royal Society of New Zealand's Marsden Fund: 'The Transformation of Everyday Life in Samoa (1800–2000)'. This project looks at two hundred years of large-scale, but ordinary, transformations in Samoa, particularly relating to social, technological, environmental and economic change. This current talk stems from part of that Marsden project. By focusing on the quotidian dimensions of Samoan life, rather than on 'politics' as most Samoan history has, many familiar topics can be re-examined anew. In this way it is striking to consider the place of Asian (especially Chinese) people and things in these everyday changes in Samoa.

People's ordinary experiences of life often drive structural change, or change in larger scales. It is also in these ordinary dimensions where changes are felt most, and might be witnessed most clearly. This has not always been helped by historical writing, which has been organised largely by focusing on individual Pacific nations or archipelagoes. It has been exacerbated by the dominant focus on governments and high politics. Many of the key experiences and key sources of human energy and development, as I have suggested, do not exist in, or overflow, those frames.

I began with the lōli as it is helps imagine a different kind of beginning for a shared Chinese and Samoan history. Typically, when people have investigated Asia in the Pacific and particularly the Chinese in Samoa, the beginning has been with the indentured workers, or the few lone Asian settlers who preceded them. That is understandable, but it works to disguise a deeper set of origins that link Asia and the Pacific and which are felt in Samoa. This has two analytical follow-ons. One, it helps us understand these deeper origins that are mediated initially through a third set of actors – Europeans. Second, it allows us to uncover the reach of Asia into Samoa, and the early ways in which they were entangled. These views deserve more consideration, as they in many ways foreshadow some of the key relationships the Pacific and Asia currently entertain.

In some ways the economic shifts Samoa experienced in the 1800s were more marked than the later changes Samoa experienced with the arrival of Chinese workers. These 19th-century economic changes were unprecedented; they represented not just the linking of local and distant markets but in some ways the actual beginning of a Samoan 'market'. By the time Chinese came in substantial numbers to Samoa, as indentured labourers, Samoa had long been a cosmopolitan society within their Pacific neighbourhood of Tonga, Uvea and Fiji. In addition to these groups, and different varieties of Papalagi, from the late 1880s there had been thousands who had come to work in Samoa from the Gilberts, Niue and Melanesia. This context of mobility from many different peoples, in a larger setting of economic change, is where Asian migration to Samoa fits in.

But the importance of Chinese migration to Samoa is unusual in the Pacific, and it should not be understated. During most of the time that the western part of Samoa was under the rule of the Germans, there were often more Chinese in Samoa than there were Papalagi (whites/Europeans). The influence we often imagine that Papalagi had in Samoa needs to be properly contextualised. While Papalagi were undoubtedly ascendant in what was often an intrusive and powerful colonialism (whether American, German or New Zealand), they did not have nearly as much control over the various kinds of ordinary exchanges that were occurring in everyday Samoa, especially the kinds of transformation that were being intimately experienced by Samoans.

Like the lōli, other instances of Chinese–Samoan connections come from the most ordinary, yet most important dimensions of Samoan life: diet and agriculture. Keke puaʻa (pork buns) and sapasui (Samoan chop suey) are two of many such Chinese-influenced staples in Samoan meals. In Samoa, as elsewhere, Chinese market gardeners and growers were renowned for their productivity and their ability to work previously marginal land, and in Samoa the few who were working as independent growers had similar reputations. A marker of this agricultural innovation is one of the flavours of contemporary Samoa, aniani saina ('Chinese onion' – garlic); there are also many accounts of Chinese farmers 'breaking in' new land.

Influentially, Ron Crocombe asked in 2007 whether Asia was replacing the West in the Pacific.[2] This question becomes far more complex when one focuses not on the actions of empires and states, but on the kinds of workings of ordinary life and more quotidian developments as suggested above. First, as lōli and sapasui demonstrate, the East and the West – Asia and Europe/America – were *already* interpolated. Second, as we have seen in Samoa as in some other Pacific locations, the Pacific had long been home to large Asian populations, in more than a few cases far larger than the European populations claiming colonial ascendancy. Rather than a case where Asia was replacing the West, in many ways the two had been entangled for decades, even centuries.

The experiences of Chinese indentured labourers have been relatively well studied. In this conference we have welcomed another distinguished contribution to this literature from Tuatagaloa Aumua Ming Leung Wai. His account, which sits in a genealogy of powerful stories of Samoan and Chinese connections, demonstrates the kind of enduring and intimate connections produced at a time, and in places, where they were established against multiple efforts to prevent them.[3] In a sense these families are one of the enduring legacies of colonialism, even of colonialisms that sought to prevent them.

When governing Samoa, New Zealand both developed and expressed views that had long been part of domestic New Zealand politics. Like Australia, New Zealand had strong restrictions specifically targeted at Chinese people, and whose purpose was to keep New Zealand white.[4] The first New Zealand administrator of Samoa, predictably, had a deep dislike and distrust of Chinese workers: consequently many of his proclamations, and those of his successors, disproportionately targeted Chinese. This included a notorious proclamation that banned not just marriage between Chinese workers and Samoan women but banned Chinese workers from being in Samoan residences.

These ordinary human relationships were ordered by, but also gave order to larger politics, as can be seen in the attempts to regulate and discipline intimate relationships. There were sustained and energetic efforts by German, and then New Zealand officials, to make it illegal for Chinese and Samoans to marry. Chinese or Samoans caught cohabiting could be prosecuted, and many were. Their commitment to these principles ensured that there were prosecutions of some of those who were married. An extraordinary amount of government energy was devoted to this problem. Colonial officials thought the consequences were real and high; that the future of the Pacific, and particularly the Samoan race, was at stake. While long-held views about the Chinese coloured the views of officials, animating these decisions was much more than mere base racial animosity. For New Zealanders the commitment to keep Samoans and Chinese apart was also of strategic concern. If Chinese people were permitted to remain in large numbers in Samoa, the future of Samoa would be forever changed – and indeed the future of New Zealand.

Intimate and personal concerns, such as interracial intimacy, could animate statecraft and policy. The reverse was equally true: these marriages, which we might see simply as private or intimate concerns, were subject to strategic, governmental and international interventions. In this sense intimate relations were not distant from or beneath explicitly political or strategic concerns, but interwoven with them: the intimate and strategic interacted in ways where they could be fruitfully understood as 'strategic intimacy.'[5]

The larger point is not to see this intersection of the intimate and strategic as exceptional. Certainly in Samoa's history, we see huge investments by empires and colonial governments into governing, interfering, intervening in intimate relationships because they think the stakes are so high. Around Samoa today we can see similar kinds of developments. In my research I have found another such set of intersections in opium smuggling in Samoa, which we might see as a precursor to the kind of alarmism around international crime. The kinds of opium smuggling cases that came before Samoan courts were models of a kind of ordinary cosmopolitanism. In cases I have analysed Fijians, Samoans, Chinese, men and women alike worked together to smuggle opium into Samoa; an ordinary cosmopolitanism worrying to colonial officials for both its illegality and its interracial cooperation.

Intimate and family histories instruct about the power of families and individuals to cross – and adhere across – states, governments and scales. Such histories, and the histories of the influence of Asian markets and Chinese workers, show that the ordinary dimensions of people and their lives, and their things, will often be decisive.

Tuatagaloa's account, here, is revealing. What he called 'the fourth generation' or 'the new Chinese', carry in their ordinary lives a defining capability: how they conduct themselves with Samoans, and particularly how Samoans understand that behaviour will have large-scale, even strategic ramifications. The future of Chinese-Samoan relations may well lie less in questions of state policy or strategic alignment, or concessionary loans, and more in the kind of affinities and ties forged in the bounds of these peoples' lives.[6]

In this conference one of the emerging themes has been around questions of Islander or indigenous agency in international affairs. In Pacific history such questions about agency have been long standing and perennial ones. And while, predictably, historians have provided no definitive answers, one of the outcomes of taking these questions seriously has been a transformation in methods (to foreground indigenous actors and archives) and a deep broadening of the stories and analyses that scholars produce. Given how narrow many of the analyses of international politics sometimes seem, and how constrained some of our ways of representing these analyses remain, it is easy to see potential. The challenge is the opportunity: to widen the horizons of our analyses so that they can fully comprehend the scope of people's humanity and cultures. The horizons are indeed broad: from lōli – gathered in Samoa and turned into commodities for Asian markets – via sapasui, a Chinese food reworked into an indigenised Samoan food – to the Samoan families made by Samoan women and their Chinese partners.

Notes

1 Ward, R. Gerard, *The Pacific bêche-de-mer trade with special reference to Fiji*, Oxford: Oxford University Press, 1972.
2 Ron Crocombe, *Asia in the Pacific Islands: Replacing the West*, Suva, University of the South Pacific, 2007.
3 Liua'ana, Ben Featuna'i, 'Dragons in little paradise: Chinese (Mis-) Fortunes in Samoa, 1900–1950', *The Journal of Pacific History* 32, no. 1 (1997): 29–48; Nancy Y.W. Tom, *The Chinese in Western Samoa 1875-1985: The Dragon Came from Afar*, Western Samoa Historical and Cultural Trust, 1986; John A. Moses, 'The coolie labour question and German colonial policy in Samoa, 1900–1914', *The Journal of Pacific History* 8, no. 1 (1973): 101–124.
4 P.S. O'Connor, 'Keeping New Zealand White, 1908–1920', *New Zealand Journal of History* 2, no. 1 (1968): 41–65; Manying Ip, 'Chinese immigrants and transnationals in New Zealand: A fortress opened', *The Chinese Diaspora: Space, Place, Mobility and Identity*, Lanham, Rowman and Littlefield (2003): 339–358.
5 D. Salesa, 'Samoa's Half-Castes and Some Frontiers of Comparison', *Tense and Tender Ties: Race and Empire in North American History*, Ann Laura Stoler, ed., Durham: Duke University Press (2004), 72–93.
6 In the week prior to the conference the 2014 Citizen Investment Bill was debated in the Samoan parliament. In debate there were two widely reported points of contention which rested on very intimate, personal matters. One of them concerned the ownership of a particular store in Vailele, and whether it was it owned by a Samoan and operated by a Samoan, or owned by a Samoan and operated by a Chinese. The other directly raised the questions to whom a certain prominent Chinese businessman was married.

China in the Pacific: Alternative Perspectives

Dr Iati Iati
Lecturer, Department of Politics, University of Otago, Dunedin

Introduction
Perspectives about China's presence in the Pacific, including Samoa, are dominated by scholars. What is largely absent from discussions about what to make of China's and Chinese presence in the Pacific are the perspectives of ordinary people. Yet, ordinary people are just as important to this discussion as scholars, if not more so. Chinese engagement with the region will, to a large extent, be determined by the politics in this region, and politics is still largely localised. When faced with pressing issues, ordinary people can and will make their voices heard. Riots in places such as the Solomon Islands, Tonga, and Papua New Guinea are blatant reminders of this. And ultimately ordinary people will be the most affected by China's or the Chinese presence in the region. This paper addresses this gap in the literature.

This paper is largely based on field research undertaken in Samoa in January and February, 2015. Fifty participants were asked about their views about the presence of the Chinese government and Chinese in Samoa. Although this was a rather small sample, some key points clearly came across. These include the recognition and appreciation of Chinese development assistance and their impact on lowering prices for consumer goods and construction, but also suspicion of Chinese motives and frustration and fear about the possibility of Chinese domination of the business sector. Mixed with this was a concern that the rise in Chinese numbers could be related to recent legislation that undermines safeguards for people's customary land rights. The paper argues that the geopolitical considerations that dominate the discourse about China's presence in Samoa are significantly detached from the views of ordinary people.

China in the Pacific: Dominant Perspectives

The Threat Discourse and Its Discontents
China's presence in the Pacific has solicited considerable attention from the scholarly community. In addition to examining the nature of China's presence, scholarly discussion and debate have focussed on two key questions: why is China here, and what impact will it have? The answers to these questions have generally fallen into two categories, which could be described as the 'threat discourse', and its counter-narratives.

The 'threat discourse' has two notable features. First, China's presence in the region is motivated by its rivalry with Taiwan; both are seeking diplomatic recognition from Pacific Island countries in order to strengthen their standing as the legitimate government of China, and to deprive the other of this position. Consequently, the betterment of the region is a secondary consideration. Thus, whatever benefits they may provide through aid and trade opportunities are treated with suspicion. Negative connotations, such as 'chequebook diplomacy', are often associated with Chinese aid.[1] Second, China's presence is motivated by a desire to fill a 'big power' vacuum in the region that has developed in the post-Cold War period. An extension of this argument is that China is now competing with the United States to be the 'pre-eminent power in the Pacific Ocean'[2]. Like the first feature, the benefits of China's presence are treated with caution because they serve an ulterior motive. The threat discourse presents China's presence in the region as something that Western and Pacific Island countries should be wary of.

The threat discourse has a counter-narrative, which manifests in at least two ways. First, it acknowledges that rivalries and tensions between China and Taiwan, and China and the United States, exist, but argues that China's role is not unexpected from a rising power in world affairs. Furthermore, China's growing presence in the region follows an unsurprising trajectory of major (and minor) power evolution[3]; major Western powers have been as expansionist in their rise to the top. Second, the counter-narrative provides different explanations for some of the key arguments within the threat discourse. For example, the lack of conditionality attached to Chinese aid is explained as respect for sovereignty and that China adheres to a different model for development to that followed by Western countries.[4] Furthermore, China is just as if not more genuine in its desire to help Pacific Island countries develop.

The threat discourse and its discontents present a useful analysis of why China is in the region and what its impact will be. However, in terms of its impact, these are blatantly deficient. How will China's presence impact on relations between the state and society, and within society itself? To be sure, these kinds of issues are touched on tangentially, such as when the Honiara riots are connected to a public backlash against perceived collusions between corrupt government officials and the Taiwanese. However, these lack any analytical depth, and are few and far between.

It is important to examine China's impact on relations within society itself and between the state and society. The Pacific is comprised of relatively new states that are struggling to adapt appropriately the democratic political frameworks that colonial administrations and the United Nations imposed on them. Even relatively stable countries like Samoa have had their fair share of problems, and these have been linked to difficulties in making the Westminster system of democracy work.

These problems stem from the inappropriateness of Western political systems for most Pacific societies.[5]. Most Pacific Island countries are still coming to terms with what the relationship between the state and society should be within these systems. The imposition of a central government on once decentralised societies and political systems has reconfigured relationships between leaders and followers, in some cases creating new categories of elites. Moreover, there is not one country in the region whose boundaries are congruent with pre-colonial ethnic groups. All, in varying degrees, are an agglomeration of different ethnic, linguistic, and racial groups, or were once part of one or more of these. At one stage more than half of Fiji's population were indentured labourers from India. Surprisingly, societal relations have remained relatively peaceful despite this. However, there are issues in relation to political and economic equality in many Pacific countries which can aggravate these divisions, resulting in crisis situations. The Pacific is made up of volatile nations, nation-states, states and societies.

China's increasing presence in the Pacific particularly complicates relationships between these countries and former colonial powers. Since Pacific Island countries gained independence, former metropolitan powers have been their main development partners. Specific development programmes focus on good governance objectives. There is a complex relationship between them as aid recipients and donors; the latter can be seen as development partners and benefactors, and/or as neo-colonialists using aid to leverage their policies in the region. China's presence, particularly as an aid donor, complicates these relationships because its aid is not subject to the conditions imposed by Western donors. China's aid is thought to undermine the objectives of Western donors and lessen their control over Pacific Island countries. Relationships between traditional partners and Pacific countries are complicated by China's presence as it eases pressure on Pacific Island countries to meet the conditions traditional donors seek to impose.

China, Chinese and Samoa

Chinese have been coming to Samoa since the end of the 19th century. The first main movement began in 1903, when the German Governor, Wilhelm Solf, authorised the recruitment of Chinese labourers to work on German-owned plantations in Samoa. Under the German Administration, from 1900 to 1914, approximately 3,868 Chinese entered Samoa. Following 1914, New Zealand continued the programme bringing a further 3,116 Chinese to Samoa. The majority were eventually repatriated to China. Over a 1,000 remained in Samoa, and many if not all of these integrated into Samoa society, taking Samoan spouses, and becoming part of Samoan extended families. Many have also helped family members from China migrate to Samoa.[6]

This paper is principally concerned with these later migrants and with subsequent waves of Chinese migration, particularly the latest wave which has been associated with China's recent push into the Pacific.

Among Pacific Island countries, Samoa has one of the longest and most enduring relationships with China. Diplomatic ties were established in 1975, a few days after China and Fiji established diplomatic relations. Exchanges between Samoa and China in the 1970s and 1980s mainly involved strengthening social, cultural and education ties.[7] After the Cold War, diplomatic relations strengthened, particularly after Samoa showed surprising support for China over incidents that drew international condemnation for the latter. In 1989, for example, Samoan Prime Minister Tofilau Eti was one of the first foreign leaders to make an official visit to China following the Tiananmen Square protests.[8] The strengthening of relations has encouraged further migration of Chinese to Samoa, and these are 'full-blooded Chinese' whose migration has less to do with family considerations and more to do with business interests. Leung Wai[9] refers to them as 'full-blooded Chinese who do not have relatives in Samoa'.

Government statistics about the number of Chinese in Samoa have been very difficult to obtain. (Personal interviews, Samoa, Jan–Feb 2015.) But some figures have been obtained from other sources. According to Leung Wai[10], the Government of Samoa issued 1,573 permits to Chinese to enter Samoa for various purposes, mostly business related. These have been made possible, encouraged and/or facilitated by closer Samoa–China relations. This group is very distinguishable; even Chinese from the earlier migration make this point, often criticising the latest lot for their business practices, and lack of integration and respect for such things as the Samoan culture.[11] These Chinese are the focus of the interviews and alternative perspectives discussed in this paper.

Alternative Perspectives

China and Chinese in Samoa: The Positives

A number of interviewed participants talked positively about the presence of Chinese from recent migrations. Most of these participants lived in urban areas and had spent time living overseas, in developed Western countries. The one participant who had not lived overseas was not as enthusiastic about the presence of Chinese. Those who had lived overseas were much more enthusiastic. Most of these participants shared another commonality; they all benefited directly from Chinese businesses. They frequented Chinese shops, and one had employed a Chinese construction company. These characteristics are interesting to note, but cautiously, given the small number of participants involved in this study.

Participants who spoke positively highlighted a number of points. First, Chinese businesses kept prices low in the retail and construction industries, largely by stimulating competition. One participant noted that there had been somewhat of a monopoly in the construction industry before companies like Shanghai Construction came on the scene.

Also, Chinese construction companies do not adhere to cultural protocols, and clients have benefited as a result. Participants noted that a significant drawback in using local companies has been the cultural expectations that filter into a business relationship. Cultural obligations are often placed on the clients of Samoan companies, such as having to take care of workers by providing food, gift exchanges and so forth. By and large, the general view among participants in this category is that cultural protocols and expectations are burdensome. They noted their increased lack of toleration for the 'special obligations', because more often than not, these were an extra burden on top of the price they paid for the goods and services. Chinese companies do not require the observance of cultural protocols; the relationship is strictly business.

This has interesting implications for culture. Culture may be squeezed out of this sphere, or at least modified to accommodate change. In general, Chinese companies have a reputation for completing projects within a shorter time frame than non-Chinese companies, and culture and religion or the lack of these are contributing factors.

The quality of Chinese products and work has received attention in some literature. The participants that spoke positively of the Chinese presence considered this a non-issue.

The Chinese appear to have a genuine desire to help Samoa develop. One particular example referred to was the agricultural projects run by Chinese in the village of Nu'u. A Chinese farming venture was initiated on plots of land that many considered non-arable. Apparently it has proven successful and is now a produce source for local markets.

Even if Chinese had ulterior motives, such as gaining economic ascendancy over Samoans, laws are in place to prevent or at least hinder this. One participant, who holds a high position in government, noted that regardless of whether Chinese do have ambitions to 'take over Samoa', this would be very difficult given the safeguards in place to prevent this. Only citizens are allowed to establish a business outside of the urban area, which currently stretches between the villages of Vailele and Vaitele. Chinese, therefore, would not be able to operate their businesses in the rural villages. This is meant to safeguard local businesses, many of which are small grocery stores.

China and Chinese in Samoa: The Negatives

A majority of the interviewed participants expressed a negative outlook on the presence of Chinese. Many of the participants in this group had not lived overseas, and most lived in urban areas, and had strong ties to their villages. Their perspectives included:

Too Many, Too Fast?

Concern exists over what appears to be a sudden rise in the number of Chinese in Samoa. Unfortunately, reliable statistics are not available.

Nevertheless, the apparently rapid increase in Chinese is causing curiosity, suspicion and insecurity. One of the most common questions asked of us was 'what is behind the Chinese assistance?' Most participants were suspicious that China had motives other than simply helping Samoa. 'What was their motive?' The participants generally believed that the motto/principle – 'there is no such thing as a free lunch' – was applicable to the aid and in particular the big Chinese-funded projects. Many believed that Samoa would one day have to pay for the Chinese aid, but none had any idea about what this would entail. The literature suggests that land may factor in this equation. This has merit; Samoa is not endowed with many natural resources apart from land and fisheries.

The Chinese – Devious?

There is a view that the Chinese are using devious and unscrupulous ways to obtain long-term residence in Samoa. One of these is through what are called marriages of convenience. Participants noted the high incidence of marriages between Chinese and Samoans, in particular Chinese males and Samoan females and that these were often short-lived. There is no statistical evidence to support these perceptions, but they appear to be widely held views; even those who take a positive response to Chinese in Samoa made similar observations.

One participant discussed a particularly interesting case that exemplifies the view of Chinese as being devious and unscrupulous. This story is unconfirmed, but is useful in providing an insight into why Chinese may be viewed negatively. The participant discussed how a Chinese businessman was using his restaurant business to bring in Chinese. After a period working for the restaurant, workers would mysteriously disappear. The owner claimed that they had run away and sought permission to bring in new workers from China. It was later discovered by this participant that the missing workers were working for the Chinese owner in another part of his business.

The Chinese – Taking Over?

Participants often expressed concerns that the Chinese would one day take over or control Samoa. There was a real sense of fear, insecurity and suspicion about the Chinese motives, with many suspecting that there was some ploy on behalf of the latter to gain greater control of the country.

Intriguingly, not all the participants who expressed this view were Samoans. One participant, a foreigner who had lived in Samoa for the best part of a decade, described how Chinese would talk among themselves about how good life in Samoa was. Samoa provided many freedoms that were not available in China. This participant noted that there was even talk among Chinese that Samoa was easy for the taking, primarily because Samoans were lazy. It was considered an easy task for Chinese to assert themselves in commerce and perhaps other spheres.

This view of Samoans was not exclusive to the Chinese. A number of participants, all Samoans, also noted the same things, particularly in relation to the cultivation of agricultural land.

With reference to agricultural production, the political opposition has noted in the past that Samoans did not work because there was nothing to be gained from it. There were insufficient markets in Samoa for agricultural production, beyond the requirements of subsistence living, to be profitable.

Few of these particular participants acknowledged the positive aspects outlined above. None of these participants associated the increase of Chinese businesses with any lowering of prices, across any industry. They acknowledged the big buildings that the Chinese government had provided, but none talked about any of these, except the new hospital building and a number of school buildings, in a positive way. Government buildings were of little interest and one even questioned the value of the newly built hospital.

Making Sense of the Negative Perspectives

Are Samoans Racist?
The subject of fears and suspicions about Chinese and other foreigners was raised in parliament by the Prime Minister in January 2015. He contended that many expressing negative attitudes towards Chinese, Melanesians and other foreigners, were racist. He defended these communities, in particular the Chinese, noting the substantial benefits they had provided to Samoa such as 'the big government buildings', 'Parliament House', 'new hospital', and 'school buildings throughout Samoa'.[12]

The Prime Minister's comments were raised with some of the participants. In response, it was argued that people who viewed the presence of Chinese as a threat were not doing it out of 'faailoga lanu' (racism/a prejudice based on colour), but 'fa'ailoga tagata' (a prejudice based on the person or people). One participant believed the fears, rather than being based on race, were based on what these Chinese brought with them in terms of culture and other practices, and what these mean and would mean for Samoan culture and way of life. There is a real question among Samoans about whether or not the new wave of Chinese will integrate into Samoan society, as earlier waves did. There appears to be a genuine fear that new arrivals may bring changes to fundamental tenets of Samoan life, such as culture and the control that Samoans have over their country. While racism should not be discounted altogether, a better explanation arguably lies in the area of culture, tradition and nation.

Samoa – A Homogenous Society, A Nation Based on the Fa'asamoa
First it is important to consider the nature of Samoan society. This is a very homogenous society. It might be argued that the Samoan nation is identifiable; its parameters are for many people self-evident. There is a language that all Samoans share, there is a history they all readily identify with, and most importantly Samoans have a unifying culture, which might be referred to in general as the fa'asamoa, and in particular as the fa'amatai. The importance of the culture, which is supported by the language and history, to the Samoan nation is critical. It permeates all facets of life in the country, from social relations, to economic transactions, to political institutions and processes. It is relevant to both rural and urban areas. As such it appears to infuse everything that is 'Samoan'. It is critical to the identity of the Samoan nation, and nation-state. The homogeneity of society means that it is very easy to identify outsiders and foreigners. They not only stand out in the way they look, but also by their lack of integration into the Samoan culture and way of life. Whether they should or not is not the issue here; it is just a fact that many foreigners, particularly those in the last wave of Chinese to Samoa, are not perceived by Samoans as integrating with Samoan society. Consequently, these foreigners solicit curiosity, suspicion, and may even be treated as a threat. This appears to have happened with the latest wave of Chinese.

A Homogenous Society Facing a Rapidly Increasing Foreign Group
The growth of this new/foreign group has been sudden and rapid, transforming feelings of curiosity and suspicions into ones of fear and threat. People's curiosity, suspicions, and fears are based in part on the 'very sudden' increase in the number of Chinese. Government policies can take credit, or at least some credit, for this sudden increase.

The Reasons for the Rapid Increase Unexplained
Secondly, the increase in the new/foreign group remains largely unexplained to the public. Many gave what might be considered wild projections of anticipated Chinese migration. People are left to their devices to determine why this is occurring.

The Increase Taking Place In An Era Of Rapid Societal Transformation And Reform
There are a number of significant changes taking place concurrently with the increase in the Chinese presence, and these are compounding some of the aforementioned feelings of vulnerability among Samoans. These include land reforms that are opening up customary lands for lease under a new system, the Torrens system. There is public speculation that this might lead to the alienation of customary lands. Compounding these insecurities are those that stem from proposed changes to citizenship rules. Parliament is currently debating The Citizenship Investment Bill 2014, which is intended to promote investment in Samoa by foreigners by allowing entitlement to citizenship through their investments.[13] Given that much of the investment in Samoa is coming from China, people are making associations between these reforms and Chinese presence in Samoa. It is an association that even supporters of the Bill are making.[14]

The Increase Taking Place in a Political Environment that Breeds Suspicion, Distrust and Fear
The Samoan political environment has been beset by a number of problems over the past several decades. Although the ruling Human Rights Protection Party government can rightfully be credited for creating what is arguably one if not the most stable country in the region, it is also widely recognised as one of the most long-serving parties in power. Apart from a two year hiatus from power during the mid-1980s, it has held the reins of power since 1982. This has led to contentions that Samoa is a one-party state.[15] States such as this are associated with a lack of democracy, in particular lack of political accountability and legitimacy. The extent to which democracy and political accountability exist in Samoa is questionable.[16] Samoa's political record is blighted with allegations of and actual cases of corruption. A political environment such as this is a wonderful breeding ground for suspicion and fear, and this would apply no less to the rapid increase of Chinese in Samoa, particularly given the associations between this and government policies.

Conclusion

Perspectives about China's and Chinese presence in the Pacific, which focus on macro-level analysis such as geopolitics, appear to have very little relevance to the kinds of discussions that ordinary people have about these issues. The threats, as construed in discourses such as the threat discourse and its counter-narratives, could not be further detached from the threats that ordinary people face. Whether China or the United States is the regional hegemon, or whether diplomatic ties with China are better than ties with Taiwan, are issues that ordinary people appear to have very little concern about. This does not mean that these issues do not affect them; there are likely to be real differences if a country aligns with one or the other; the level of aid that country receives, for example, is likely to be different. The Pacific world would arguably have a different experience with China as opposed to the United States being the regional hegemon. While the discourse at this level is extremely important and relevant to the Pacific region, countries and its peoples, the necessity of taking into account the views of ordinary people should also be recognised.

Although this study is based on a very small sample of participants in Samoa, it strongly suggests that the perspectives of ordinary people are just as important as those of scholars and policymakers concerned with geopolitical issues. They provide insights into issues that are also critical to the Pacific–China nexus. Although Chinese entrance into the Pacific might be welcomed at the government level, in order for this to have any success it must also be accommodated at the societal/local level. Based on the interviews for this study, this is likely to be very problematic. There are a number of critical issues that need to be resolved in order for the new wave of Chinese to be integrated, or at least accepted, into Samoa. They are not insurmountable, but are formidable, not only because of the characteristics associated with the two communities (Samoans and the new wave of Chinese), and their perspectives and expectations of each other, but also because of the sociopolitical factors pertinent to Samoa.

Although a relatively new nation-state, Samoa is a homogenous society, where foreigners that easily stand out and appear to pose a threat are unlikely to be welcomed. A rapidly increasing Chinese population, with apparently little interest in integrating with Samoan society yet beginning to dominate economically fits the bill. The lack of transparency about these developments, amid rapid and significant social and political transformation within a political environment conducive of suspicion, distrust and fear, compounds these problems. Ultimately, what this demonstrates is that a study of these alternative perspectives produces different analytical foci. Like geopolitical analysis, the political emphasis remains, but it is politics at a different level and between different actors. Some of the problems are politically derived, lack of transparency, accountability and so forth, and therefore can be politically addressed. Policies dealing with China's and Chinese presence in Samoa, and one might argue the Pacific as a whole, need to also cater for this level.

Notes

1. Henderson, J., 'China, Taiwan and the Changing Strategic Significance of Oceania', in S. Levine and T. Sage, Contemporary Challenges in the Pacific: Toward a New Consensus, Vol 1, special issue of *Revue Juridique Polynesienne*, 2001; Spillius, A., 'China's chequebook diplomacyruns deep in the Pacific', The Telegraph, 11 November 2011. Available at: http://www.telegraph.co.uk/news/worldnews/asia/china/8883910/Chinas-chequebook-diplomacy-runs-deep-in-the-Pacific.html accessed14 April, 2015.
2. Henderson, J., 'Dragon in Paradise: China's Rising Star in Oceania', *The National Interest*, No. 72, Summer 2003; Windybank, S., 'The China Syndrome', *Policy*, Vol. 21, No. 2, Winter 2005; Shie, T., 'Rising Chinese Influence in the South Pacific', Asia Survey, Vol. 47, No. 2, 2007
3. Crocombe, R., Asia in the Pacific Islands: Reolacing the West (Suva: IPS Publications, 2007); Wesley-Smith, T., China in Oceania: New Forces in Pacific Politics (Honolulu: East West Center, 2007, p 27)
4. Zhang, Y., 'China and the Emerging Regional Order in the South Pacific', *Australian Journal of International Affairs*, Vol. 61, No. 3, 2007
5. Henderson, J., 'The Future of Democracy in Melanesia: What role for outside powers?', *Asia Pacific Viewpoint*, Vol. 44, No. 3, December, 2003, 228–232, 227–8; Wesley-Smith, ibid.
6. Crocombe, R., *Asia in the Pacific: Replacing the West,* Suva: IPS Publications, 2007, 33.
7. Iati, I., 'China and Samoa', in T. Wesley-Smith & E A Porter, eds, *China in Oceania: Reshaping the Pacific?*, New York: Berghahn Books, 2010.
8. Iati, I., 2010, ibid.
9. Leung Wai, 'Reflections on the Experience of the Chinese Community in Samoa', 2015, Paper presented to Conference 'China and the Pacific: The View of Oceania', Apia, 25–27 February 2015.
10. Leung Wai, 2015, ibid.
11. Leung Wai, 2015, ibid.
12. Tupufia, L., 'P.M. Cautions Against Racism', *Samoa Observer*, 22 January 2015. Available online at: http://www.samoaobserver.ws/home/headlines/12690-pm-cautions-against-racism, accessed 14 April 2014.
13. *Samoa Observer*, 'What Citizenship Bill Says', 19 January 2015. Available at: http://www.samoaobserver.ws/home/headlines/12666-what-citizenship-bill-says accessed 14 April 2015.
14. Radio New Zealand, 'Samoan Exporters Argue for Citizenship Investment Bill', 26 February 2015. Available online at: http://www.radionz.co.nz/international/programmes/datelinepacific/audio/20168816/samoan-exporter-argues-for-citizenship-investment-bill, accessed 14 April 2015.
15. Toleafoa, A., 'One Party State: The Samoan Experience', in D. Hegarty & D. Tryon, eds, *Politics, Development and Security in Oceania*, Canberra: ANU E Press, 2013, 70; Radio New Zealand, 'Samoa opposition concurs with US view of Samoa being a one-party state', 15 March 2006. Available online at: http://www.radionz.co.nz/international/pacific-news/160897/samoa-opposition-concurs-with-us-view-of-samoa-being-one-party-state accessed 14 April 2015.
16. Iati, I., 'Samoa's Price for 25 Years of Political Stability', *Journal of Pacific History*, Vol. 48, No. 4, pp. 443–463, 2013.

China and the Pacific: A View from Tonga

Pesi Fonua
Publisher/Editor, Matangi Tonga Online, Tonga

The Increasing Role and Influence of China in the Pacific
Thank you for the opportunity to talk on the topic of 'The increasing role and the influence of China in the Pacific', and within this very short presentation I'll try to give you a glimpse of China's role and influence in Tonga.

Tonga's relationship with the People's Republic of China is relatively young. Our diplomatic relationship was formalised 16 years ago on November 2nd, 1998. On that date Tonga launched its so called 'Look East Policy', when the flag of the People's Republic of China was raised during a ceremony to formalise the establishment of diplomatic relations between the two countries, at the Royal Palace, Nuku'alofa.

Simultaneously, about one kilometre to the east – at the Taiwanese Embassy on the Nuku'alofa waterfront, the flag of the Republic of China was lowered, at the termination of Tonga's diplomatic relations with Taiwan.

Tonga established diplomatic relations with Taiwan in 1972, but by 1998 the Tonga government was convinced that there was only one China and that Taiwan, the Republic of China, was a part of the People's Republic of China.

It is worth noting that Tonga established diplomatic relations with Taiwan a year before Tonga became fully independent from the United Kingdom in 1973. Before that, Tonga had been a British Protectorate since 1900.

The British established their first consulate in Nuku'alofa in 1862, but on February 2nd, 2006, the Union Jack was lowered for the last time at the residence of the British High Commissioner.

During those years, from 1862 to 2006 Tongans had assimilated many British and Western ideas and called them their own. The British missionaries had earlier introduced Christianity along with formal education, and assisted in the establishment of a constitutional monarchy system of government.

So Tonga switched its diplomatic relations from Taipei to Beijing in 1998. The British had returned Hong Kong to China in 1997. Macau went back to China in 1999.

Leading up to and during the return of these territories to China, Tonga embarked on what became known as its Passport Sales Scheme. The scheme made it possible for Chinese who did not want to live under the People's Republic of China – Communist China – to seek a new life outside of China.

The scheme went out of control, and the millions that Tonga was supposed to have collected from the sales of these passports were lost because of the mishandling of public funds. The end result was that about 400 Chinese nationals became Tongan citizens.

Currently, it is estimated that more than a thousand Chinese have become Tongan citizens, and some of them are still living in Tonga with their families today. Many of these Chinese immigrants live and work in tiny stores known as 'Fale Koloa', selling basic goods at cheap prices and found in almost every village.

When Tonga became a member of the World Trade Organization in 2006, the business of running Fale Koloas was set aside for only Tongans, but because many Chinese had become nationalised Tongans they also had the right to own Fale Koloa, and today the Fale Koloa business in Tonga is dominated by Chinese-Tongans.

Soon Tonga wanted to turn its new diplomatic relations into a more practical relationship with China. In 1999, as an independent photo-journalist for *Matangi Tonga* magazine, I covered the State Visit to China by King Tāufaʻāhau Tupou IV and his delegation. A bilateral trade agreement was signed in Beijing on 7 October 1999, and the agreement made it easier for Chinese investors to invest in Tonga and for Tongan investors to invest in China. At the time there were high hopes that Tonga and the People's Republic of China were going to be in a partnership to develop an international satellite telecommunications network.

Today, the increasingly complex role and influence of China in the Pacific and in Tonga is still in the making. In trade and investment it appears to be definitely a one-way traffic. The only Tongan company, that we are aware of, that had a branch in China was TongaSat, a company owned by the daughter of Tupou IV and others, that was the agent for leasing the Tongan government's orbital slots. At the time, the Hong Kong office of Pacific Asia Global Holdings Limited marketed Tonga's claims to six orbital slots that covered China. Tonga's main client was APSTAR, a company in which China was said to be a major shareholder. TongaSat played a role in brokering the normalisation of the relationship between the two countries, a process that accelerated after Tupou IV gave Princess Pilolevu a mandate in 1996 to normalise Tonga's relations with China.

A decade later, the China-Pacific Islands Countries Economic Development and Cooperation Forum first met in Nadi in 2006 when USD 492 millions in concessional loans was made available to Pacific countries.

A second, similar, China-Pacific Islands Countries Economic Development and Cooperation Forum, was held in 2013 and USD 1 billion in concessional loans was made available.

The increasing influence of China in Tonga came about through a mutual understanding that through a diplomatic relationship and a bilateral trade agreement both countries would achieve their development goals and in Tonga's case, hopefully raise its standard of living.

On November 16th, 2006, a riot broke out in Nukuʻalofa and the central business district was destroyed, including the businesses of many Chinese nationals. To finance the reconstruction of Nukuʻalofa, the government took a concessional loan from China, the equivalent of $233.3 million Pa'anga, which included $138.9m for the reconstruction of the Nuku'alofa CBD, $91.8m for a road project and $2.6m for the renovation of the now defunct Dateline Hotel.

The repayment of only the 2% interest on the loan, which was scheduled to start last year, has been deferred for another five years to 2018. The 20-year loan was signed for by the, then, Minister of Finance Siosiua 'Utoikamanu on 9 November 2007.

There was also an on-lent portion of the loan, whereby government offered loans to businesses, whose premises were destroyed during the riot, at a higher interest rate of 5%. All these borrowers are having problems repaying their loans, and today one has still not signed its loan agreement with the government.

Apart from these constraints China continues to give Tonga millions to develop the country and its economy.

In September 2010, two Chinese warships called into Nuku'alofa on a goodwill visit, the first to arrive on our shores. Most recently, a Chinese navy hospital ship stopped over for a week on a humanitarian visit to the Pacific Islands, offering free medical treatments, including complex surgical operations, to Tongans who queued at the wharf over several days to receive consultations and treatments. Official visits between the two countries have become commonplace. In 2013 a new bank, a Chinese-Tongan venture was set up in Nuku'alofa.

Meanwhile, the USD 15 million MA60 aircraft that China gifted to Tonga in 2013 has become a foreign relations dilemma for Tonga, particularly with Western-allied nations such as New Zealand, Australia, USA, UK and the EU – countries that have not certified the MA60. Tonga has certified the aircraft, but following a survey of the standard of safety of Tonga's transport sector, funded by the World Bank and New Zealand, ICAO demanded Tonga upgrade its aircraft certification process and also its aviation engineering competency. A deadline was set for December 2014, which Tonga did not meet, and therefore the Tongan government has taken the MA60 out of service. The only solution to the issue that the Prime Minister Hon 'Akilisi Pohiva could offer was for 'China and New Zealand to talk it over'.

There have been goodwill visits by the Chinese navy, Tongans taking up scholarships to China, and continuing gifts of infrastructure and airplanes. Nevertheless, it is clear that the increasing role and influence of China in Tonga today basically revolves around finding ways for Tonga to be able to repay its loan to China. It is a debt collector's influence, and Tonga has no option but to satisfy the demands of the debt collectors.

References:

Fonua, Pesi, 2000. 'China switch sparked top ministerial resignations,' *Matangi Tonga,* Vol. 15, no. 1 January-April 2000, pp16-17; 1999. 'State Visit to the People's Republic of China by HM King Taufa'ahau Tupou IV . . . ' *Matangi Tonga,* Vol. 14, no. 4 December 1999, pp22-43; 1998. 'China switch brings Tonga closer to UN dream,' *Matangi Tonga,* Vol. 13, no. 4 December 1998, pp26-29.

Fonua, Pesi, et al. in *Matangi Tonga Online,* matangitonga.to:

2015, February 19, 'Tonga's external debt a worry', http://matangitonga.to/2015/02/19/tonga-s-external-debt-worry

2015, February 17, 'McCully releases 2013 development funds for Tonga', http://matangitonga.to/2015/02/17/mccully-releases-2013-development-funds-tonga

2015, February 12, 'Tonga struggles to meet ICAO demands', http://matangitonga.to/2015/02/12/tonga-struggles-meet-icao-demands

2015, February 12, 'China and Tonga strengthen friendship', http://matangitonga.to/2015/02/12/china-and-tonga-strengthen-friendship

2014, September 27, 'Tonga's Aviation struggles to abide by international standards', http://matangitonga.to/2014/09/27/tongas-aviation-struggles-abide-international-standards

2014, September 5, 'Tonga fails to write-off China loan', http://matangitonga.to/2014/09/05/tonga-fails-write-china-loan

2014, August 7, 'Govt denies MPs' spin on orbital slots sales' http://matangitonga.to/2014/08/07/govt-denies-mps-spin-orbital-slots-sales

2014, June 11, 'Tonga's biggest national budget depends on aid' http://matangitonga.to/2014/06/11/tongas-biggest-national-budget-depends-aid

2013, November 11, 'Tonga gets $15 million grant from China', http://matangitonga.to/2013/11/11/tonga-gets-15-million-grant-china

2013, July 10, 'New commercial bank a Chinese-Tongan venture', matangitonga.to/2013/07/10/new-commercial-bank-chinese-tongan-venture

2013, May 24, 'Chinese visit prompts Tonga government to review business investment policy', http://matangitonga.to/2013/05/24/chinese-visit-prompts-tonga-government-review-business-investment-policy

2011, September 30, 'Tonga pledges support to China in international forums', http://matangitonga.to/2011/09/30/tonga-pledges-support-china-international-forums

2010, September 5, 'Chinese navy ships make first visit to Tonga' http://matangitonga.to/2010/09/05/chinese-navy-ships-make-first-visit-tonga

2007, October 19, 'PM signs USD 56m loan from China for Nuku'alofa reconstruction', http://matangitonga.to/2007/10/19/pm-signs-usd56m-loan-china-nukualofa-reconstruction

2007, April 11, 'Tonga Govt pursues $100 million loan from China', http://matangitonga.to/2007/04/11/tonga-govt-pursues-100-million-loan-china

2006, April 27, 'Tonga seeks $60m loan from China to buy back Shoreline's electricity assets', http://matangitonga.to/2006/04/27/tonga-seeks-60m-loan-china-buy-back-shorelines-electricity-assets

2006, March 12, 'Can China replace the British influence in our lives? Editor's Comment, by Pesi Fonua', http://matangitonga.to/2006/03/12/can-china-replace-british-influence-our-lives

2004, July 26, 'Tonga appoints first ambassador to China', http://matangitonga.to/2004/07/26/tonga-appoints-first-ambassador-china

Pesi Fonua

Dr Graeme Smith

The Drivers of Current Chinese Business Migration to the South Pacific

Dr Graeme Smith[1]

Research Fellow, State, Society and Governance in Melanesia Program, School of International Political and Strategic Studies, Australian National University, Canberra

The impact on Pacific economies of investment associated with small-scale retail investors appears to be substantial but is completely unmeasured in Chinese statistics, as these rely on self-reporting to the Chinese Ministry of Commerce. Only large state enterprises in the Pacific report their investment activity. On the other side, when you talk to government officials from the Investment Promotion Authority in Papua New Guinea about the impact of this sort of activity on the domestic economy they say that cumulatively, Chinese investment in the retail and wholesale trade is probably greater than its investment in the resources sector or the construction sector, but no one adds up the investments undertaken by each of these shops, many of which are opening in areas where there were previously no trade stores.

What Pacific citizens do focus on – and this is a large part of their resentment – is that the money ends up mostly back in China. An email, which was widely circulated by the organisers of anti-Asian demonstrations in Port Moresby in 2009, which eventually led to nationwide riots targeting Asian-owned stores, summed up many of these concerns:[2]

> ... None of the so called leaders seem to understand how the inflow of illegal Asians are stealing business opportunities and jobs from helpless PNGans. It's costing the country simple storekeeper jobs and denying the privilege of simple PNGans owning these businesses. Competition among the Asians themselves has left not a chance for would-be PNGans. One just simply needs to walk down the street corner stores at Gerehu, Erima, Kundiawa Town, Kiunga, Lae Market stores, Rabaul Town, Alotau, Madang, you name the rest! In every one of these locations, you will see a takka box store being managed by three to four odd looking Asians who can't even speak proper pidgin, let alone English! What the hell is happening with the laws of this country?

These concerns and the media reaction that they have generated have been well documented by other participants at this conference, in particular Patrick Matbob.[3] What I want to get to in this paper is: what drives this investment from the perspective of the Chinese business investors, and why do they work so hard?

It's a question that might have occurred to you on many occasions when you see Chinese shopkeepers in the Pacific working until 7.30, 8 o'clock at night and staying on despite the fact that they get robbed so regularly.

There have also been a number of attacks on shopkeepers as a group, specifically anti-Asian riots that have played out in the Solomon Islands and Tonga (2006) and Papua New Guinea (2009). In Tonga, even though the Chinese shopkeepers dominate the retail trade to a greater extent than any other Pacific nation, you can't quite make a direct case that the 2006 riots specifically targeted these new arrivals. There were other factors at play, particularly protests against the monarchy. A mixture of resentment, poverty, the shops acting as a proxy for dissatisfaction with the regime, be it the monarchy in Tonga proving unwilling to cede its power in a timely manner, or the inept Somare administration, which barely governed PNG towards the end of its final term. There's also an element of opportunism. At the time of the Sandline affair when there were similar riots in Port Moresby, looting Chinese shops was colloquially referred to as 'going shopping'.

But it's not to say that these communities are unaware that their reputation is bad, and that it's getting worse due to the actions of a minority in their community. They're very well aware of this, as this quote indicates:

> After they were caught [two Fujian migrants who bungled an attempt to assassinate Jason Tan, the owner of J Mart in Port Moresby], it affected everyone. People would say that the worst sorts of people are here; Chinese killers have come into our country. Our reputation was destroyed. Wherever Chinese people go, particularly Fuqingese, our name is worse than pig shit. There's too much illegal migration, and there are too many new arrivals.

Some scholars, particularly Benjamin Riley, John Henderson and Susan Windybank back in the early 2000s, tried to draw a link between this migration and the Chinese state.[4] In the case of wealthier countries, such as Japan, you do see state support for migration because it earns large amounts of remittances that feed back into the Chinese sub-national economy. From the perspective of China's diplomatic representatives in the embassies throughout the Pacific, these new migrants are far from a welcome manifestation of Chinese power, soft or otherwise.[5] Interviewees in Port Moresby complained that: 'Even when someone gets killed, they're no use. They'll just send out a notice telling you to take extra care, and not to go out.' While barbed wire, guard dogs and security guards are part of life for these new arrivals, particularly in Melanesia, they often look back to an idyllic time of about fifteen years ago when there weren't quite so many Chinese, when 'people used to get up and give me their seat on the bus, and that doesn't happen anymore.'

One interviewee tried to explain this apparent lack of concern from their embassy in structural and historical terms: 'All they can do is host visitors, conduct ceremonies, there's no capacity to do much in PNG. China is still too poor ... and besides, this country isn't that important. It was only after Taiwan [tried to] buy their allegiance that they gave it some attention.' A report entitled 'China's Emergence: Implications for Australia' tabled by the Australian senate in March 2006 claimed that: 'China has a stronger diplomatic presence in the South Pacific than any other country . . . This indicates that they have more diplomats than any other country, rather than more diplomatic missions.'[6] Despite relying on Windybank and unnamed DFAT officials as the source of this revelation, a range of subsequent writers unquestioningly cited it. In interviews with Chinese embassy officials, it becomes apparent that China's diplomatic representation in the Pacific is paltry, and they are woefully understaffed. In many Chinese embassies in the Pacific, there are less than ten occupants, including support staff such as drivers and cooks. In PNG, the Economic Counsellor's Office, which is meant to oversee all of China's trade, investment and development assistance, had just two staff when I visited with a research team in February 2014.[7]

Where do all of these new migrants come from? The majority of migrants to the South Pacific, particularly PNG and Tonga, come from Fujian. One reason why this province only makes up less than 3% of the Chinese population but accounts for nearly one third of Chinese migrants abroad is recent history. If you head east from Fujian, you hit Taiwan. Under Mao there was a lack of investment in Fujian because he feared that it would become a staging post for Taiwan reinvading the mainland. So there was no investment in rural infrastructure that formed the basis for the economic boom that occurred in the rest of China during the 1970s and 1980s. In Fujian, they were left to fend for themselves. Their economy was in poor shape, so what options were available? Migration.

The main source of recent migration to the Pacific is a city called Fuqing, not far from the provincial capital of Fuzhou. Migration to the Pacific from Fuqing is a relatively recent phenomenon, following earlier waves of migration to Japan, the US, Canada, Australia, South Africa and Argentina. Here's their take on the Chinese central government's level of support for them:

> It was the millennium, China was boasting about having met the basic needs of society, but then your English countrymen wanted to know, if life over there is so great, why are people risking their lives to come here? [Then President] Jiang [Zemin] was furious. He got on the phone to the Customs Bureau and told them to crack down on people smuggling. If two or three people from your village were caught, then no one in the village could get a passport. That's what our government is like. One person does something, and another one pays for it. In the past, the emperor would issue a decree to punish a clan for one person's treason. Now, damn them, it's the whole village. The ban stayed for 7 years.

This was in response to a tragedy that unfolded on the docks at Dover, where 54 men and four women – largely from Fuqing – suffocated to death in an 18-metre long container. This unfortunately happened at the same time that President Jiang Zemin was visiting Great Britain. It didn't play well, but nor did it stop the wave of out-migration, as banned villagers used informal channels to access the required passports and visas. These migrants aren't afraid to break a few regulations, and a cavalier attitude to the laws of their home country extends to the Pacific. In Madang, a ban on the sale of home brew was largely ignored in their shops, to the annoyance of lawmakers and the pleasure of *spakman* (drunkards) throughout the province.

Above all, these migrants are frontier capitalists. They embody a spirit of raw entrepreneurialism that perhaps hasn't been seen since the United States in the 19th century. During the course of most of my interviews, when they judged I'd spent some time in the Pacific, the conversation would usually be guided to whether I knew of any region or country where Chinese migrants hadn't yet arrived. I may have been responsible for sending one the way of Saidor, on the Rai Coast, and for this I am truly sorry. This willingness to go where others will not venture was captured perfectly in recent interviews conducted by Chinese researchers in Japan, who were told:[8]

> All you need is courage. The one thing the [Fukushima] earthquake and radiation zones have is work, and the wages are higher. Because of this, lots of us went there to find jobs . . . On any given day in the earthquake zone, you should be able to find two or three jobs. If you sleep five hours a day and don't rest, aside from one hour spent eating, you can work for the rest of the time and earn 400,000 yen per month, which is about twice your average wages. And because of the GFC, in other areas, it's almost impossible to get a full day's work.

Another source of support for these migrants might be the subnational state, which has benefited handsomely from remittances and donations. The Fuqing City government received over two billion *yuan* in overseas donations from 1978 to 2011.[9] But in the Pacific this doesn't seem to be the case. As one interviewee noted:

> The Fujian Province Overseas Chinese Affairs Office[10] has no eyes for this place [PNG]; they just don't see it. They only see Japan, America, Australia and Canada. They look down on PNG. It only has five million or so people, after all . . . There are hundreds of thousands of Fuqing migrants in Japan, and if each of them sends back 5000 yuan ($800) per month, that's hundreds of millions in remittances. In PNG, there might be over a thousand migrants, and they earn less.

So in terms of both the central state, and the local state, migrants from Fuqing are left to fend for themselves. There's an established discourse in China around quality or *suzhi*, which has been used to argue that people targeted in anti-Asian riots, such are the ones which have flared in the Pacific, are of low quality and they don't deserve the full protection of the Chinese state.[11] Fujianese migrants don't care much for the state either; the feeling is mutual.

Migration from Fuqing to the Pacific challenges many of our assumptions – that migration is a relatively linear process, either from rural to urban areas within a country, or from poorer countries to wealthier ones.[12] For many Fuqing migrants, their journey involves a shift from an urban life to a remote rural existence, and from a country where all their material needs are met to villages without power or running water. Another common sense notion, that there is always a conscious decision to migrate, is also challenged by this research. Among Fuqing migrants, there's agency but not full agency. A final story to illustrate this.

On Karkar Island, a remote volcanic island off the north coast of Madang province, I met a shopkeeper called Loki. After working for a couple of years with a relative in Madang town, he set up a shop in an area that had no power and no water. Loki is an interesting character; thoughtful, fleshy and a touch melancholic. Sitting in a shop for twelve hours a day, surrounded by barbed wire, keeping an eye out to make sure he wasn't being robbed. This was not how he'd hoped his life would pan out; he wanted to be an architect, and he even trained to be one in Xi'an. He's an extremely intelligent man, but there's a narrative around what it means to 'be a good man' (*haohan*) in this part of China. *Haohan* goes forth and makes a fortune to support a big family, something you can't do on an architect's salary. When everyone around you is pushing you to do it, you sit in the shop for twelve hours a day. So what's driving you? As is the case in much of China, providing the best education and best life you can for your children. Loki, like many people from Fuqing, was in breach of the one-child policy, with three sons and two daughters. You pay your fine and you're done with it, but providing them all with education, health care and a house is not cheap.

It's also driven by status. Successful rural-to-urban migration within China will typically involve building a two- or three-story house back in your home village. But in Fuqing, these are six- or seven-storey dwellings, often with a spire on top to make it slightly larger than the structure next door. Until the neighbours rebuild, a few years later. It's doubtful that anyone needs a six-storey house. Typically, the first two floors have some furniture, usually hidden by dust covers. The top floors are just dust. Another trend found in other parts of China, but taken to an extreme in Fuqing, is that they provide their own rural infrastructure, right down to the village school, health clinic, and even the main road. Each entrance to a village in Fuqing features a plaque commemorating the building of the village road, and individual donations are in the order of 10,000 *yuan*, rising to over 50,000 *yuan* ($10,000).

Many are also driven by faith, not something many in Samoa would be aware of, but certainly something Samoans would understand. A significant number of Fuqing migrants send money back to their village church, and some grand structures are the result – not a common sight in nominally communist China. The mystery of why Fuqing migrants labour so long and hard is partly down to a blending of the Protestant work ethic with traditional Chinese mores of respecting your ancestors and prioritising male heirs. It's a heady combination that drives much of this entrepreneurial activity.

An earlier paper introduced the phrase 'assimilable stock', which was used to appraise the worth of the first generation of Chinese migrants to the Pacific. Perhaps the main fault line for these new arrivals is the question: are they real migrants or just sojourners? Will they stay in the Pacific and make it their home? A lot of the resentment these migrants face arises from this doubt, and it runs up against a persistent sentiment in mainstream Chinese culture, 'a fallen leaf returns to its root' (*luo ye gui gen*). Aside from being the title of an endearing film, where a construction worker tries to bring the corpse of his dead friend from Shenzhen to a village near Chongqing, it refers to a custom of Chinese expatriates returning to their hometown to die. As was the case for an earlier generation, it is likely that Pacific communities will start to embrace the new arrivals when they see evidence that they are looking to contribute to Pacific communities and put down some roots.

Notes

1. I would like to acknowledge the assistance of DFAT's Australian Development Research Award in supporting this research, and the support of Divine Word University, particularly Mr Patrick Matbob. All errors in this paper are of my own making, and I can be contacted at graeme.smith@anu.edu.au.
2. PNG Grassroots, 'All Asian-Owned Cottage Businesses Must Cease Dateline 31 December 2009.' Online: http://asopa.typepad.com/files/anti-asian-propaganda.pdf.
3. See also Jonathan Sullivan and Bettina Renz (2012) 'Representing China in the South Pacific', *East Asia*. 29, 377-390; and Graeme Smith (2012) 'Chinese Reactions to Anti-Asian Riots in the Pacific', *The Journal of Pacific History*. 47(1), 93–109.
4. John Henderson and Benjamin Reilly (2003) 'Dragon in Paradise: China's Rising Star in Oceania,' *The National Interest*. 94-105; Susan Windybank (2005) 'The China Syndrome: China's Growing Presence in the Southwest Pacific,' *Policy*. 21(2), 28–33.
5. Graeme Smith (2012) 'Chinese reactions to anti-Asian riots in the Pacific.' *The Journal of Pacific History* 47(1), 93–109.
6. Australian Senate Foreign Affairs, Defence and Trade References Committee (2006) *China's Emergence: Implications for Australia*. Canberra: Senate Printing Unit, 183.
7. Graeme Smith, George Carter, Mao Xiaojing, Almah Tararia, Elsie Tupou and Xu Weitao (2014) *The Development Needs of Pacific Island Countries*. Beijing: UNDP China. Online: http://www.cn.undp.org/content/china/en/home/library/south-south-cooperation/the-development-needs-of-pacific-island-countries-report-0/.
8. Sheng Lin and Zhu Yu (2014) 'Fuqing migration activity in the context of the Global Financial Crisis [guoji jinrong weiji beijingxia Fujian Fuqing de haiwai yimin huodong],' *Journal of Fujian Normal University (Philosophy and Social Sciences Edition)*, 186(3), 144–150.
9. Xingan Lin (2013) 'A Cultural Explanation for Donations from Fuqing Overseas Chinese since Reform and Opening Up [Gaige kaifang yilai huaqiao huaren zai Fuqing qiaoxiang juanzeng xingwei de weihua jieshi],' Overseas Chinese Journal of Bagui [Bagui Qiaokan]. 4, 15–21.
10. The Fujian Province Office for Overseas Chinese Affairs is the agency responsible for looking after Fujianese migrants abroad. In the case of PNG, most migrants are from Fujian, so the Fujian Office looks after it. In the case of the Solomons, they are mostly from Guangdong, so the Guangdong provincial office takes responsibility.
11. Smith, 'Chinese reactions to anti-Asian riots.'
12. Michael Kearney (1986) 'From the Invisible Hand to Visible Feet: Anthropological Studies of Migration and Development,' *Annual Review of Anthropology*. 15, 331–361.

A Pacific Island Student in China – Reflections

Dr Rebecca Bogiri
Port Vila, Vanuatu

Good afternoon and *xin nian kuai le* or happy Chinese New Year. Firstly, thank you for the invitation to speak.

My name is Rebecca and I spent five years in Beijing, China, from 2009 to 2014. During that time, I studied towards a Master's and a PhD in Economics at the University of International Business and Economics. The China Scholarship Council (CSC) sponsored my scholarship. During my first year in China there were twenty ni-Vanuatu students, over fifty Papua New Guinean students, over twenty Fijian students, over twenty Tongan students, and over thirty Samoan students. The number of Pacific Island students in China has increased greatly over time and there is an increasing number of students who are privately sponsored in China as well. For example in Vanuatu, CSC scholarships were first awarded in 2006, when two students were the first recipients of the CSC scholarship. By 2007, they were awarding five per year, an increase of 150%. And in the last year, nineteen students were awarded CSC scholarships in Vanuatu, an increase of 280%.

I will talk about my experience and the experience of my Pacific Island colleagues of studying in China. My talk will focus on the handling of Pacific Island students by Chinese universities, and how the experience of studying in China is beneficial to Pacific Island students.

First Impressions
Upon arrival in China, I did not speak a word of Chinese. The only words I knew were *ni hao*. I immediately felt out of place. Other new Pacific Island students also felt out of place. Notices and signs were written in Chinese. All taxi drivers spoke only Chinese. Few Chinese spoke English. It was difficult to go shopping, sightseeing, or travel without having someone who spoke Chinese to accompany us. Knowledge of basic Chinese prior to arriving in China would have been very helpful in settling down and adjusting to life at the university.

Medical insurance was provided but it differed between universities. For example, in my university, only basic medical insurance covering basic health issues was covered. In other universities, comprehensive medical insurance was provided, including all kinds of treatment and surgery needed.

The establishment allowance offered by universities arrived at different times, too. I received mine two weeks after I arrived. For some of my colleagues studying at other universities it was given even later. Others were lucky and received theirs

Dr Rebecca Bogiri

immediately upon arrival. Furthermore, the amount of the establishment allowance received differed by university. As such, there appears to be no harmonisation of the medical insurance policies and establishment allowance policies of universities hosting CSC students.

Allowances were given at different amounts depending on the level of study. Degree students were given RMB 1,400 per month which is equivalent to USD 223. Master's students received RMB 1,700 per month which is equivalent to USD 271. PhD students received RMB 2,000 per month which is equivalent to USD 319. Given that the RMB has continued to appreciate, these amounts of money are no longer sufficient to sustain students at the current price levels. For example in 2009, you could easily buy a packet of sliced bread for RMB 4 or around USD 0.64. Now the price has risen to about RMB 7 or about USD 1.10.

The grading system

Chinese universities have very stringent grading systems. Any mark below 60% is considered a fail mark. To get an A, you had to get between 92–100%. I studied earlier when any mark below 50% was considered a fail and you could easily gain an A grade if you gained between 85–100%. So you can imagine my surprise and horror when I learnt about this at orientation week. This forces international students, especially those from the Pacific, to work harder to be able to pass comfortably. It is also a requirement to attend all classes. If a student misses three classes in a semester without a medical report or sick leave, the student has immediately failed. Students are also marked for general behaviour during class, such as respect for the teacher and other students, punctuality in attending classes, and attempting all assignments.

Chinese students are generally very academically competitive. They usually aim for a grade of 90% or over. They spend long hours in the library studying and completing their assignments and they complete all work long before the set deadline. Living, studying, and hanging out with these Chinese students means that the competitiveness and study habits rub off on their classmates who are international students.

Teachers

Teachers in China also serve as mentors and role models and they are always concerned for their students' education, health, and life at the university. It is common to find a class of students and their teacher enjoying dinner together at a restaurant at the beginning or end of a semester. A teacher will also go out of her or his way to visit a student who is hospitalised or bring lessons to a child who cannot attend classes due to illness. I myself was hospitalised once, and it was a comfort to have my teacher visit me, and my department administrator call up to check on me. In return, a student displays a very respectful attitude towards a teacher.

General Culture

Chinese are very hardworking and respectful people. They live frugally and are also very efficient in their work. So the next question is – how can these features benefit Pacific Islanders? Pacific Islanders who study in China are exposed to competitiveness and efficiency during their studies. They learn to be efficient in their work and not to waste time. They learn to work hard and be respectful. This is useful for Pacific Islanders, who often have a generally laid-back and relaxed attitude. Students also learn to build networks and maintain relationships to grow these networks.

They also learn to live frugally on a small monthly allowance. They learn to budget and save up to meet medical expenses that will not be covered otherwise by medical insurance. But most importantly, they learn the Chinese language and how to deal with Chinese people. This is especially beneficial as we see an increasing Chinese presence in the Pacific region. Pacific Island students who return to their home countries have additional career options such as translators, business consultants, immigration consultants, property consultants, tour operators, policy analysts and policy planners at a government level, as well as in other careers that cater for the needs of incoming Chinese investors, Chinese tourists, and the increasing Chinese presence in the Pacific.

Recommendations

I would like to make comments on the handling of students by Chinese universities and authorities. Based on my experience and the experience of other CSC awardees from the Pacific, the following are recommendations to improve the way students are handled by Chinese universities or authorities.

First, it is recommended that students be given classes in basic Chinese prior to their departure for China to assist them in settling down. Some universities organise airport pick-ups, while others don't, and it is very important to ensure the student does not get lost and can settle down comfortably into university life. Classes in basic Chinese can be organised at Chinese Confucius Institutes set up in Pacific Island countries.

Secondly, it is recommended that students be given establishment allowances upon their arrival at the university or prior to their departure.

Thirdly, it is recommended that the monthly stipend be increased to take into account the appreciating RMB, which is causing a general increase in prices in China.

Thirdly, it is recommended that universities hosting CSC students in China harmonise their medical insurance policies and establishment allowance policies.

Conclusion
I would like to thank the Chinese government for providing opportunities for Pacific students to study in China. The number of scholarships has continued to increase over time and they complement traditional donors in the Pacific to educate students in priority fields. It is my humble opinion that the increase in the number of Chinese scholarships is timely as it not only assists Pacific Island countries in developing their human resources but also prepares us indirectly to better understand and play an active role in the increasing Chinese presence in the Pacific. Thank you.

Non-Traditional Security and Global Governance: China's Participation in Climate Adaptation in Oceania

Associate Professor Wang Xuedong

Deputy Director, National Centre for Oceania Studies, Sun Yat-sen University, Guangzhou

Climate Change and Global Governance: China's Development Assistance in the South Pacific Area

Ladies and gentlemen, thank you. It's my pleasure to be here. Actually I just modified my title for this presentation a little bit. I think the new title is more accurate. My title is 'Climate Change and Global Governance: China's Development Assistance in the South Pacific Area'.

We know human beings live in a very complicated society, which means our world is full of uncertainty, and full of continuity and change. Continuity means we, all countries, are still struggling to find a way, a solution, a resolution to deal with traditional security issues such as the Ukraine crisis, the Russian–American strategic conflict, and North Korea and South Korea. At the same time we have to turn our minds to non-traditional security issues like ISIS terrorism, energy issues, and of course climate change.

We know we cannot deal with climate change issues without global cooperation and global governance. This means that countries with high capacity such as the US and China should provide assistance to the very sensitive, vulnerable countries like small island states.

Small island states in this area are right now facing a tough job but, fortunately, they are not alone because countries inside and outside this area, like the USA, EU, Japan, China, Australia and New Zealand, are standing by them.

When we talk about development assistance and climate adaptation, generally, there are two kinds of approaches. One approach is 'climate mitigation' which means all countries cut greenhouse gas emissions and try to reverse or even stop the trajectory that causes global warming. Another way is 'climate adaptation' including trying to promote vulnerability reduction and encourage capacity building. Studies show climate adaptation requires more and more urgent adaptation in this area, the South Pacific area. At the same time, development is a form of adaptation because development in any society can lead to increased adaptive capacity.

Associate Professor Wang Xuedong

China takes action. We know China is a world-leading carbon emitter since 2007 and China takes its responsibility on climate change mitigation based on the CBDR ('Common But Differential Responsibility') principal. Last November, our President signed an MOU with President Obama about our pledge to have carbon emissions peak in 2030. At the same time, China is always encouraging climate adaptation, always promoting the capability and capacity for development.

That's some background for the question.

If you read the White Paper issued by the Chinese government about foreign assistance, or what we call development assistance, the statistics show China provided a lot of money to other developing countries, especially in this area, and we have pledged further assistance in the near future. We founded the Pacific Island Forum Cooperation Fund and we encourage environmental protection here, providing solar power generators and biogas equipment. We encourage the use of energy-efficient technology and renewable energy here. One example is China's help for the use of clean energy in Tonga, the 'mass gas utilisation'. China has set up programmes to train and educate people from developing countries on energy efficiency, renewable energy and to provide information on climate change, while at the same time trying to promote agriculture development.

I think you know that President Xi Jinping proposed the idea one and a half years ago of a 'One Belt, One Road' policy. It encourages cooperation with world partners, especially countries from the south, meaning in our country, developing country cooperation. President Xi Jinping visited the South Pacific last November and our government is expected to build on his commitments here, and at the same time provide solar power and other assistance.

Questions are raised by the quick growth of China's foreign assistance, prompting some debate. These concern China's resource diplomacy, its political push against Japan, the issue of the political legitimacy of Taiwan and even strategic resistance to US dominance.

On resource diplomacy, China comes to the region not only for energy resources, although we do need energy resources. (But after 2030 China should be less thirsty for energy resources.)

On China versus Japan: I think it is easy to overestimate Japanese influence and at the same time this concern underestimates China's relevance in the UN system. My opinion is that enhancing political influence is not necessarily a zero-sum game. You can win political support. And in the South Pacific, we can win support too.

On Taiwan, well, the world is changing rapidly; we know Taiwan cannot compete with the mainland anymore.

Finally, on resistance to American dominance, I would argue that it's still too early to count the eggs before the chicken grows up. Right now, China is not powerful enough to compete against America in this area

So the question is: why does China assist? China is always promoting ideas, always making it clear that taking action and utilising technology are very important. These have to be the major factors in dealing with climate change. The small island states have the will to act because they are very vulnerable, very sensitive to climate change and global warming. They need help. China takes this as an opportunity to be a responsible power. At the UN conference on climate change in Copenhagen, China agreed to share its experience on energy conservation and emission reduction with other developing countries and promised increased assistance.

Some will argue that China actually is reluctant to cut its greenhouse gas emissions. That's true. Actually, China is very reluctant to cut its greenhouse gas emissions because it is unfair. Why is China's assistance so controversial and contentious? Is Japanese assistance here controversial and contentious? The Americans? Well, I would say China's intensified foreign assistance does have a lack of transparency. China's government always prefers minilateralism over multilateralism. Finally, China never imposes any political conditions on its aid and the USA criticises China for that.

Australia is very cautious about China's intent here. Why do they criticise China's assistance? Probably two reasons: firstly, China always provided foreign aid or development assistance abiding by the principle of not imposing any political conditions. Secondly, it's something like a growing pain. You know, China's aid seems different from traditional donors like the USA or other countries. People from Western societies say: 'your aid, your assistance will corrupt the system of liberal democracy.' But my question is . . . you know Fukuyama, the author of *The End of History*, published a brand new book last year called *Political Order and Political Decay*. Fukuyama presents a very open question, a very good question: 'is liberal democracy a developmental universal?' America supported Pinochet in Chile; Americans supported Saddam Hussein. Human beings cannot play God. We always make mistakes and always learn from these mistakes.

In China's white paper we say we never impose political conditions. That's not true. You know, before the 1980s, China's foreign assistance to Korea, to Albania, to East Pakistan . . . always imposed political conditions. But it failed and failed and failed again. So when Deng Xiaoping came to power he said no, not anymore, we don't want to impose political conditions – that's very bad. So the history of American foreign aid and Chinese development assistance teaches us lessons. Confucius is a great expert on Chinese history. He said do not do unto others as you would not like to be done to you and treat others as you would have them treat you. Don't point the finger at other people. Let other people make their own decisions.

There's also the issue of growing pains. China's participation in this area brings a kind of growing pain. Xi Jinping, when he delivered an address last November to the Australian parliament, said, 'we are a big power, we are a big guy, of course . . . decades ago we were a little boy, and now we grow up as tall as Yao Ming. We are the big guy in the club so naturally when we move around people say "wow, look out, big guy coming in".'

One question is, how big is big enough? The Pacific Ocean is big enough to hold all of us. This meeting room holds all of us here and not only the USA, China, Australia and New Zealand, but also Samoa and its island neighbours and France. The Pacific Ocean, in my mind, should be a shared area. It cannot be someone's private backyard.

To conclude: South Pacific Island states expect to be very vulnerable and sensitive to climate change. They need help. China takes the opportunity to provide assistance to this area. At the same time, China is playing a very active role as a responsible power. Hillary Clinton is right. She is very smart. She is right; she is not stupid. Right now, Taiwan is not so much a factor, but the South Pacific is important. She said Taiwan is not an important point anymore for China's assistance here. In the future, of course, after our President Xi Jinping's undertaking, China will be providing more help here. Here are some points about China's aid in the future. Firstly, there will be more input. Secondly, there will be more transparency. Thirdly, China will actually try to find a way to shift from minilateralism to multilateralism. And last but not least, there will be more sharing the stage with NGOs domestically.

Ladies and gentlemen, I know you are sleepy and tired. I promise you, we will have a beer soon. I believe China will have transparency soon, like a cold beer. Just be patient waiting for both.

We are providing more development assistance to this region – and it is increasingly transparent. China is a new power on the world stage. You need patience. You need to encourage. I think countries like America and Australia are very experienced in foreign assistance, so we need to encourage China to move on the right track, in the right direction. So my conclusion is to be patient. Thank you.

5. DEVELOPMENT COOPERATION

Professor John Overton, Victoria University of Wellington

The Context of Aid in the Pacific – and Its Effectiveness

Professor John Overton
Professor, School of Geography, Victoria University of Wellington

Introduction
China has become an increasingly prominent part of the aid environment in the Pacific Islands region. To a large extent, its involvement in development cooperation in the region – at least until recently – has been seen as out of line with traditional donors in the Pacific (Australia, New Zealand, France, USA and even Japan). It has not been a part of the international aid consensus built around the Millennium Development Goals and the OECD-brokered Paris Declaration of Aid Effectiveness in 2005. China's position, instead, has been met with suspicion by other donors and seen to be heavily motivated by its own economic and geopolitical concerns. Yet since the global financial crisis of 2007–08 – and the Busan meeting on aid effectiveness in 2011 – there has been a marked shift in the approach to aid by Western donors. This has seen a lessening of emphasis on poverty alleviation as the central motivation for aid and a much more explicit embodiment of donors' own economic and political interests within their aid programmes. The result has been a significant change in the aid 'landscape' in the Pacific Islands region.

This paper presents a summary of these changes in development co-operation in the region since 2000, at first contrasting the approaches of traditional donors with China. It concludes, however, that since 2008 there has been a noticeable convergence – and even cooperation – between the two in their implementation of development cooperation programmes and projects.

The Paris Consensus 2000–2008
Between 2000 and 2008 there was a remarkable degree of consensus amongst Western aid donors. Driven by public campaigns such as 'Live Aid' and 'Make Poverty History' and facilitated by a prolonged period of prosperity and growth in Western economies, donors agreed not only to increase their aid budgets substantially but also, guided by the launch of the Millennium Development Goals (MDGs) by the United Nations, to focus their aid policies on poverty alleviation. Critically, also, they subscribed to a concerted effort by the Development Assistance Committee (DAC) of the OECD to improve the effectiveness of aid and aid delivery.

The issue of development effectiveness was tackled through a series of international meetings ('high level forums') – successively in Rome (2002), Paris (2005), Accra

(2008) and Busan (2011). Initially these meetings were driven solely by DAC and the major Western donors who belonged to DAC – effectively the Western aid 'club'. Subsequently efforts were made to also involve recipient countries and, later, non-traditional donors, civil society and the private sector.

The most important of these meetings was that in Paris in 2005. This resulted in the Paris Declaration, a statement, amongst other things, of five key principles of aid effectiveness:

1 Ownership: Developing countries set their own strategies for poverty reduction, improve their institutions and tackle corruption.
2 Alignment: Donor countries align behind these objectives and use local systems.
3 Harmonisation: Donor countries coordinate, simplify procedures and share information to avoid duplication.
4 Results: Developing countries and donors shift focus to development results and results get measured.
5 Mutual accountability: Donors and partners are accountable for development results.

The Paris Declaration was notable for two main reasons. Firstly, the recognition of country ownership as the central principle was a remarkable step, at least at the rhetorical level, for it acknowledged that donors should, in effect, cede control over aid and development to developing countries. This gave a far greater explicit role for recipient country governments. They were asked to develop their own development plans – Poverty Reduction Strategy Programmes (PRSPs) – and lead the disbursement of aid through their own institutions and procurement systems.[1] Secondly, in agreements and documents that followed the Paris Declaration, donors acknowledged that aid modalities had to change; rather than discrete and often short-term aid projects, effective development assistance required long-term support that used and strengthened local institutions and delivery systems. Thus there was a strong push to move from projects to mechanisms such as Sector Wide Approaches (SWAps) and ultimately General Budget Support (GBS)[2]. Put together, these agreements saw an era of aid that was centred on the MDGs and the Paris Declaration and largely orchestrated by DAC and the Western aid 'club'. It represented a sharp reversal of the former hard-line neoliberal approaches of the late 1980s and early and mid-1990s, which sought to limit the size and scope of the state and promote the market as the central development mechanism. Poverty alleviation was uppermost, there was a marked shift towards the use of state institutions, there was support for long-term programmes in health and education in particular, and there was a significant increase in real aid volumes – especially to sub-Saharan Africa – in the first decade of the new millennium (Figure 1):

This era of development cooperation received criticism at the time. For some, the increases were still far too small, underlying causes of underdevelopment were not being addressed (the MDGs focused only on a few symptoms), and the reality was

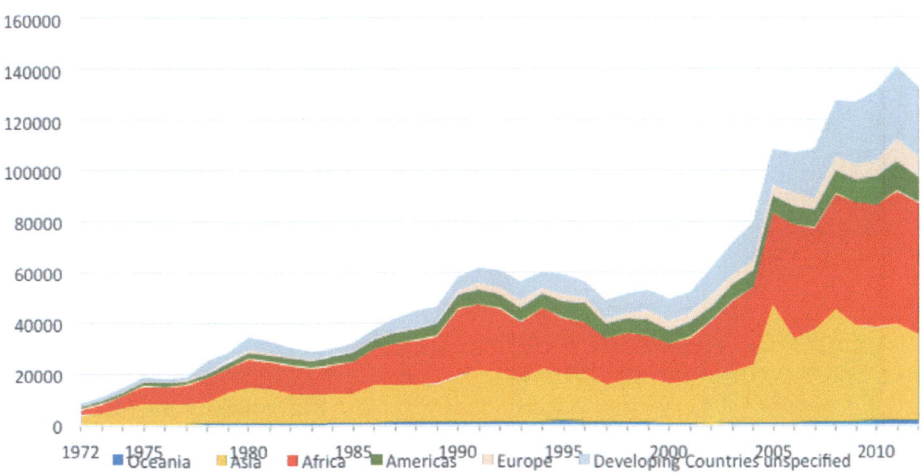

Figure 1: Total aid to all regions 1972–2012 (USD mill current prices)
Note: DAC donors only
Source: http://stats.oecd.org/ accessed 9 October 2014

not of country ownership and poverty alleviation but rather a continuation of the old market-led approaches of neoliberalism under a new guise. For others it went too far. Donor interests should have been taken into account more openly and there was continuing mistrust of state institutions.

We have termed this aid regime of the early 2000s 'neostructuralism'[3], a term which draws on Latin American usage[4,5] and which recognises a new more populist approach mixing continuing market-led approaches with a strengthening of the capabilities of the state to provide the environment for economic growth and poverty alleviation.

Aid in the Pacific 2000–2008

These global aid trends were directly reflected in patterns of development cooperation in the Pacific. Firstly, however, we can portray the overall features and patterns of aid. Using OECD Official Development Assistance (ODA) data[6], a clear picture of aid contrasts and commonalities emerges. Key features are:

- A small number of donors dominate: Australia, Japan, New Zealand, USA and France. See Figure 2 for a summary.
- Each of these donors has a marked 'sphere of influence' where they are the dominant donor. France (as far as we can estimate from non-OECD data) is a very large donor in New Caledonia, French Polynesia and Wallis and Futuna. Australia accounts for the majority of aid in Papua New Guinea, Solomon Islands, Vanuatu, Fiji, Nauru, Kiribati and Tuvalu and is the largest overall donor in the region. The USA is most in evidence in Micronesia (FSM, Palau, Marshalls, Northern Marianas) as well as American Samoa. New Zealand

is dominant in Tokelau, Niue, Cook Islands and is a major (though not the largest) donor in Tonga and Samoa. Japan's aid is rather more diffuse but it is notable in Fiji, Samoa and Tonga and the Micronesian countries.
- The patterns, with the exception of Japan, reflect former (or in some cases continuing) colonial relationships. The former colonial power has maintained a dominant role in a Pacific country through aid. The exception here is the United Kingdom, now largely a minor aid player, its dominant position having been replaced by Australia.
- There are major inequalities in the geography of aid. Within the region, the highest aid volumes are channelled to the large Melanesian countries: Papua New Guinea, Solomon Islands, Vanuatu and, with interruptions, Fiji. By contrast, some smaller island states receive small volumes: in 2012 Papua New Guinea was the largest Pacific Island ODA recipient with USD 665 million whilst Tokelau was the smallest with $18.7 million.
- When per capita aid receipts are shown, however, the inequalities are reversed. Small island states receive much higher amounts of aid per capita: in 2012 each person on Tokelau received the equivalent USD 13,280 whereas in PNG the figure was only USD 93.
- Furthermore, it is apparent that per capita receipts are strongly influenced by political status. Those countries and territories that maintain forms of close political ties (whether fully integrated or in 'free association') with a metropolitan 'patron' (again usually the former colonial power) appear to receive much more in aid, albeit from a single source.

With regard to the neostructural era of aid in the Pacific, we can see from Figure 2 that real aid volumes increased steadily in the region, though perhaps these increases were not as great as those to other regions of the world deemed to have higher rates of poverty, especially sub-Saharan Africa, or (given the post 9/11 concerns about security and the war on terror) deemed to be of high geostrategic importance, such as Iraq and Afghanistan.

One notable shift during the period, however, was the way the adoption of the poverty agenda helped redirect ODA. In general – and we can see this most markedly in the data for New Zealand aid – there was a shift from the smaller but rather better off (as defined by the MDGs) island states of Polynesia to the larger states of Melanesia, particularly PNG and the Solomon Islands where the MDGs pointed to significant poverty-related concerns around literacy and maternal and child health. Given these concerns and the post-Paris Declaration efforts to improve aid effectiveness, there were efforts to promote longer-term aid-supported programmes in health and education. There were the beginnings of SWAps in Solomon Islands and PNG – though the rather stronger government systems meant that SWAps and even forms of GBS found a firmer footing in Samoa and Cook Islands.

Indeed, the issue of recipient state capabilities became crucial during this era. For some, notably Solomon Islands with the RAMSI intervention, the reconstruction

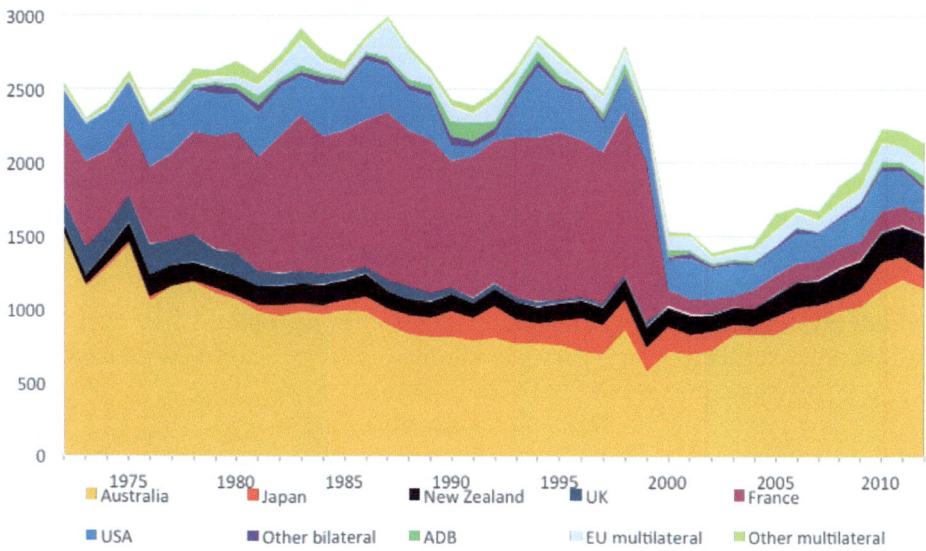

Figure 2: ODA to the Pacific region by donor 1972–2012 (USD mill current prices)
Note: DAC donors only. The apparent sharp decline in French aid in the late 1990s was the result of a reclassification of flows to French Polynesia and New Caledonia; they were no longer regarded as ODA.
Source: http://stats.oecd.org/ accessed 9 October 2014

of the state and its institutions became a major priority of donors. Solomon Islands received a major increase in aid with RAMSI, and in PNG, Australian concerns about the ability of the public sector to manage their day-to-day functions, let alone increases in aid, led to direct 'investment' in state-building operations. Paradoxically, though, and with the exception of Solomon Islands, some perceived weaker states with poorer poverty indicators actually experienced declines in real aid volumes – PNG amongst them. On the other hand, countries such as Samoa, which were able to demonstrate that they had robust financial management systems and good governance, persuaded donors to sign up to SWAps. It seemed then that in practice, state efficiency and 'clean' governance was an effective way for Pacific states to attract aid, rather than rely on poor poverty indicators to open the purse strings of donors.

Whilst these changes were occurring amongst the traditional donors in the Pacific, new donors were appearing. Aid delegations from India, Malaysia and Indonesia were seen in Fiji and the Republic of China (Taiwan) was active in trying to court, through aid, political backing from Pacific countries with seats at the United Nations and other international bodies. But it was the People's Republic of China that attracted the most attention, and occasional disapprobation. China, it seemed, did not play by the rules – at least those used within the DAC club. China did not seem to be guided by the MDGs, nor did it particularly embrace the Paris Declaration. Statistics on China's aid were opaque at best, a well-kept secret at worst

– unlike the apparently transparent ODA monitoring system of the DAC. Instead, people in the Pacific saw the new imprint of China's aid in quite visible ways: new government buildings, sports complexes and, in many corners of the rural Pacific, roads and bridges – all being built by Chinese contractors, Chinese labour and Chinese equipment and materials. The little that leaked out of government circles in the Pacific hinted at large concessional loans being the mechanism for these new forms of development assistance – they were commercial transactions, albeit on concessional terms, that brought benefits to Chinese state-owned enterprises as well as to Pacific governments and communities. The established donors in the region mostly quietly fumed at this new entrant, though their disapproval rose when China was seen to offer aid to Fiji – a pariah in the eyes of Australia and New Zealand after the military coup of 2006.

The 'Retroliberal' Turn 2008–

The aid world was fundamentally reshaped after 2007. The so-called Global Financial Crisis (GFC) of 2007–08 hit severely the economies of Europe and North America and their close trading partners. Yet the crisis was not evenly 'global', for the Chinese economy and those of its close trading partners (including Australia) avoided severe recession. The crisis for many countries was met with a sort of neo-Keynesian response: Western governments put bailout and stimulus packages in place that avoided the worst effects of economic crisis.[7] They also struggled to balance their budgets and cut many items of public expenditure.

Yet what is surprising is that aid budgets largely survived intact (see Figure 1). The United Kingdom presented the most remarkable case here: it cut its overall budget quite sharply, including even defence, in 2008. Yet its ODA was relatively unscathed. In fact the Cameron Government remained committed to increasing its aid and achieving the 0.7% of GNI target for ODA. New Zealand and Australia (the latter at least initially) also did not cut ODA, a budget head that surely would be vulnerable when the economy went into recession.

The other change that affected aid in the West – and arguably also a consequence of the global financial situation – was the election of several right-of-centre governments. In New Zealand (2008), United Kingdom (2010), Canada (2011 – re-elected), the Netherlands (2012) and Australia (2013) conservative administrations were elected to power. Many of these governments talked of austerity and a smaller state sector and some tended to anti-immigration rhetoric and a more assertive and self-interested foreign policy. Yet most maintained or increased their aid budgets.

However, despite largely protecting ODA budgets, all undertook fundamental reform of their overseas development assistance programmes. What is remarkable is the similarity between these countries in the way they reformed their programmes. Firstly, governments moved quickly to distance themselves from the poverty agenda – or at least away from the idea that it should be the central or leading objective. Nearly all articulated a new vision of 'sustainable economic growth'. Trade and economic growth moved up the policy agenda whilst poverty slipped down. The private sector has been actively promoted as a key agent of change. Secondly, there were swift moves to restructure aid agencies. Nearly all had previously worked through government aid agencies largely autonomous and with direct ministerial control. Soon former such agencies, such as NZAID, AusAid and CIDA were disbanded and aid departments instead were constituted within wider foreign affairs ministries and departments. This allowed for the articulation of a new aid mission which emphasised national self-interest with aid as part of a suite of foreign policy instruments that were coordinated by the government. There were also a variety of other changes including relationships with civil society and changes in contracting systems.[8]

A new mantra of 'shared prosperity' has emerged, found in the mission statements, policy notes and strategic plans of many bilateral and multilateral organisations. Shared prosperity talks of aid budgets producing win-win outcomes: economic growth at home stimulates trade and investment in developing countries whilst supporting economic growth overseas again encourages trade. Shared prosperity has also provided the *raison d'être* for the aid budget being used to support companies from donor countries in putatively development-related activities off-shore.[9]

Many observers – myself included [10] – focused on the dramatic changes that occurred within separate donor countries. However, it has gradually become apparent that such changes are not unique to one donor or another. They are strikingly similar: so much so that other observers have pointed to very close similarities between, say, Australia and Canada[11,12,13]

Looking across these changes, it is possible to discern a new aid regime in the wake of the global financial crisis. Generally, some have seen a new era of capitalism emerge;[14] others have analysed this new aid approach[15,16] and suggest we may be seeing the start of a 'post-aid world' where the old understandings and practices of aid – and the old DAC-centred structures – have been largely cast aside. We however argue that it represents a reworking of aid approaches that hark back to an era of modernisation – perhaps even with origins far before that – when economic growth, infrastructure, Keynesianism and aid as an explicit instrument of foreign policy defined donor aid approaches. We call this 'retroliberalism'[17]. Furthermore, we suggest that driving such retroliberal aid policies is a mindset that has been shaped by GFC experience; domestic enterprises had been bailed out and local economies stimulated by Western states during the GFC. In the years after, such open state subsidy for the private sector would be politically unacceptable, especially for such ostensibly right-of-centre governments. But what the 'shared prosperity' approach to aid has done is open the way for what might be termed 'exporting stimulus': the use of public funds in the aid budget to support and promote the operations of the donor's private sector off shore.[18]

The retroliberal turn has been matched by changes in the development effectiveness agenda. The firm definitions and commitments of the Paris Declaration were challenged and softened at subsequent High Level Forums, most significantly at Busan in 2011. The Busan meeting produced two major changes. Firstly, there was a strong push to include the private sector in the conversation around development effectiveness; it was recognised that any efforts to promote economic development had to have private sector involvement. Secondly, there was a strong desire to bring in non-DAC donors to the consensus around development effectiveness principles. In the end, China observed and its views were heeded but it decided to remain outside the club. A consequence of Busan has been recognition that China (and India and other non-traditional donors) are now very much part of the aid scene and the old *modus operandi* centred on DAC, the MDGs and the Paris Declaration has weakened considerably.

China (and Others) in the Pacific 2008–

The Pacific Islands region experienced the changes to the global aid regime somewhat rapidly after 2008. Largely this was because the main donors changed their orientation and purpose with ODA in the region, though aid from China has also seemingly shifted to adjust to the new aid landscape.

To a great extent, development cooperation from China, though, has continued on its pre 2008 trajectory. Although we lack comprehensive data, it seems as if there has been a continuation of an approach that has focused on infrastructure development and construction. We term this a 'state capitalist' aid regime.[19] It is characterised by some key features. Firstly, its focus is on state-state relationships with little involvement of civil society, and the private sector seems to be involved only insofar as donor (largely state-owned) corporations are contracted as construction forms. The recipient country private sector is largely excluded. Furthermore, there is not a major concern for addressing the issues of recipient state legitimacy: China had few qualms in dealing with the Bainimarama regime in Fiji prior to the 2014 elections when traditional donors were imposing sanctions. Secondly, the focus of this regime is not so much 'aid' (implying a net flow of resources from donor to recipient in order to promote development and welfare) but 'development cooperation' (joint activities to promote forms of development that bring benefits to both parties). The modalities for this form of cooperation are largely soft loans, together with some grants, that are then often spent on Chinese contracting firms. Thus, this form of development cooperation sees the donor party acting as a type of broker linking demand in recipient states with providers from donor countries. Finally, the regime is one that is largely focused on infrastructure and construction, rather than service provision, capacity building and sectors such as health and education – the key elements of the neostructural aid approach of traditional donors. This model of Chinese development cooperation is perhaps best framed as south-south cooperation[20,21] rather than ODA or 'aid'.

These features can be seen in a brief examination of Chinese development cooperation in the Cook Islands (Table 1). This example is one of the few in the region where such data is available publicly (here through a transparent recipient country budget process). As can be seen, most of the development cooperation assistance has come in the form of construction or equipment, supplemented by some cash grants to fund special events. The Cook Islands example is an interesting one for the region: China is now the second-largest donor behind the historical 'patron', New Zealand, and there are moves for these two donors to cooperate in jointly-funded activities, an important sign that China is now being accepted as a key donor with whom both recipient states and other donors can work. The context for such cooperation might not have been provided by the Paris-consensus (neostructural) era, but it does signal a new way for China and traditional donors to use complementary strengths and resources to address the objectives of Pacific Island development. It is suggested here that such cooperation between China and other donors is symptomatic not only of a slight shift in the Chinese position but also, and more so, reflects the retroliberal turn amongst traditional donors.

Funded projects 2001–2014	$NZ mill
Heavy machinery	6.9
Courthouse	4.7
Police HQ	3.9
Pearl equipment	2.1
Tractors	1.5
MoE furniture	1.3
Cash grants (Pacific Games & Leaders Forum)	2.8
Anticipated projects 2015–	
Agricultural equipment	1.5
Apii Nikao (new school)	10.0
Atiu airport upgrade	3.9
Building repairs	0.8
Cash grants (50th celebration)	2.7

Table 1: Chinese-funded projects in Cook Islands 2001–2014
Source: Cook Islands 2014/15 Budget http://www.mfem.gov.ck/images/20141027_Budget_Breakfast_Ministerial_Slides.pdf accessed 12 February 2015

Since 2008, the main established donors in the Pacific have instituted some fundamental changes in their aid policies in the Pacific. For Australia, this has come relatively recently with the Abbot/Bishop government elected in 2013. As well as the general retroliberal recipe outlined earlier, this government has signalled that Australia's previous aid 'investment' in Solomon Islands and PNG has not produced adequate returns and major cuts in these programmes have been announced.

It has been New Zealand's aid policy since 2008, however, that has changed most significantly. Overall, the Key/McCully government policy has pushed for a greater emphasis on the Pacific, so within its overall aid portfolio, spending in the Pacific has been increased whilst that in Africa and Latin America has been cut. Within the Pacific, though, there have been changes. The so-called 'realm' countries (Tokelau, Niue and Cook Islands) have received greater attention, reflecting both a withdrawal from the poverty focus of the overall programme and a desire to concentrate the aid dollar on where it can make the most impact. Some elements of the former neostructural approach have remained – spending in PNG and the Solomon Islands and on health and education programmes there have fortunately continued. But the policy priorities have shifted. Infrastructure and agriculture, together with tourism, have become key foci, with health and education falling down the priority chain. The New Zealand aid programme's draft strategic plan for 2015/16–2018/19 (recently released for public consultation) outlines twelve 'investment priorities'.[22]

This represents a major shift from the neostructural approach for New Zealand aid in 2000–2008. Health and education remain but are relatively low priorities and the term 'poverty alleviation' has diminished greatly in prominence. Instead there is an emphasis on infrastructure and driving economic development: energy, agriculture and ICT are listed as 'flagship' priorities and fisheries, tourism and labour migration are included. The phrase 'shared prosperity' now figures prominently. Such a strategic plan has clearly reflected current retroliberal thinking – using the state and aid budgets to promote economic growth and deliver benefits to both parties. It also facilitates the use of the New Zealand private sector (companies such as Meridian, Fonterra etc) in aid delivery.

Conclusions: A New Convergence?

This paper has examined major shifts in global aid regimes over the past 15 years and the way these have been reflected in the Pacific Islands region. We have seen how the previous approach of Western donors was anchored in two key global agreements: the MDGs and the Paris Declaration. This defined a poverty focus for aid, put emphasis on building the capacity of recipient states to deliver long-term investments in welfare and poverty alleviation, and reconfigured aid in the Pacific towards those countries such as PNG and the Solomon Islands where MDG indices pointed to greatest need. It also excluded China, in that China was depicted as a donor not part of the DAC club, with different and self-serving motives and a lack of transparency.

Since 2008, however, this dualism has become less marked. China has engaged more, as in the discussions around the Busan forum on aid effectiveness, and has become a more stable and visible presence in many parts of the developing world – a leader in so-called south-south cooperation. This paper argues, though, that the greatest change in the global aid regime has come because Western donors have substantially reformed their approaches to aid. The poverty focus has become blurred and sometimes almost invisible. The enthusiasm to progress neostructural capacity building and provide long-term support for states through SWAps and GBS has waned. Rather we see much more explicit statements tying aid programmes to the promotion of donor economic and political interests in the developing world. Support for donor companies operating overseas has increased and the shift to promote economic growth and trade has been marked.

For the Pacific, this transformation is still taking place. We are likely to see much less support for state-building – especially as Australia cuts back – and, at best, static levels of expenditure on health and education. Instead the vision of 'shared prosperity' sees much greater expenditure on building infrastructure and supporting key economic sectors in which donors have either a strategic interest or perceived expertise. What then is emerging is a convergence: a convergence between the retroliberal and state capitalist aid regimes. China is no longer a pariah as a donor. Indeed, traditional donors seem to have learned from the approach of China – especially in infrastructure development – and have shown signs of a willingness to cooperate. These are first small steps but they reflect the fact that the great divide in development cooperation in the Pacific – and elsewhere – is much less marked than it was before 2008.

Notes

1. The rhetoric of country ownership however was accompanied by practices that maintained donor control, especially as they had to approve the PRSPs and be satisfied with local financial management systems and the like before releasing funds.
2. Koeberle, S., & Stavreski, Z. (2006). 'Budget support: Concepts and issues', in S. Koeberle, Z. Stavreski & J. Walliser (Eds.), *Budget Support as More Effective Aid* (pp. 3–27). Washington DC: World Bank.
3. Murray, W.E. and Overton, J. (2011a) 'The inverse sovereignty effect: Aid, scale and neostructuralism in Oceania' *Asia Pacific Viewpoint* 52,3 272–284; Murray, W.E. and Overton, J.D. (2011b) 'Neoliberalism is dead, Long live neoliberalism. Neostructuralism and the new international aid regime of the 2000s' *Progress in Development Studies* 11,4 307–19.
4. Leiva, F. (2008) 'Toward a critique of Latin American neostructuralism' *Latin American Politics and Society* 50, 1–25.
5. Grugel, J. and Riggirozzi, P. (2012) 'Post-neoliberalism in Latin America: Rebuilding and Reclaiming the State after Crisis Post-neoliberalism in Latin America', *Development and Change*, 43(1), 1–21.
6. Such data exclude development assistance from China and some other non-DAC donors as well as forms of development assistance such as preferential trade agreements, immigration concessions and military support. There are also flaws in the data to do with reclassification of ODA, most notably no longer counting French expenditure in New Caledonia and French Polynesia as ODA after 1999 (see Overton et al, 2012).
7. Stiglitz, J. E. (2010), *Freefall: America: Free Markets, and the Sinking of the World Economy*, WW Norton.
8. McGregor, A., Challies, E. Overton, J. and Sentes, L. (2013) 'Developmentalities and donor-NGO relations: Contesting foreign aid policies in New Zealand / Aotearoa' *Antipode* 45,5 1232–1253.
9. Mawdsley, E., Murray, W.E., Overton, J, Scheyvens, R. and Banks, G.A. (2015) *Sharing Prosperity? A Comparative Analysis of Aid Policy in New Zealand the United Kingdom in the 2010s.* NZADDS Working Paper 2015/1. Wellington: NZADDS.

10. Banks, G., Murray, W.E., Overton, J., and Scheyvens, R. (2012), 'Paddling on one side of the canoe? The changing nature of New Zealand's development assistance programme' *Development Policy Review* 30,2 169–186.
11. Smillie, I. (2013) 'How to Hijack an Aid Program: An open letter to Australian Prime Minister Tony Abbott' http://www.mcleodgroup.ca/2013/10/29/how-to-hijack-an-aid-program/ accessed Dec 2013
12. Davies, R. (2013), Dismantling AusAID: taking a leaf out of the Canadian book? http://devpolicy.org/o-cida-dismantling-ausaid-the-canadian-way-20131115/ accessed 30 October 2014.
13. Sharma, Y. (2014), Aid mergers in Australia and Canada could hit poor regions, warn experts http://www.theguardian.com/global-development/2014/may/08/australia-canada-aid-merger-poor accessed 30 October 2014
14. Altvater, E. (2009), Postneoliberalism or postcapitalism? The failure of neoliberalism in the financial market crisis. *Development Dialogue*, 51, 73–86.
15. Harman, S. and Williams, D. (2014), 'International development in transition', *International Affairs* 90,4 925–941.
16. Mawdsley, E., Savage, L. and Kim, S-M (2014), 'A 'post-aid world'? paradigm shift in foreign aid and development cooperation at the 2011 Busan High level Forum' *Geographical Journal* 180,1 27–38.
17. Murray, W.E. & Overton, J. (2015), Retroliberalism and the new aid regime of the 2010s. MS, Victoria University of Wellington, Wellington.
18. Mawdsley et al, (2015), ibid.
19. Murray H E and Overton (2015), ibid.
20. Mawdsley, E. (2012), *From Recipients to Donors: The Emerging Powers and the Changing Development Landscape*. London: Zed.
21. Mawdsley E et al (2014).
22. MFAT (New Zealand Ministry of Foreign Affairs and Trade) (2015), 'New Zealand Aid Programme Draft Strategic Plan 2015/16-2018/19', Wellington: MFAT.

Mapping Chinese Aid in the Pacific

Dr Philippa Brant

Research Associate, Lowy Institute for International Policy, Sydney

Dr Brant's remarks at the Conference should be read in conjunction with the interactive mapping tool she created and describes here:
http://www.lowyinstitute.org/chinese-aid-map/

Thanks everyone. As we've been discussing in the past day, it's very clear that China's engagement in the Pacific region over the last decade has increased. There is a lot of interest and concern in Australia, NZ, and within Pacific Island communities. Much of the focus, as we've been discussing, is on its foreign aid programme.

The challenge, though, is that China doesn't provide data about its foreign aid programme at a country level or project level, and many Pacific Island governments themselves don't have comprehensive information about the aid they receive from China. This can lead to misperceptions about its aid. We know it's growing. But how much it actually gives, where, and in what form, has remained unclear.

Today I'm revealing a project called 'Mapping Chinese Aid in the Pacific'. It will be officially launched on Monday. I was planning to show you the actual map but we're having some Internet problems so luckily I've got some back-up snapshots. The intention of the project was to provide information about Chinese aid funded projects in the Pacific region. It is the first time this data has been collected and mapped in a comprehensive way. It covers the eight countries with which China has diplomatic relations: the Cook Islands, Federated States of Micronesia, Fiji, Niue, Papua New Guinea, Samoa, Tonga, Vanuatu, as well as Timor-Leste. There are six countries in the region that recognise Taiwan and therefore don't receive official Chinese aid. The map includes all bilateral aid provided by the Chinese government as part of its aid programme since 2006.

Importantly, only projects that have been completed or are in the process of being implemented are included. It does not include projects that have been pledged, announced or agreed, but are as yet not underway.

The map is designed to be fact-based and neutral. Its core purpose is to provide information about Chinese aid projects and to display it in an interactive and accessible way.

But given China hasn't published this data, all of it had to be collected, verified and analysed. Finding information, as you all know, is more challenging regarding China than for other donors. The data has come from over 500 sources. This includes Pacific Island government budgets, parliamentary acts and congressional agreements, Chinese government tender documents, project announcements, reports from Chinese contractors that are implementing aid projects, interviews and site visits in the region, and a number of direct email requests with government officials, project managers, and other key stakeholders.

This information was cross-checked across multiple sources. Official Chinese and Pacific Island government sources and documents were privileged over media reports. Sometimes media reports can be unreliable – often projects are announced more than once, and sometimes there is confusion over the currency of the aid.

The map is designed to be dynamic and interactive. I will briefly take you through what I think are its three most powerful features.

First, the project level information. There are 169 individual Chinese aid projects in the map and it can be easily updated to add new projects. For each project, there

Dr Philippa Brant

is information about its cost, the time frame, the type of aid, the sector it belongs in, and the Chinese contractor that implemented the project. The example here is the Navua Hospital in Fiji. Where possible I've included a nice photo of it as well.

The second great feature of the map is its filtering function. You can filter all of the projects by the type of aid, the sector, status, and country. This can be done at a regional level or within an individual country. So for example if you filter in concessional loans, it tells you the total amount of concessional loan funding since 2006. Here, looking at Samoa, you can filter by the education sector and it will show all the projects funded in that sector by China.

The third feature of the project is the country-level snapshots and its comparative data. On the very first slide you will have seen a regional comparison table that gives you a high-level overview of how China's aid in each country and in the region compares with other major development partners.

At a country level, too, I've provided an overview of how much China has given since 2006, the number of projects, what sectors are funded, and if you click on the 'more info' button down in the corner there's a handy two-page PDF that gives you a snapshot of China's aid in the region: what the main sectors are, how much of it is funded through concessional loans vs. grants, and how it compares with the other major donors.

Just briefly I'll take you through a couple of the key findings of the map. Firstly, China is now on track to overtake Japan as the third-largest provider of foreign aid in the region. But Australia still dominates. Between 2006 and 2013, Australia provided more than six times the amount of aid that China did. In some countries, however, the amount of Chinese aid is rivalling that of traditional development partners. Again between 2006 and 2013, China was actually the largest donor in Fiji and the second largest in the Cook Islands, Samoa, Papua New Guinea, and Tonga. The third interesting finding is that since 2006 some 80% of total Chinese aid in the Pacific has been in the form of concessional loans. This is something I know we are all slightly concerned about.

My hope is that this will be a valuable tool for researchers, policymakers, officials, and journalists who are interested in China's engagement in the Pacific. I welcome any comments and feedback you may have. Thank you.

Soft Loans and Aid:
China's Economic Influence in the Pacific

Dr Biman Prasad
Leader, National Federation Party, Fiji; formerly Professor of Economics, University of the South Pacific, Suva

Thank you, it's a pleasure to be here. Let me begin by thanking the organisers. I'm very pleased to be present here for this very important conference. I contested the elections in Fiji last year and I'm now in parliament, making a transition from academia to becoming a politician, and I hope I can speak more like an academic rather than a politician. I know politicians like to be misquoted; I hope I am not misquoted by the media.

I agree with Philippa Brant with respect to data availability and the willingness of governments in the Pacific as well as, I must say, Chinese embassies in the Pacific to provide information. From my own experience there is a big reluctance to release data on Chinese loans, projects, and other details that one might be interested in. I think Philippa's project is a very good one and I'm sure it will be of a lot of interest to us and to policymakers.

We had some very useful presentations yesterday. Most of it tried to examine recent developments in economic relations between China and the Pacific Island Countries (PICs) in relation to soft loans, trade and investment. Many of the presentations did identify factors that drive or hinder bilateral trade or investment in the Pacific by China. I also think that many of the presentations did pinpoint specific areas of strategic importance for PICs in expanding economic cooperation with China. But I also think that we perhaps are missing the point with respect to our deeper engagement with Australia and New Zealand, and how we may be able to derive more benefits from not only development partners like China but many others who are trying to get into the Pacific (and I'll dwell on that a little bit more as we move on).

The key point that I would like to concentrate on is perhaps looking at why China's economic relations with the Pacific have grown so rapidly. Indeed, there are other countries, like India, for example, recently trying to expand their links into the Pacific. In fact India has announced an India Pacific Summit later in the year in India. There are other countries that we ought to look at as well. One of the reasons for the growth is, I think, China's concentration on infrastructure projects, big projects, or what I call 'hard aid' (versus 'soft aid'). I think in the late '80s and the '90s, our traditional donors seemed to have shifted – they became reluctant to engage in hard aid and moved to more soft aid. This was an important area – capacity building, good governance, poverty reduction strategies and so forth. But I think Pacific Island countries saw a gap with respect to support for infrastructure development in a big way. Some have taken the opportunity to build that capacity and gone to actively seek aid from China to fill that gap.

The other point that Pacific Island countries are also looking at is the increasing integration of both Australia, New Zealand and traditional partners with China, particularly Australia and New Zealand (NZ having signed a Free Trade Agreement (FTA) with China and Australia being in the process of negotiating one now) so many of them think it is logical that they ought to forge closer ties with China as well.

I think when we talk about China's support to the Pacific, it sometimes appears that maybe it's China trying to get into the Pacific in an especially big way – but I think it's part of China's global strategy. Look at some of the new initiatives such as One Belt, One Road, the Asian Infrastructure Investment Bank and more recently the creation of Free Trade Areas. The Free Trade Area of the Pacific is basically China's alternative to the Trans-Pacific Partnership. Increasingly, what you see is China trying to be part of international organisations while at the same time trying to look at alternatives – regional and global forums to push its global ambitions in a way that it thinks may be in the long-term interests of China.

In the area of security, again you see China is trying to strengthen or revitalise some of the organisations to build that kind of influence. Of course, there are other countries that are also trying to do similar things to China, such as India.

I think many of the PICs are also using their sovereignty or their jurisdiction as a resource. The fact that China has issues with Taiwan may be one of the reasons why Chinese integration into the Pacific is being pushed more vigorously by China. It may be a factor, but I think the bigger issue is China's own global issues. But also, in the absence of hard aid from traditional donors, many of these smaller PICs and those who might be considered or might have been considered 'rogue states' like Fiji have used their sovereignty or what I call 'jurisdictional resource' to actively seek Chinese participation in various sectors of their economy, and, indeed, some are going beyond China. If you look at Fiji's diplomatic activity over the last several years, it's actually going beyond China and trying to woo non-traditional donors and players into Fiji.

I think that is an important factor we need to consider. I'm sure PICs will continue to look at other partners and play their sovereignty or jurisdictional power to actually get resources for themselves.

If you look at China's trade with the PICs, essentially you can look at two groups: fish and sea products, and minerals and timber; obviously the Melanesian countries are most involved in the last. More fish is exported to China. I think there are implications for the fishing infrastructure and China's involvement in the new fisheries management regime. Chinese exports to PICs have been increasing significantly: by 608% between 2002 and 2011.

China's trade, of course, with PICs is very imbalanced and I think that's understandable. If you look at the MFN tariff rates, if you look at countries like Vanuatu and Samoa that have duty-free access to Chinese markets, 95% or 97% of the products are covered, but the 3 or 5% that are not covered is very important for PICs. It includes fish, minerals and forestry products. China has given duty-free access to markets for a large percentage of products, but in fact most PICs don't export anything except those that attract some duty and there is the possibility for that to be decreased. For example, the Chinese tariff on its fisheries is around 10% – it's not covered in the 95% or 97% duty free access to China. Among the five countries that qualify for zero tariffs for LDCs, only two (Vanuatu and Samoa) actually receive the treatment, while the others, because they have ties with Taiwan, don't benefit from it.

Besides the tariff on the small range of products that PICs *are* able to export to China, they're also faced with technical barriers to trade (TBT), technical restrictions. So in terms of actual export potential, while it's there, I think we are still restricted by high duty and also non-tariff barriers to China. Perhaps that's one area that PICs could take up with China if they feel they are able to export more to China.

But I think the real issue is the capacity of PICs. Chinese importers are looking for big volumes. I don't think many PICs, even big ones, have the capacity to produce those big volumes for export. So the potential would still lie with our traditional markets.

I think there's been in increase in foreign direct investment and there are examples of projects – Ramu Nickel is probably the largest project of foreign investment in the Pacific. There are possibilities for investment in services, trade and banking.

But let me just come to soft loans. Soft loans have become important tools for expansion. In the case of Fiji, 66% and 65% loan disbursement respectively in 2012 and 2013 came from the Exim Bank of China. And you can see external debt in Fiji has risen from 16.8% in 2009 to 28.3% of GDP. Of course it doesn't just include Chinese loans, but they form the bulk of it. There is a need for proper cost benefit analyses and priority setting – I think many of the countries have not actually done that yet.

There are implications for debt and the burden on future generations that we need to consider. I think there are risks associated with trade, soft loans, and foreign direct investment and we need more analyses of those risks and more understanding of those risks.

One final point. I think the issue of integration with Australia and NZ needs to be considered. They have a combined GDP of USD 1.6 trillion; they are the countries from where we get most of our tourists and most of our remittances. I think they will remain very, very important economic partners for the future, for most PICs. In fact, it might be desirable for PICs to seek much deeper engagement, deeper integration, with Australia and New Zealand because by doing that we may be able to benefit more from their engagement with the East Asian region and Asia in general. And I think the flow on from that kind of engagement would be much more beneficial to the Pacific than what they might get directly from China and other partners who are now engaging in the Pacific.

One final point with respect to Fiji. The view of the Fiji government right now that Australia and NZ should not be part of the Forum I think lacks economic logic, lacks understanding of our history, and perhaps the future economic link that we will continue to have with Australia and New Zealand. Thank you.

China's Aid: A Melanesian Perspective

Dulciana Somare-Brash
Deputy Director, Pacific Institute of Public Policy, Vila

Good morning everyone.

Firstly I'd like to thank the organisers for inviting me to speak today, and the National University of Samoa for this ideal venue.

When I listened to the presentations on China's diplomatic, economic and investment presence in these Pacific Islands yesterday, I was in the throes of completing what was my original presentation for today on Chinese aid in Melanesia. Overnight I thought of the notion of 'island agency' that Professor Wesley-Smith and Dr Jim Rolfe put forward yesterday. At great risk of sounding somewhat fickle, and in the interest of time, I will look at the single proposition of island agency in a very general sense.

In relation to development assistance from China, the most prominent of the non-traditional players emerging in our islands, I will not look at the emerging and prominent challenges but instead emphasise that the onus on us as Melanesians is to enhance achievable governance ideals and standards in the face of increasing interest in our sub-region.

It must be said that yesterday's discussions reminded me of how I often feel in a room when my own country, Papua New Guinea, is being dissected, analysed, and categorised. We have always been more than the seemingly universal rules available: narrow categories, measurements, discourse and generalisations.

We heard yesterday that we are all here talking right now because Western political influence is being challenged. We were told yesterday that since 2000 China reached out to the developing world (as itself a developing nation) with the capacity to trade, aid and compete proactively with other global giants. We heard of the diplomatic truce between Taipei and Beijing from 2008. As a professional, I understood this to mean that the heady days of chequebook diplomacy had ended. As a Melanesian, I still beg to differ.

My strong view is that Melanesia can't entirely be figured out enough for Island agency to occur during the window when the world wants a lot of what we have. We can't be judged entirely on institutional standards that by design assume yet ignore so many things about us. I speak as a Melanesian who wants to understand the many cultural, social, economic and of course intensely political transitions in our member countries. Many of the transitions in Melanesia since before our nations gained independence were subject to external interventions, remembering that as a sub-region in Melanesia there are French-speaking Melanesians, Portuguese-speaking Melanesians, English-speaking Melanesians, and Bahasa-speaking Melanesians. I go back to many of the transitions in Melanesia since before our nations gained independence subject to external interventions: Christianity, the cash economy, colonisation itself, then decolonisation. In the years before our indigenous folk gained the education and the requisite exposure to global ideas, principles and rules, we seemed to track along a path guided by innate urgency to be in charge of our own future. What we lacked in uniformity we made up for in strong extended cultural links and familial ties that, like school rules, attached coded penalties for a series of identified civic and other breaches.

The *pasin*, as we say, or 'custom', seemed to find its way into early administrations guiding our young leaders. Assisted by trained experts and traditional donors, we forged our way. We built institutions, political parties, infrastructure, established diplomatic relations, filled our courts, schools, and parliaments with our own indigenous people. And the whole time we maintained our ways, our links to our land and our identity, and we resisted external pressure not to entertain others isolated and sometimes ostracised like us.

My point is that existing structures don't adequately measure us; not according to the institutions we adopted at independence. This is perhaps also true of socialist China today as it emerges, attempting now to have a hand in influencing the rules by providing alternatives in development in our countries. Historian Michael Howard said recently, 'we need greater understanding of China's environment, history and culture including its political system – but understanding does *not* imply that we like that system, but that we are able to work effectively with it.'

Nostalgia is a remarkable feature of human imagination. It allows us to remember our collective journey fondly, maybe excluding difficult dynamics and hard battles. So how will we look back and remember this period of transition? Will we blame those we ourselves engaged with diplomatically for setting standards too high, so that we were forced to accept lower ones? Should we blame our own voting patterns and governing systems, or each other? Or do we blame our own resilience for the calibre of leaders we now have in place? Or will we improve how we relate to each other first in Melanesia, so that one day our conduct becomes self-regulating enough to be remembered well, not just for our plans and priorities but for our achievements?

The point here is that a stocktake is needed. We know certain things already. We know that Chinese development assistance involves grants, interest-free loans, aid in kind and concessional loans. We know the gaps in the traditional donor sphere where demands for multiparty cooperation and aid coordination are most critical. China is here to stay. This, too, is reiterated in emerging literature, and the general consensus here yesterday suggests the same.

An interesting distinction was made in a recent UNDP Australian aid joint report on the development needs of Pacific Island countries. It noted that while Chinese policymakers are interested in adopting some aspects of the OECD approach to development, it is clear that they wish to maintain a different brand of aid built on China's own identity as a developing country. In November 2013 at the China Pacific Islands Economic Development Forum, a commitment was made by China to increase trade and share expertise in areas such as healthcare, education, tourism and disaster relief to PNG and Fiji. Both meetings saw a substantial commitment to concessional loans for infrastructure development.

In our Melanesian sub-region we boast diverse economic growth rates, markets, raw materials and valuable natural resources that China wants as its expanding middle class demands incrementally more. China is the second-largest economy in the world, producing over USD 10 trillion in output per year, up to ten times from 1998. The population of 1.36 billion trades 4.2 trillion worth of goods annually, and China is in the middle of a slow process of opening up its capital account. The opening up of the capital account will mean ample savings accumulated over the past decades will more aggressively fund their way across the globe and certainly into Melanesia.

This makes us in Melanesia relatively influential yet also very vulnerable, particularly where we have been slow to evolve our formal institutions of state and its processes to match the potential gains of growing and evolving populations, and importantly, our change in cultural dynamics. Australia's foreign policy through consecutive governments has been aligned firmly with US interests, particularly in military and defence cooperation in our region. For some time the US has been a Pacific power, albeit militarily remote and less visible in Melanesia. Recently, observers commenting on the changing regional dynamic suggest that 'maintaining authority remotely will pose challenges for any competing power'.

So what does this mean to a new order if non-traditional inputs in our economies are visible and welcome in the face of what one speaker called 'the China alternative' yesterday? Chinese foreign direct investment, diplomatic ties, scholarship programmes and, yes, the concessional loans and increased development support are almost on par with traditional donor support today. The presence of Western industrial nations through the Bretton Woods Institutions has justifiably guided a collective Western push for universal standards and transparency ideals through governments, including fiscal accountability. The World Bank and the IMF support core infrastructure projects in partnership with our traditional donors in Melanesia, underpinned by adjusted governance ambitions for recipient nations. Structural adjustment programmes and other public sector reform agendas weren't always welcome in Melanesia, let alone achievable within the weak implementing frames of our adopted institutions.

I said recently in an IPS interview that development cooperation requires a facelift that begs support from traditional and non-traditional donors whose record of increasing support, even to the detriment of recipient nations, continues. Equally, the unwillingness and incapacity of our past and current Melanesian leaders to halt the debilitating political mentality of aid dependence has ultimately created insurmountable debt, and may continue to undermine the appeal of ownership and self-determination so essential to this notion of island agency.

As a final and brief reference, in PNG for example, our debt-to-GDP ratio has not only exceeded the permissible legal limit of 35% through various means of legislative tweaking and commercial dealings. The problem is that our current decision-makers are reducing the ingrained transparency mechanisms and therefore weakening institutional standards to accommodate poor planning and worse implementation.

In conclusion, in Melanesia our development outlook must be updated with our own understanding as Melanesians and with our knowledge of political, economic, sociocultural and politico-economic motivations of donor states, in particular the not-so-altruistic agenda of donor aid programmes. Thank you.

The Samoan Experience of China's Aid

Mrs Peseta Noumea Simi
Assistant Chief Executive, Ministry of Finance, Apia

Talofa lava. I am happy to share our experiences and how we have engaged with China over the last 40 years. I'd like to say at the outset that how we engage with our partners, including China, in developmental operations is very much premised on a robust policy framework, systems, processes and commitments to ensuring continuing dialogue and consultations. This will ensure accountability, coherence and transparency.

Along the way, the government of Samoa has undertaken extensive and numerous reforms that have strengthened how we do business with our development partners. I'd like to briefly reflect on the ongoing and continuing work under the umbrella of the Pacific Islands Forum Secretariat. I look to all our member countries in this process, although we are at varying stages of progress.

As the Honourable Prime Minister said yesterday in his opening statement, our diplomatic relations with China started in 1975. Then a Chinese embassy was established in Samoa in 1978. Likewise, we established our embassy in Beijing in 2009. Since then, we have given unwavering support to a One-China Policy. This year marks the 40th year of Samoa–Sino relations.

I would like to give a brief background to the nature of the work we do in terms of aid management. In the case of our relations with China, the grants and the interest-free loans are processed through the China Development Bank while the concessional loans are executed through the Export/Import Bank of China. As I said before, it's a partnership relationship. In preparation for the deepening of this relationship Samoa has adopted a policy for effective development cooperation since 2010 as well as an immediate-term Debt Management Strategy and a formal system for aid coordination.

Different forms of aid are provided by China. First of all we have had interest-free loans for use for public facilities and projects that improve people's livelihoods. One of the features of interest-free loans is that the repayment terms can be renegotiated and outstanding debts can be cancelled, as was the experience for Samoa and a number of other Pacific Island countries in 2006. There was a debt cancellation programme for the Pacific in that year. Some of the examples of the activities and programmes that we have had funded under interest-free loans include the construction of sports facilities and a vegetable project, the government complex which now houses the seat of government in town, and also the office for the Ministry of Community and Social Development. These are clear landmarks in Apia.

The second form of aid that we receive from China is grant aid. These are usually provided for small to medium-sized projects that include social welfare, humanitarian aid, or other similar assistance. The grants are usually given in kind, commonly in amounts not more than RMB 20 million or around USD 4 million. Small cash donations are also made, usually in response to emergencies, and we have benefited from this in the last decade when we had the tsunami and also Cyclone Evan in 2012. The process is this: the signing of the technical and economical operation agreement, and then there's a dialogue on what will be funded under the related agreement.

Since the year 2000, Samoa has signed twenty economic and technical cooperation agreements with the government of China to fund projects that came from the education, sports, agriculture, health and meteorology sectors. On average in any one year, Samoa would be signing grant agreements to the value of RMB 100 million.

I thought it would be important to at least provide information on some of the challenges, some of the issues we face in the implementation and delivery of the different forms of assistance from the government of China. Around grants, it is usually difficult to get a clear decision on what China will and will not fund, particularly if there's a long list of projects from the government's side. What we've tended to do is ensure that when we do provide a list of things to be submitted for consideration by the government of China, we prioritise. I hope that that facilitates the decision making on the part of the government of China. Secondly, it is very difficult to try and reconcile records with payment advice from the agency of the Chinese government that is designated to work in this area. The actual payments made per approved project do not always correlate with the actual financing agreement of the related agreement. So as a result, the government no longer compiles a pipeline list of activities that could be funded from grants, and consideration for any new activities will only be made when current activities are completed.

It's also a fact that when we implement grant activities, and what is funded under loans for that matter, a financial commitment is required of the counterpart recipient agency. Community activities such as schools and proposals from NGOs are not encouraged, as they cannot afford to pay counterpart costs, unless of course there is an arrangement for the government to pay for those commitments.

In accordance with our aid policy, the government of Samoa clearly articulates a preference for grant aid. The option of loans is only taken up when we know that there will be economic returns involved. Another means by which we try to impress on China the importance of grant assistance to us is that we often ask if there is the possibility of up-scaling grant assistance because of debt sustainability issues in the case of Samoa. And for good planning we have also requested the embassy to consider the possibility of putting in place a regular grant aid programme with a set ceiling. This would greatly facilitate how we plan and programme over a number of years.

The third form of aid we receive from the government of China is, of course, concessional loans. These are usually provided to fund larger projects through the Exim Bank under the designation of the Chinese government. Unlike interest-free loans, concessional loans aren't easily cancelled or rescheduled. In 2004, as most of the Pacific would know, a RMB 4 billion Pacific Loans Facility was announced following the first Pacific Leaders Meeting in Beijing. And as most of you are also aware, in December last year a similar facility was also announced in light of the visit of the President of China. To date, Samoa has taken out concessional loans to the total amount of around 250 million under the Pacific Loans Facility.

The loan terms are uniform for all concessional loans. The average interest rate is around 1.9%. The average repayment period is 15 years, exclusive of a five-year grace period. There is a 2.5% commitment fee as well as a .25% administration fee. Indeed, the loans are concessional, but we face challenges all the same. These include conditions such as a short maturity period and fast-disbursing features of the loans. These will result in the rapid increase in the total debt stock as reflected in a rising GDP-to-debt ratio, elevated fiscal deficits, and increased levels of debt surfacing. There is also currently inflexibility in terms of payment dates. For those of you who understand how these things are managed, these are all very important considerations when you are working with loans. These loans add to the existing loan stock repayments, resulting in unusually deep repayment periods in any financial year.

This is how we have looked at the aid that the government of China has extended to the government of Samoa. It provides both opportunities and challenges. The advantages include being a readily available financier of projects. They can fund projects like infrastructure that other traditional donors are not involved in. The advantages with China's aid are that the processes are simple compared to our other development partners and that there is delivery on a timely basis and according to the needs of recipient countries.

In the execution of Chinese assistance, non-policy conditions are imposed, such as the fact that the contractor must be a Chinese company and that at least 50% of goods are imported from China. Of course, only countries that adhere to the One-China Policy receive this form of aid. I will go on to add that there is now a greater use of local labour and local companies to procure supplies and goods. Chinese companies, as you are aware, are state-owned companies and they are important actors in China's foreign aid programme, often being the face of China in recipient countries. Together with the Exim Bank they have both an executing and implementing role.

China's aid is very much aligned to recipient national priorities. The challenges lie in the negotiation process because the contractors have the tendency to negotiate directly with political leaders, hence bypassing the civil service that could provide the appropriate technical advice. The contractual arrangements are often not so clear, and there are also construction quality issues.

The potential for political involvement often contributes to suspicion of Chinese assistance, sometimes unfairly. Contractors tend to approach ministers with assurances that they could arrange Exim Bank financing despite construction funded by such loans needing to go through specified processes. Some have also promised forgiveness of loans when it is apparent that under the Exim Bank arrangements, this is no longer an option.

So what do we do? We strongly believe in ensuring there are strong aid coordination mechanisms, which would help to increase transparency and ensure that government is informed about development assistance, and the involvement of civil servants in decision making. This is very important to us if we are serious about central planning and debt sustainability. The involvement of central agencies in this process, such as the Ministry of Finance, will ensure that government objectives are met through close links to political leaders, and that there is capacity relative to sector ministries so there is the ability to provide a broad assessment of the impacts of projects as well as provide advice on debt sustainability.

We also know that oversight funding is not provided by China. Our capacity to oversee has varied across projects and across sector ministries. Where this has been strong, construction quality issues have been minimal and we have had practical examples of these situations in Samoa. The prioritisation of infrastructure works for China's assistance needs to be done in connection with ongoing and/or proposed works by our other development partners, as this can provide an option for co-financing of agreed-to objectives of the government and will promote trilateral cooperation.

What is the way forward? There is opportunity for the development of a regular aid programme to be delivered annually. It supports the government's forward planning and regular policy dialogue processes. There is also the possibility of trilateral cooperation involving our other development partners. There should be consideration for greater involvement in the tender processes if concessional loans are to be the financing modality going forward. There is an urgent call for consideration of the Paris Declaration and the Forum Compact Principles of effective development cooperation and use of country systems. There is also a request for more South–South cooperation training opportunities in relation to technical and economic cooperation. We are looking towards durable partnerships through:
- facilitation of the development of private sector initiatives,
- the provision of Technical Assistance to the Samoan private sector,
- study tours,
- other capacity building initiatives tenable to China, and
- exploring opportunities for private/public partnerships.

Given the transition of Samoa to a low-income status country as we graduated out of least-developed country status last year, it's likely that China would prefer that we look more towards the use of loans, despite the fact that we have always impressed upon them the importance of grant assistance. It would be very much in the interests of the government of Samoa to provide space for itself to reduce current loan stocks for a period of two to three years before it looks to consider further borrowing and to be vigilant about using the most competitive loan rate facilities. The ability to renegotiate loan terms, therefore, is essential in this regard.

China's Development Aid to Fiji: Motive and Method

Professor Lyu Guixia

Research Centre for Pacific Island Countries, Liaocheng University, Shandong

My name is Lyu Guixia and I come from China. At the same time I am a visiting fellow at ANU. Paul d'Arcy is my tutor and coordinator. This is my first time taking part in an international meeting abroad. I am quite nervous.

My topic is China's development aid to Fiji. Development aid, also called Official Development Assistance, or ODA, is financial aid given by governments and other agencies to support the economic, environmental, social and political development of developing countries. In the past, most development aid came from Western industrialised countries, especially from the 28 members of the Development Assistance Committee of the OECD, such as the US, Germany, Japan, Australia and NZ. But China, India, Brazil, Russia and other emerging economies have also joined them in recent years.

It looks like breaking the tradition . . . Western countries took the lead in the developing aid area and made it their exclusive domain. Many Western scholars and officials question the motivation and message of development aid offered by these countries. But in my opinion, it is a symbol of societal progress in the context of globalisation. In this article I have been focusing on several aspects.

One is the progress of China's development aid to Fiji. China's development aid to Fiji began in the 1970s, but it did not catch people's attention because of its restricted scope. After Hu Yaobang visited Fiji in 1985,[1] economic cooperation between China and Fiji grew in scale and scope. Through this visit, China and Fiji were fully aware that both sides belonged to the Third World and had another significant shared interest. Both sides would enlarge and deepen economic and technological cooperation.

In 2006, Chinese development aid increased considerably for two reasons: First, Chinese Premier Wen Jiabao visited Fiji and issued a joint communiqué in 2006 with Pacific leaders. Wen was the first Chinese head of government to visit island governments in the Pacific. The joint communiqué marked a new stage in Sino–Fiji relations.[2]

Another reason for the increase in China's aid was Fiji's December 2006 coup and changes in the international situation. After the coup, Australia and New Zealand imposed sanctions on Fiji. At the same time, Fiji was suspended from the Commonwealth and from the Pacific Islands Forum. In this situation, China gave priority to Fiji and maintained its full range of aid programmes.

Frank Bainimarama of Fiji aimed to increase Fiji–Chinese relations and adopted a 'Look North' policy. For its part, China increased its aid to Fiji and Bainimarama visited China. A bilateral agreement between China and Fiji was signed and, under it, China provides aid to Fiji for special activities.

According to the White Paper on China's foreign aid released by the State Council Information Office in 2011,[3] complete foreign aid programmes include help in recipient countries with construction projects in production and civilian areas by providing aid through interest-free loans and the like. This is the largest category of China's foreign aid and accounts for 40% of China's official expenditure overall. In the case of China's aid to Fiji, the percentage is perhaps higher. There is a focus on human resources and development cooperation, emergency humanitarian aid, relief, student scholarships and other similar forms of assistance.

Motivations for China's development aid to Fiji – as far as China's motivations are concerned, many Western officials and scholars provide all kinds of statements, but in my opinion, the motivation of Chinese aid to Fiji includes the following four main aspects.

Firstly, it is the continuation of internationalist thought. China is a developing country but it has begun to undertake corresponding international obligations and provide assistance to other developing countries that require assistance.

Secondly, aid can contribute to establishing a good international image. Any country or organisation wants to create a good image in the international community. As a responsible power, China is playing a role in international affairs, and is providing aid to more and more developing countries, including Fiji.

Thirdly, political motivations are a very important factor. First of all, Fiji's adherence to the One-China Policy is the most important.[4] In fact, China's aid to Fiji is conditional; that is, Fiji must persist with its One-China Policy. In addition, China seeks Fiji's support on issues related to China's core interests and major concerns.

Fourth, China's development aid to Fiji will benefit both Fiji and China.[5] The two economies are highly complementary; Fiji is economically backward but boasts rich tourist, marine, mineral, agricultural and forestry resources. And China has the advantages of capital, technology, market and human resources. So I think China's aid to Fiji is killing two birds with one stone.

How effective is China's aid?

First, I think China's aid to Fiji has played an important role in Fiji's economic development. It is not only improving the economic environment but also enhancing Fiji's ability to be independent and reducing dependency on imports.

Second, Chinese aid to Fiji is suitable to local custom and practice while enhancing the people's living conditions, improving their living standards, and increasing their incomes.

Third, China's aid to Fiji is also improving the status and employment rate of women, which enhances their confidence. The All China Women's Federation provides assistance to the Ministry of Women in Fiji. This helps provide the opportunity to walk from welfare to workfare.

Fourth, China's aid to Fiji plays an important role in the process of democratisation in Fiji. China provided support to make the holding of elections in Fiji in 2014 possible.[6] This support included the provision of $1.42 million and police and law enforcement equipment.

In the end, China's development aid to Fiji deepens and enlarges Chinese–Fijian relations. This rests on mutual respect, the enhancement of understanding and the deepening of trust. China respects Fiji's sovereignty, unlike countries that continue to bully Fiji. China believes Fiji has the right to resolve its own issues as a sovereign nation. China will not take sides in continuously condemning and pressuring Fiji to make decisions like Australia and New Zealand. China will be pro-Fiji and support Fiji and treat Fiji like a friend as long as it supports the One-China Policy.

In turn, Fiji appreciates China's principle of non-interference in other countries' internal affairs and its understanding for the changes in Fiji's political situation. When Fiji's leader Voreqe Bainimarama visited China, he said China was the one country that understood the reforms he was trying to implement.[7] China is willing to work with Fiji to lift bilateral ties to a higher level.

Different Voices

Certainly there are different voices. Some think Chinese assistance does not provide urgent assistance for balance of payment difficulties since the vast bulk of payments are made overseas. In Australian opinion, China's aid to Fiji has been an apparent effort to use money as a persuasive diplomatic tool, undermining international efforts to isolate Fiji's military government.[8]

Some think a potent Fiji navy with new Chinese vessels and an army with Chinese arms and vehicles could present New Zealand with a potentially dangerous and unusual military threat. I don't think so. Is Tonga's defence force also a threat?

The United States had created a firewall around much of the Pacific from Guam to Hawai'i, to American Samoa and Australia, and by renewing ties with New Zealand. And what is the purpose of America? Apparently, it was fear of China and was meant to lock the Chinese out of the South Pacific or lock them into Fiji.

Problems

It is recognised that there are many shortcomings in China's development aid to Fiji. They include a lack of transparency as to the volume of aid, a focus on infrastructure, which means little contact with the public, and also a focus on construction in infrastructure projects while giving too little attention to follow-up maintenance and upgrading.

Notes

1. Zu Qichen, 'General Secretary Hu Yaobang visited five countries in Oceania' *World Affairs*, Vol. 7 185, p.2.
2. 'China, Fiji pledge to establish important cooperative partnership', *Xinhua News Agency*, 4 April 2006.
3. 'The State Council Information Office', *China's Foreign Aid*, Beijing, People's Publishing House, 2011, p.1.
4. 'China makes grant to Fiji, praises one-China policy', *BBC Monitoring Asia Pacific*, 10 May 2005.
5. 'China-Fiji ties of cooperation continue to grow', *Xinhua News Agency*, 22 December 2011.
6. People's Republic of China commits $1.42 million to Fiji election', *MENA Report*, 9 June 2014.
7. 'China respects Fiji's sovereignty: envoy', *Asia Pulse*, 14 June 2011.
8. 'Australia urges China to stop supporting Fiji 's military government', *Asia News Monitor* 27 April 2009.

The Trend Towards Chinese Triangular Development Cooperation: The Cases of PNG and Timor-Leste

Denghua Zhang
PhD candidate, Australian National University, Canberra

My presentation today will be in two parts. The first examines the features of Chinese foreign aid in recent years. The second is based on my recent fieldwork in PNG and Timor-Leste, and discusses the new phenomenon of Chinese triangular development cooperation.

Features of Chinese Aid in Recent Years and the Scale of Chinese Aid

China, a rising power, is also a rising donor, which is exerting substantial influence on the international aid regime. Foreign aid presents an excellent example of China's growing economic strength.

Chinese foreign aid has been growing rapidly over the last decade, and this trend continues. China has become one of the main donors. According to China's White Paper on Foreign Aid released in April 2011, the first official aid document clarifying in detail Chinese foreign aid since 1950s, China's cumulative overseas assistance reached USD 41.5 billion by 2009, covering 161 countries and over 30 regional and international organisations. In particular, the annual increase averaged 29.4% from 2004 to 2009[1]. China's second White Paper on Foreign Aid records a continued momentum of growth from 2010 to 2012, totalling 89.34 billion yuan (USD 14.53 billion).[2]

Chinese aid to Africa and Oceania are good examples to illustrate its magnitude. In 2012, Chinese President Hu Jintao pledged to provide USD 20 billion in loans,

30,000 technical training opportunities, 18,000 scholarships and the dispatch of 1,500 medical practitioners to Africa in the following three years. In April 2014, Chinese Premier Li Keqiang visited Africa and promised that China would provide an additional USD 10 billion in loans to Africa. To date, cumulative Chinese aid to the Pacific has reached USD 1.54 billion and an additional concessional loan of USD 1 billion was announced in November 2013.

According to a recent report from JICA Research Institute in June 2014, China's foreign aid reached USD 7.1 billion in 2013. China's rank among donors has jumped from 16th in 2001 to 6th in 2012 and 2013[3].

The rapid growth of Chinese aid has aroused growing interest and concerns on the part of traditional donors regarding the scale, operations and motives of Chinese aid. It is worth noting however, that progress is being made: China issued its first two white papers on foreign aid since April 2011 and transparency is gradually improving.

Comparison of China's Two White Papers on Foreign Aaid

China's two white papers on foreign aid provide useful information to help in predicting the trends of Chinese aid in the future. It needs to be cautioned here that, while the second white paper focuses on a three-year period, the first white paper covers a much longer timeframe without disaggregating data into shorter periods, making exact comparison difficult.

Impressively rapid growth

Chinese cumulative foreign aid from 1950 to 2009 reached 256.29 billion yuan (USD 41.7 billion), while Chinese aid from 2010 to 2012 was 89.34 billion yuan (USD 14.53 billion), more than one-third of its cumulative aid for the six decades prior to 2010. By the end of 2012, China had provided 345.63 billion yuan (USD 56.22 billion) in aid, among which aid for the period 2010–2012 accounted for 25.8% (Figure 1).

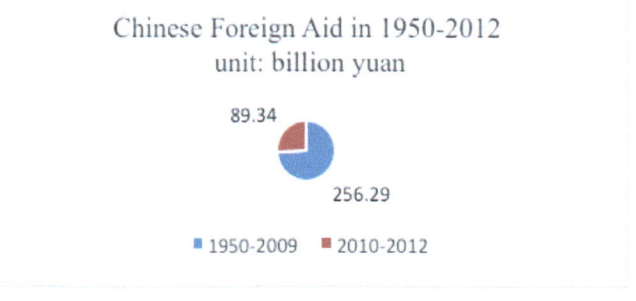

Figure 1 Source: Collated by author based on China's two white papers on foreign aid.

Drastic Change in Aid Components

From 2010 to 2012, there was a big increase in concessional loans which accounted for over half of Chinese aid, and a big fall in interest-free loans which accounted for less than 10% (Figure 2). Compared with grants or interest-free loans, the use of concessional loans expands the scope of Chinese foreign aid as it raises funds from the financial market. It reduces the financial burden on the Chinese government, which only covers the interest difference between concessional and commercial loan rates. The recipient country is required to pay back the debt. Though in practice some concessional loans are changed to grants and forgiven, this happens to a lesser extent than the write-off of interest-free loans. The focus of concessional loans on productive projects and infrastructure is meant to strengthen the revenue-generating capacity of the recipient country and its ability to pay back the debt. These advantages explain why this form of aid has grown in importance since 1995, as China is facing greater demand for aid from the developing world.

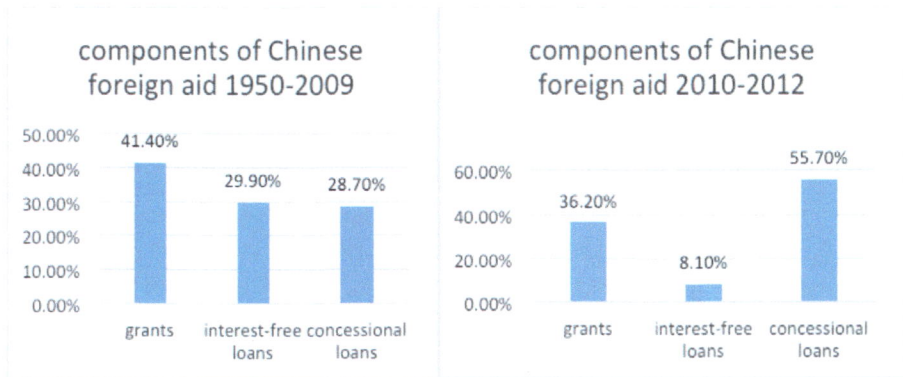

Figure 2: Source: Collated by author based on China's two white papers on foreign aid.

Africa and Asia as the Main Focus

From 2010 to 2012, China provided aid to 121 countries, including 30 in Asia, 51 in Africa, 9 in Oceania, 19 in Latin America and the Caribbean, and 12 in Europe. Africa and Asia continued to be the two largest recipients of Chinese foreign aid. Aid to Africa exceeded half of Chinese aid in the period, while Asia accounted for nearly one-third of the total. The consistency of Africa and Asia as top priorities for Chinese foreign aid highlights the ongoing significance of the regions to China from both political and economic perspectives. The proportion of Chinese aid to other regions, including Latin America and the Caribbean, Oceania and Europe remain small. For instance, China's aid to Oceania accounted for 4.2% of its aid over the period 2010–2012. But given the small population, the Pacific Island countries have received high per capita Chinese aid. Since the inaugural meeting of the China-Pacific Island Countries Economic Development & Cooperation Forum in 2006, China has trained over 2,500 officials and technicians from Pacific Island countries.

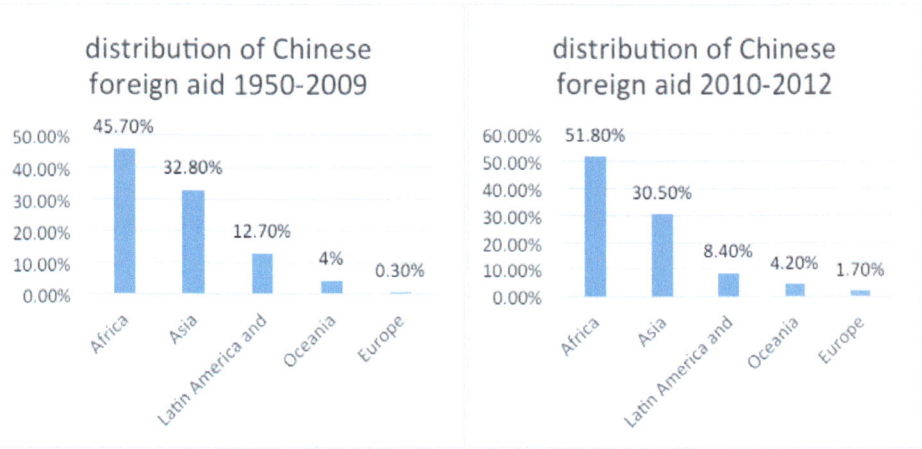

Figure 3 Source: Collated by author based on China's two white papers on foreign aid.

China's Growing Trilateral Aid Cooperation: a New Phenomenon
A close examination of Chinese foreign aid over the past decade reveals an interesting phenomenon: Chinese foreign aid, both in terms of norms and practice, seems to differ greatly from that of traditional donors. The Chinese government takes great pride in having created a new aid model with Chinese characteristics. To elaborate, Chinese aid has no political strings attached, emphasises equality and mutual benefits, and focuses on 'hardware' aid projects, infrastructure in particular. Despite ranking as the second-largest economy in 2010, China insists it is still a developing country and its foreign aid falls within South–South cooperation. By contrast, traditional donors highlight 'software' areas including democracy and good governance, attach conditionality to promote accountability, and prefer aiding programmes rather than projects.

Yet, despite their considerable differences, more recently China has signalled a greater willingness to work with other donors. An increasing number of discussions and aid projects have been conducted in partnership with traditional donors and international organisations, covering diverse areas such as agriculture, environmental protection and technical training. Since 2012, aid cooperation has been included in the China-US Strategic and Economic Dialogue meetings, the highest-level dialogue between the two nations. Chinese leaders met with UNDP administrator Helen Clark during her visits to China in 2009 and 2013, and promised to join hands for more aid cooperation in other developing countries. In the Pacific, China has reached agreements with New Zealand and Australia in August 2012 and April 2013 respectively to conduct trilateral cooperation. The China-New Zealand-Cook Islands trilateral aid project on water supply (called *Te Mato Vai*) claims to be China's first trilateral aid project with traditional donors.

Figure 4 Source: made by author based on China's two white papers on foreign aid and online information. Errors may exist.

China-Australia-PNG Trilateral Project on Malaria Control

Malaria remains a serious public health problem in PNG. The PNG government has requested help from China and Australia to combat malaria. Consequently, discussions have been held among the three countries on several occasions.

In April 2013, Australia and China signed a Memorandum of Understanding on development cooperation. This MOU stands as a milestone on aid cooperation. Under the rather broad terms of the MOU, Australia and China agreed to conduct trilateral cooperation. Malaria control was later identified as a pilot project and joint delegations were dispatched to PNG to flesh out the design of this project.

This project will officially start in 2015. It has two main objectives: to strengthen PNG's health system by improving PNG Central Public Health Laboratory (CPHL) services and malaria diagnosis, and to strengthen PNG malaria research by assisting the PNG Institute of Medical Research (PNGIMR). As research is the core of the PNG National Malaria Strategic Plan, this trilateral project will support operational research in accordance with the plan.

Australia will provide AUD 4 million to support the project. Joint research projects between Australian universities and PNGIMR may follow in the future. China will provide technical experts to work at PNGIMR headquarters in Goroka and CPHL at Port Moresby General Hospital. As the host country, PNG government will facilitate the operation of the project.

China–US–Timor-Leste Trilateral Project on Agriculture

This project was initiated by the US and China in conjunction with the Ministry of Agriculture and Fisheries (MAF) of Timor-Leste. At the fourth meeting of the China-US Strategic and Economic Dialogue in Beijing in May 2012, Chinese State

Councillor Dai Bingguo and US Secretary of State Hillary Clinton agreed that the two countries would conduct development cooperation in agriculture, health and human resources in other countries. In the follow-up meetings in 2013, consensus was reached between China and the US to conduct trilateral aid cooperation on agricultural development and food security in Timor-Leste. A Memorandum of Understanding was signed in October 2013.

This small pilot project ran from November 2013 to December 2014. It was designed to strengthen capacity building in Timor-Leste's agricultural sector. Specifically, China and the US agricultural experts taught Timorese farmers the knowledge and skills to increase production of selected crops. China focused on maize while the US focused on beans and onions. Regular short-term classroom and in-field demonstration sessions were held at the agricultural demonstration plots. As is the common practice of human resources training, China and US contributed to the project by covering the training costs rather than providing direct financial support to the Timor-Leste government. The Timor-Leste government contributed to the project by providing the field site for demonstration plots and training facilities, as well as organising farmers to participate in the training activities. Chinese and US trainers worked side by side. More than 100 farmers, MAF extension workers and UNTL agriculture students participated in the training.

Reasons for Growing Chinese Trilateral Aid Cooperation?
Engagement Imperative
In recent years, the engagement between China, traditional donors and recipient countries has been growing, which facilitates their mutual understanding and learning. For instance, Australia is the first Western country to provide foreign aid to China since Oct 1981. The two countries, especially China's Ministry of Commerce and former AusAID (now DFAT), regularly exchange views on each other's foreign aid policy and practice as well as potential aid cooperation. The signing of an MOU on development cooperation in 2013 marks a new stage of their partnership. Aid communication and cooperation between China and the US is growing at both government and academic levels. The inaugural US–China Global Development Dialogue was held in Beijing in April 2014. Aid cooperation has received strong high-level political buy-in from both countries and is increasingly regarded as a key component of the broader China-US bilateral relations. Currently, the two countries have conducted or are conducting trilateral aid cooperation in recipient countries including Liberia, Afghanistan, Timor-Leste, and promised to expand the cooperation to Myanmar and some other developing countries.

Desire for Mutual Learning
China, as the largest emerging donor, has achieved remarkable progress in eradicating extreme poverty and promoting economic development. About 600 million Chinese people have been lifted out of poverty in the last three decades.

China has the capacity to contribute to development in other developing countries by providing practical expertise. Likewise, traditional donors have rich experience in areas including aid management and evaluation. Trilateral cooperation presents a good opportunity for China and traditional donors to learn from and complement each other in aid delivery. For the China-Australia-PNG trilateral project on malaria control, Australia values China's expertise in malaria control, in particular the development of effective artemisin-based treatments, while China values Australia's broad knowledge of PNG, gained over many decades. For the China–US–Timor-Leste trilateral project on agriculture, China and the US chose their areas of comparative advantages by focusing on maize and beans respectively.

Support from Recipient Countries
Promoting aid effectiveness has been a top priority for recipient countries since the Paris Declaration on aid effectiveness was adopted in 2005. This is an arduous task as many obstacles persist. A number of officials from the PNG government, especially the Department of National Planning and Monitoring, emphasised that promoting aid coordination and reducing aid duplication has been a headache for the PNG government. Trilateral aid cooperation has the potential to relieve the burden on PNG's limited institutional capacity and increase aid efficiency by guiding China and traditional donors to provide aid to the areas of their comparative advantage. Likewise, aid coordination is an ongoing challenge in Timor-Leste, with more than 40 donors working in the country. The pilot trilateral project between China and the US is embraced by the Timor-Leste government as a way to strengthen aid ownership and reduce duplication.

Global image building
Creating and sustaining a good image by providing foreign aid is a natural objective for both traditional donors and China as an emerging donor. The rise of emerging donors and their distinctive ways of pursuing aid policy and delivery have triggered mixed reactions from some traditional donors, including frustrations and even suspicions. How to find ways to accommodate both traditional and emerging donors becomes a heavy task, which is directly linked to the international development agenda, and the image of donor countries. Trilateral aid cooperation is tested as a new type of partnership between the two different types of donors and recipient countries, which seems to have more potential than bilateral aid to enhance image building as constructive and responsible partners.

Policy Implications
At a time when the global and regional aid landscape is evolving so quickly with the rise of emerging donors, trilateral aid cooperation is a healthy phenomenon. As one interviewee noted: 'Traditional and new donors are still a long way apart, but they are coming a bit closer through trilateral cooperation.' Trilateral cooperation builds

up the mutual trust between traditional donors and China, and promotes mutual learning. It also has the potential to strengthen harmonisation and ownership in recipient countries. Of course, it is worth noting that trilateral aid cooperation also brings challenges, including rising coordination and transaction costs, which need to be carefully addressed.

In order to promote further trilateral cooperation in the future, traditional donors and China should:

- Focus on current trilateral projects and do them well. Successful pilot projects will pave the way for future cooperation and attract the attention of more donors and recipient countries.
- Strengthen the engagement between China and traditional donors. Mutual trust arises from engagement. As one interviewee said: 'the trilateral partnership signifies the maturity of relations among Australia, China and PNG'.
- Identify areas of natural synergy. The China-Australia-PNG trilateral project on malaria control and the China–US–Timor-Leste trilateral project on agriculture are such projects. Donors need to find out more areas in which they can complement each other, and also align with the development priorities of recipient countries.
- Start from less sensitive public welfare sectors. Cooperation in areas such as agriculture, public health and water management seems easier to start, and these sectors are closely linked to the development needs of recipient countries.

Notes

1. Information Office of the State Council of China. 2011. 'China's foreign aid' <http://news.xinhuanet.com/english2010/china/2011-04-21/c_13839683.htm>, viewed 18/10/2013.
2. Information Office of the State Council of China. 2014. 'China's foreign aid' (2014) <http://news.xinhuanet.com/2014-07/10/c_1111546676.htm>, viewed 11/07/2014.
3. Kitano, N. & Harada Y. 2014. E'stimating China's foreign aid 2001–2013', Tokyo: JICA Research Institute.

The Tripartite China/New Zealand/Cook Islands Project in the Cook Islands – A Cook Islands Perspective

Hon Mark Brown
Minister of Finance of the Cook Islands

Let me say how delighted I was to be invited to this conference.

I will start with the Cook Islands context. The Cook Islands is a sovereign nation in free association with New Zealand since 1965. On 4 August 2015 we will celebrate our 50th year of self-governance. To date we have diplomatic relations with over 42 countries around the world, and membership in quite a number of international and regional agencies. When I came into the job of Finance Minister in early 2011 I was struck by the absence of clear policy directions or operating parameters for development assistance and development financing. As a result, on many occasions development partners didn't really meet the development priorities of the Cook Islands.

One of the first things we did in 2011 was to convene a roundtable meeting, which I chaired, which involved a panel made up of the heads of different government ministries and also development partners. A dialogue started on the list of priorities that the country considered important. Two weeks ago we finished convening our fifth Development Partners Meeting, and at that particular meeting, the table at the front was filled by private sector, NGO and community representatives from our island communities. Department heads sat with the development partners and ministers and listened to the views and concerns from the wider community. It's that inclusive and collaborative approach that we've undertaken over the last four years that has shown some really good results. There's been innovative, creative thinking on how best we can overcome what could otherwise be insurmountable challenges in addressing development needs. By taking this type of approach we've come up with some very innovative solutions, one of which I'll talk about – the Te Mato Vai Project.

One of the outcomes to come out of this collaborative approach is that we've found it essentially reduces costs in a number of ways; it increases the sustainability of a number of projects we've put in place; and thirdly, it delivers tangible, pragmatic results on the ground where it's needed.

The Cook Islands' relationship with the People's Republic of China was established in 1997. China then became a development partner when it commenced its grant pledges in 2001. The Cooks' unequivocal One-China Policy has been a very strong component of our diplomatic relations.

In the course of developing the relationship we have with the PRC, we are engaging on the basis of the processes China uses and the processes the Cook Islands uses. One of them was mentioned by speakers yesterday – our invitation to include China in the peer review process that we have been undertaking, an opportunity for PRC officials to understand how our systems work and to understand the sorts of processes that we incorporate in trying to push forward our development agenda. Professor Wang mentioned yesterday that what we're going through is a learning process. That's precisely the approach the Cook Islands is taking. We are learning, but also our development partners are learning – not just China, I might add, but also our other development partners.

In the course of this process, it's taken some time for the Cook Islands to start utilising what is a considerable amount of grant funding. The reason has been a lack of strategy or cohesion on the part of the Cook Islands to put this money to work. Since 2011, we've tried to ensure that we have a more strategic approach towards handling our assistance from China, as we have with other development partners. One of the initiatives we've undertaken between the Ministry of Finance and China is to develop a three-year strategy between the two nations that outlines the priorities that we both work on. Additionally we've tried hard to understand the Chinese budget process (its planning and procurement cycle) to ensure that we can work with their processes as best we can.

Early use of these grants involved, in 2002, the Rarotonga Courthouse followed by the construction of the Rarotonga police station. Both of these particular projects were driven more from the donor side. Oversight of their implementation was inadequate. As a result, there were a number of maintenance issues. This demonstrated the importance of having robust oversight and monitoring, and setting the standards before any work is done.

Grant assistance from China has also been used for goods and equipment, in recent years particularly tractors for farmers, furniture and equipment for the Ministry of Education, pearl farming equipment for Northern Group pearl farmers, and most recently, heavy machinery for all of our outer islands. People ask, 'why do you need heavy machinery for the outer islands?' Well, the simple answer to that is the outer islands all have airstrips, ports, roads, and they all need to be maintained. So a basic machine like a roller or grader makes a big difference to whether an airport is going to be open and available for flights or whether it's closed. It's just part of the capital machinery that's required to maintain these very significant infrastructures that we have in the outer islands where there are very small communities.

Again, the purpose of the grant funding being utilised in capital projects is that it reduces the upfront capital cost to the government of purchasing a number of these capital requirements. Grant funding reduces cash flow requirements that may be associated with borrowings or loans that a country might have to take out to get this kind of capital. And it allows for a higher tolerance of risk in our projects.

The Tripartite China/New Zealand/Cook Islands Project

Hon Mark Brown with Luamanuvau Hon Winnie Laban

Grant funding has also been used to assist in a number of regional events, most recently the Pacific Mini Games, which the Cook Islands hosted in 2009, and the very successful Pacific Leaders Meeting which took place in 2012, attended by Secretary of State Hillary Clinton and a senior Chinese representative, really lifting the profile of that particularly forum meeting.

The government has taken out loans from the Exim Bank to fund construction of the Telecom Sports Arena in 2009 (about NZ$12 million) and also the construction of the new Ministry of Education building. The most recent loan with the Exim Bank, of course, is to do with the *Te Mato Vai* Project, the Rarotonga Ring Water Mains replacement project. That is approximately NZ$21 million.

China is not the dominant lender to the Cook Islands. We have had concessional borrowings through the Asia Development Bank going back to the 1980s. There is a residual loan we have with France for work that was done in the 1990s on our power station. Then there are small commercial loans, mostly taken out by SOEs for upgrades that they require.

Originally donors and lenders to the Cook Islands were New Zealand and maybe the odd UN agency that did some work with family planning and so forth. Today we have over a dozen development partners ranging from China to Japan, Korea, India, Turkey, Cuba, and also the support of development partners through international organisations such as the EU, the Asia Development Bank, and numerous UN agencies.

As for the Cook Islands' debt position, we have a very comfortable lending position. Once the final Chinese drawdown is taken for the *Te Mato Vai* Project we will be at about $100 million gross debt. Once we take up the ADB's loan for renewable energy projects in the southern islands, that'll push us up to about $110 million – still well below the parameter of 35% of GDP that we use to provide ourselves some resilience in terms of debt. We have a loan reserve of $16.9 million – that is money the government has put aside specifically for the purpose of debt settlement. That was built up over a number of years with loans originally taken out with the ADB that had a grace period of five years, but the government decided to start putting aside money to repay this debt over time. Last year the government passed legislation to create a debt service account, a loan reserve account. This essentially ring fences this money. It cannot be touched by any sticky-fingered Finance Minister for any purpose other than for servicing debt. So it protects that fund, but also shows an assurance to international assessors that this is actually money that is put aside, and it strengthens the net debt position in the country's books. On top of that, there are unencumbered cash reserves. As one of the countries that is most at risk from climate change, you have to be prepared for a rainy day. It's very important, I guess, that small countries that are susceptible to physical disasters are prepared in many ways.

Just yesterday, Standard and Poor's rating of the Cook Islands was released which leaves our position unchanged at B+/B with a described debt burden as 'modest', which is very good.

Now to the *Te Mato Vai* Project. The island of Rarotonga is 30 kilometres around. The amount of pipe we will be laying to replace the ring main which circles the main island, and also a secondary ring around the inner island, is about double that. The project came about from the High Level Forum on Aid Effectiveness at Busan in 2011 with the theme on partnerships. The Cooks was looking very closely at how we could finance this particular project of significant importance to us without putting ourselves into a debt position that wasn't good for the country.

It's been mentioned before, and I confess I hadn't heard of this term 'islander agency' before. It's the role the country or island has in pushing forward its development agenda, really owning those projects and taking a lead role in negotiating with development partners about what it wants and how it wants projects to be implemented. So aspects of ownership are important, as well as a focus on results, the need to look at partnerships and a collaborative approach, and the requirement for transparency and shared responsibility. For us, the push for transparency wasn't to demonstrate to development partners that the Cook Islands was a country that was operating well. The primary push for transparency was to demonstrate to our own taxpayers that their money is being used well. If we could use that and demonstrate that model to development partners, then, hey, why not use the systems we've created for your money as well? And I'm happy to say that this is all progressing well after a great deal of discussion over many years with various officials and politicians from other countries.

As I said, the Cook Islands defined its needs. We had nearly 40 different individual reports pointing out the need for the country to have an upgraded water supply. These had been done by numerous agencies and many consultants over many, many years. The need was identified – let's get it done. The government also recognised that in these reports it was important that we didn't just fix one part of the water system – we had to look at the whole lot. A holistic approach was taken. This was a large project, yes. But it was what one would call an intergenerational project. It would last. We've looked at a timeline of 50–100 years for the benefits that would accrue from this type of project.

Sustainability is the important thing. This is a project that will deliver water to the country for many years. There was neglect for many years on a number of assets, not just water, which I could go on for a while about but I won't. It was clear that water was essential not just for our people on the island but also because one of the country's key economic drivers is tourism. So we must have a good, clean, consistent water supply.

I learned when I came into office that the approaches that the different partners had were very divergent. NZ and China had their approaches. Typically NZ had the North–South approach while China, as we've heard, had more of the South–south approach. What was clear to us was that we had to develop a model that suited us. What we came up with was an innovative approach that was more a South–North–South type of approach. The way I first explained it to our development partners when we sat down was: 'The Cook Islands would like a bicycle. We've got the frame and the driver, but we need a back wheel and front wheel. One of you guys provide the back wheel, one of you provide the front wheel, and then we've got a bike we can go around the island on. But the wheels have got to be the same. You can't provide a different wheel for this one and a different wheel for that one. And I'm going to be the driver, not you guys.' So that's how we got from there in 2011 to what we see now: a fairly good project moving forward.

As I mentioned, transparency is the key. Now all of government financing now is transparent, and all development finance comes through what I call an 'aid window'. We have a clear aid policy, a strong push for using national systems that we've put in place and made sure we've strengthened. All costs are available freely online. You can go onto the Ministry of Finance website and see the latest fiscal figures. The half-year update for December will be out in a couple of weeks. It's all there online and very transparent, very open. It will tell you how much money is coming in, who the development partner is, what project it's going to be used for, and when the project will be completed. The only downside I didn't like about that was the fact that politicians like myself will be very exposed to the public, because they'll look at this and say, 'hey, you said this would be done by this time – how come that hasn't happened?' Well, I have a foolproof plan. I say, 'go see the head of the Ministry, that's his job. My job is to get the money so it's done now.'

The financing of the *Te Mato Vai* project: the concessional borrowing through the Exim Bank is $21 million. The Cook Islands is looking to contribute $15 million and then there's a NZ government grant of around $15 million. For us, one of the key drivers and components was the inclusion of the local Cook Islands private sector in this project. That was a discussion we had at the political level and fortunately that filtered down to the officials' level and into the contract itself. So out of that $21 million, one third goes to the local contractor who does the trenching and digging work. One third goes to the cost of materials, the pipes which were sourced out of China, and I have to say those pipes also had a quality assurance measure where we took independent quality assurance teams to make sure what we were getting was the right thing. That testing on quality assurance continues right throughout the life of the project. And one third would go to the Chinese contractor (in our case CCECC) to provide the technical and expert engineering. So out of that particular project, the $21 million, you'd say that two-thirds of those funds remain in the country with the local contractor and the pipes themselves.

In negotiating the second part of the project with the Cook Islands and New Zealand just recently, one of the things that we have insisted upon is that although NZ will use an international tendering process, as much as possible local companies will be given the opportunity to be able to bid for this particular type of work. Traditionally, the international tender process puts in place conditions that are out of reach for local companies because of the size and scale of our small businesses. But combined together, a number of small companies have more than adequate competence and can acquire any required specialist competence to be able to deliver a project of this size in their country. So our discussions at this stage on the second component of *Te Mato Vai* are along those lines.

A governance group that oversees the project involves senior officials from China, New Zealand and the Cook Islands. That's been working very well. Down from them is a project steering group. These people are more involved in the operational aspects of the *Te Mato Vai* project. As we've said, it's a learning process for everybody. Chinese construction companies have a certain way of doing things. Our oversight companies want to insist on certain compliance measures and standards. On a number of occasions we've had to stop work and say: 'look, guys, we're not happy with the way things are going – these things are not being done. Take a step back.' Everybody looks at the problem, looks at a resolution to the problem, and then we start moving forward again. We've had a couple of occasions where we've had to go through this process but it's been really good. It means we've identified an issue early before it becomes an issue down the line, and then we have to go and dig up pipes again.

I guess this is an example of how, for us, it's more of a case of necessity. Small countries really do need to take the lead in terms of development financing, work closely with development partners, and make sure our house is in order so that the systems we use can provide an assurance of strong, robust finance management. It took a little time, we're still working on it, but it's an important project for us that will last for over 50 years.

Someone asked the question yesterday: is Chinese engagement in the Pacific based on a Pacific policy, or is it a basic international policy template that is adapted to the consequence of the way the Pacific operates? I thought it was a very good question. I'm not too sure about the answer, but I can tell you that from my view, specifically from the Cook Islands, that in the absence of any strong policy direction, especially in regards to development finance, development will just meander along.

I think one of the things I've discovered as a Minister of Finance is that on numerous occasions the attempts to look at a 'one model fits all' approach has failed miserably. It doesn't work – not in our country, anyway. We've had to take the approach of designing or coming up with solutions, ways of doing things, that are unique to the challenges that *we* have. In some cases they make no economic sense. If a banker looked at it, it would make no financial sense at all. But when we cast our eye on it from our perspective it has something that we called – at our Development Partners Meeting – 'island sense'. And you've got to look at innovative ways to find out how 'island sense' projects work. One of the things I've found in my dealings with the People's Republic of China is that there is an emerging flexibility, a way to adapt to approaches to find solutions. But it requires (behind the good, strong financial management systems you have in place) good, strong country leadership and ownership especially of those systems, and a strong ownership of the development agenda. I guess that's what was being referred to as 'islander agency' in some cases. You know, in a lot of ways when we first started off it was a bit of the tail wagging the dog, if you know what that means. It's still a bit like that with other development partners. But it's slowly turning around now; it's slowly working.

As we've done this in terms of development finance, the new challenge for us (a different area, but we can talk about it – and I'll finish off here) is in terms of climate financing and how we can get that sort of funding down at the grassroots level to get things moving, particularly for those countries most at risk from the effects of climate change.

But thank you very much for your attention. I will finish here.

The Tripartite China/New Zealand/Cook Islands Project – A New Zealand Perspective

Peter Zwart
Ministry of Foreign Affairs and Trade, Wellington

I wish to start with a couple of apologies and acknowledgements, certainly to acknowledge as others have done the organisers of this conference for bringing together such an array of perspectives and good analysis on the issue that we're looking at. Also to National University of Samoa (NUS) – many speakers have commented on the very fine venue and the organisation of the conference itself. It feels in this very beautiful fale that we are together under one roof, yet we are transparent to the world. I think that is something of the spirit of the conference and I think of the spirit of the people here today. Due acknowledgement to NUS for the venue.

The apologies . . . those of you that follow New Zealand politics might be aware that about a year ago a prominent New Zealand politician, in the context of a discussion on the rates of domestic violence in New Zealand, apologised for 'being a man' and caused quite a flurry of public discussion and media discussion. I don't plan to do that today but I do want to apologise for not being Jackie Frizelle, Her Excellency the High Commissioner for New Zealand, despite numerous signage that suggests that I am. Jackie also very much sends her sincere apologies. She was very much looking forward to being here today to join in the discussion and also this presentation, but she has unfortunately had to travel. So I am a ring-in from Wellington trying to fill some very large shoes.

My second apology is that I am not in the line of management within Foreign Affairs for the Cook Islands programme or for the *Te Mato Vai* project so I just offer that as a bit of a caveat on my presentation. I'm presenting the work of others, and if you're looking for a source of truth on *Te Mato Vai* I think you probably need to look to the eminent speaker, the Hon. Minister Brown, who was there at the inception of *Te Mato Vai* and continues to provide leadership for that programme.

Inevitably, because we're presenting on the same subject there will be a little duplication, but I guess I'm happy to say that the only duplication in *Te Mato Vai* is our two presentations, *not* in the work on the ground. I think that is one of the big benefits of this exercise and engagement that we have entered into with our two partners, the Cook Islands and China. I'm not sure whether I'm the tail or the dog but I just want to point out that the Cook Islands is doing the wagging in this project.

I'm very mindful that John Overton commented on our branding which I see heads up the presentation that I'm going to make today. It's not an ad for the coming All Blacks / Manu Samoa game, but I would point out that if you haven't booked your tickets or your accommodation then you should do so now. Whether that branding is a sign of retro-liberalism within the aid programme, I'll let others debate after the presentation.

In terms of what I'm going to do, some of that duplication will be in the project overview of *Te Mato Vai*. I did ask coming into this fresh what the significance of the name '*Te Mato Vai*' was, and unfortunately I got a number of competing explanations and translations and maybe I'll defer to my Cook Islands counterpart to enlighten us but it seemed that the ideas present ... well, one of them seemed to have Biblical connotations around 'water from the rock', Moses pulling water from the rock. The other said that '*Te Mato*' also signifies 'foundations' and I guess either way, it seems like a very appropriate title both for the project itself and for the exercise that it represents of cooperation and partnership in a triangular way.

What follows is the text of a paper prepared in the Ministry of Foreign Affairs and Trade in Wellington for this Conference.

Triangular Partnerships
'Triangular partnerships' are those between DAC donors and providers of South-South Cooperation to implement development cooperation programmes or projects in developing counties. They are characterised by three types of partners (facilitator, pivot and beneficiary). Triangular partnerships are often linked to bilateral relationships, and can yield synergistic results from the combination of partner experience, knowledge, innovation and resources. However, there are also challenges inherent in triangular partnerships, particularly communication, coordination, systematisation and evaluation, which make it difficult to demonstrate partnership results.

Triangular partnerships are a recent form of collaboration to assist developing countries to meet their development goals. The international development community considers such partnerships can offer effective complementary assistance through knowledge-sharing, technical assistance and different funding modalities. Global experience with triangular partnerships is limited, although international interest in them has been significant over the past three years.

Te Mato Vai Project Overview
The Water Partnership project (*Te Mato Vai*) is a NZ$60 million collaborative development project between the governments of the Cook Islands (CIG), China and New Zealand. The project is a key component of the Cook Islands National Sustainable Development Plan, and will upgrade ageing infrastructure to improve water quality and reliability for Rarotonga's population of approximately 11,000 residents and around 115,000 tourists who visit each year. It will also underpin

improvements in public health, improve drought resilience, control network leakage, improve firefighting capability, reduce risks to the tourism sector and contribute to Cook Islands' economic development.

The need for the project arose out of investigations funded by New Zealand and the ADB in 2009, which highlighted poor water quality, intermittent supply and excessive leakage, and estimated that the necessary upgrade work would cost NZ$60 million. This led the Cook Islands government to turn to its established development partners for financial and technical support to deliver the upgrade.

At the Busan Fourth High Level on Development Effectiveness, the Cook Islands

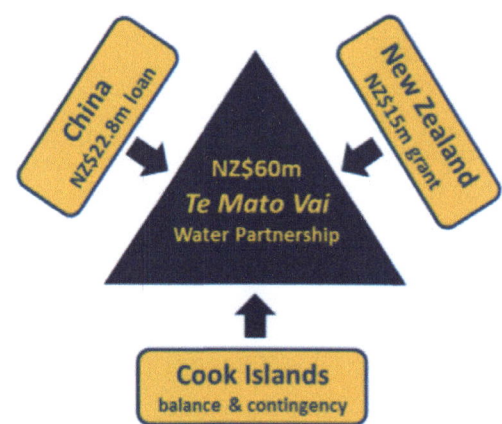

Figure 1 – Triangular Partnership Funding Arrangements

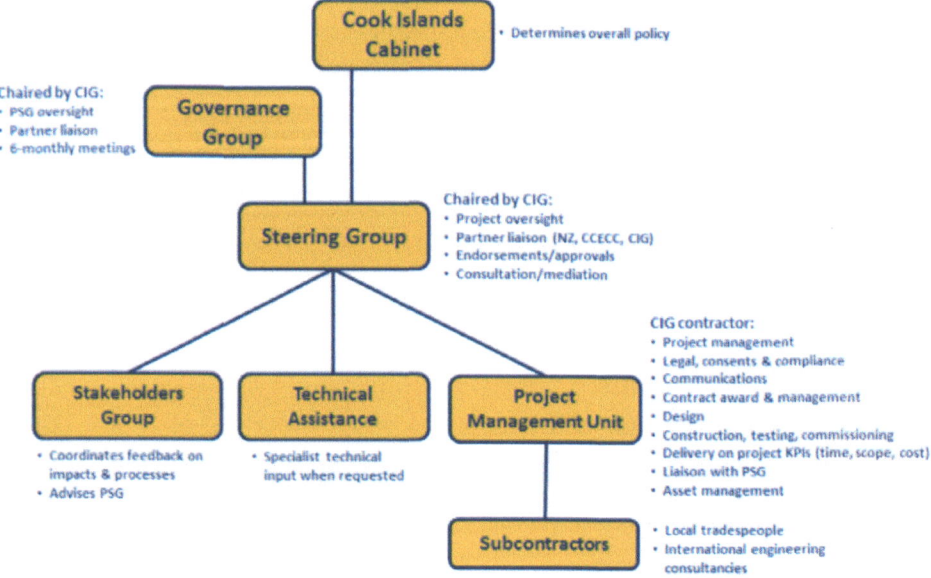

Figure 2 – *Te Mato Vai* Project Delivery Structure

Foreign Minister, Mark Brown, informally proposed a possible joint partnership between China, New Zealand and the Cook Islands. Over the following few months the three countries entered into a dialogue to determine what form this might take.

Although the Chinese embassy in Wellington services both New Zealand and the Cook Islands, remote communications proved challenging, and it was not until all partners met in Beijing that it was possible to agree common language and a process to establish the triangular partnership (illustrated in Figure 1). The partners agreed that both negotiations and the project should be led by the Cook Islands, supported by New Zealand and China, in order to enhance ownership and encourage capacity development. Each of the partner countries were encouraged to contribute according to their means and comparative advantage.

China and the Cook Islands signed a Framework Agreement on Cooperation in 2009, and China's Exim Bank agreed to provide a NZ$22.8 million concessional loan that was sufficient to replace the ring mains around the island. CCECC has built several significant buildings in Rarotonga in recent years, resulting in established ties and familiarity between officials. Noteworthy was agreement by China to have Cook Island's contractors involved with the construction of the new education ministry building, following an open tender process.

New Zealand has particularly strong ties to the Cook Islands via its special relationship and shared history. The New Zealand Aid Programme has a well-established bilateral relationship with the Cook Islands government, and utilises a combination of sector support and grant funding to deliver jointly agreed development outcomes. New Zealand offered NZ$15 million in grant funding to help the Cook Islands government to design and upgrade all other network components, and to enable access to technical assistance. New Zealand's involvement also contributed to an increased focus on sustainable delivery of a critical public utility.

This triangular partnership provided sufficient finance and support to proceed, and the *Te Mato Vai* water partnership project was announced publicly at the Pacific Islands Forum on 30 August 2012. All upgrade work is currently scheduled to be completed by 2017.

Figure 2 illustrates the project implementation structure, in which all three partners are represented on the project governance group and project steering group. CIG appointed the Samoa-based company Kew Consult Limited to project manage the planning, design and construction work, and has a 'client side representative' who oversees performance of this project management unit.

Project Design
Preparatory work for the project involved data collection to characterise the existing network, its condition and performance. This information was used to develop a computer model for the entire network. This model enabled confirmation of the Chinese ring main design, optimisation of all other network components. Information arising out of the modelling was used to develop a Master Plan for the

network upgrade, which confirmed the concept design and project cost.

Project Governance

In the spirit of partner led development, the Cook Islands government proposed the project governance structure, and chairs both the project steering group and the project governance group. The project steering group is supported by a project management unit, on contract to the Cook Islands government, whose performance is monitored by the government's 'client side representative'.

The governance group has played a significant role in maintaining the triangular partnership, by providing an opportunity for high level engagement to reaffirm commitments to the partnership, and guide implementation. The Cook Islands delegation is represented by the Secretary of Finance and its High Commissioner in New Zealand. China is represented by the Economic & Commercial Counsellor from its embassy in Wellington, while New Zealand is typically represented by the Deputy Secretary of the International Development Group of the Ministry of Foreign Affairs and Trade.

The project steering group has been pivotal in directing the project to date, which has required close involvement from all partners. It has been particularly effective at sharing information between partners and utilising technical assistance where necessary, to supplement the resources and capability of the project management unit. Interestingly, the Chinese ring main contractor (CCECC) participates in project steering group meetings. This is an unusual arrangement for such construction projects, but demonstrates the high degree of trust that permeates this triangular partnership.

Project Implementation

The *Te Mato Vai* project was formally launched at an unveiling ceremony in Rarotonga on 20 February 2014, following endorsement of the project Master Plan by the Cook Islands Cabinet. Work then commenced on two parallel fronts. The Chinese Civil Engineering Construction Corporation (CCECC) began its replacement of the two existing ring mains that run around the island. Pipes and labour were sourced from China, although other components such as valves came from New Zealand. At the same time, New Zealand and the Cook Islands government initiated the detailed design work for all other parts of the water supply network (i.e. stream intakes, storage tanks, water treatment systems, trunk mains, water conservation measures) and provided technical assistance as needed to support the project management unit and project steering group.

Approximately 30% of the new ring main has now been laid, while the detailed design work has been completed and tenders invited to build all other network components. This is slightly behind the original work schedule, which can largely be attributed to a longer than anticipated public consultation process and distractions associated with the Cook Islands general election held on 9 July 2014. It is currently

The Tripartite Chna/New Zealand/Cook Islands Project

anticipated that all construction work will be completed and the new network operational by early 2017.

Although funding for the ring main upgrade component required Chinese labour and pipes, all other aspects of the project have utilised Cook Islands government procurement systems to source necessary research, consultancy and construction services. In many instances, the Cook Island Government has also lodged tenders on the New Zealand Government's electronic tendering service website, to improve the visibility of these opportunities. This use of partner procurement systems will also provide local contractors with the opportunity to bid for work on components of forthcoming (non-ring main) construction work.

Project partners have exhibited a high degree of collaboration at an operational level. Examples of this have been New Zealand's willingness to help CCECC resolve administrative barriers related to customs clearance and work visas, and providing technical assistance for tender evaluations and to help resolve questions about contracts, standards and policy settings. In return, CCECC has shared its ring main design documentation, and been very responsive to help resolve ambiguous roles and responsibilities regarding construction supervision, jointing standards and testing methods. The Cook Islands Government has actively encouraged information sharing by inviting CCECC to participate in project steering group meetings, and providing ready access to contract and technical documentation.

A recent demonstration of how effective a triangular partnership can be was the speedy resolution of quality concerns associated with pipe jointing for the ring main. This issue arose when it became apparent that partners had different expectations regarding the inspection and testing method for pipe joints, and resulted in adverse media coverage. However, the issue was quickly resolved by the combination of prompt technical assistance and a high level commitment to agree common performance standards.

Development results

Te Mato Vai is a first 'Triangular Partnership' involving China and a Western development partner collaborating in an international development project. As such, it has attracted considerable interest from those in diplomatic and development professions.

The project has been progressing well, and has been notable for the high level of collaboration and commitment by all three parties to a successful outcome, as demonstrated at Governance Group meetings. Key achievements have been completion of the project Master Plan, commencement of construction work on Stage 1 (ring mains being installed by CCECC) and completion of the detailed design for Stage II (intakes, treatment, storage, distribution mains).

The *Te Mato Vai* project has enabled a development project that no one partner was able to fund at the time. It has also provided all partners with the opportunity to learn more about their respective approaches to development and

project management, and provided them with opportunities for sharing and mutual learning. Experiences have largely been consistent with the conclusions reached in a 2012 Brainstorming Meeting on Triangular Cooperation in Lisbon, namely:
- Leadership from the developing country partner is critical to success of the partnership.
- Mutual trust and respect are fundamental to overcome different operating styles and cultural contexts.
- Partners need to focus on the partnership's outcomes, and not just the process of engagement.
- Establishing the partnership significantly benefited from the trust and familiarity arising from existing bilateral relationships.
- In addition to the above, the *Te Mato Vai* project has revealed the following about the dynamics of triangular partnerships:

It is essential that partners identify and agree common delivery criteria at the outset (which include arrangements for funding, timelines, quality standards, procurement methods, monitoring and reporting procedures, roles and responsibilities etc.). This will avoid the risk that partners are unwittingly working at odds with each other.

Strong political commitment by all partners is fundamental to an effective partnership, and can overcome challenges that might otherwise slow or derail a project during design or implementation.

The 'facilitator' role is not limited to establishment of the partnership, but continues throughout implementation to ensure the partnership remains effective. It also goes beyond providing financial and technical support, by anticipating and overcoming the many administrative and procedural barriers to international collaboration.

Partners can have multiple roles, which may change over time. The Cook Islands has remained the 'beneficiary' to date, while China has remained a 'facilitator' (by the provision of a loan). However, New Zealand's role has shifted from 'facilitator' during establishment (by providing grant funding and encouraging partnership) to 'pivotal partner' today (by providing technical assistance for project management and implementation).

Timely technical assistance is essential to maintain project momentum where in-country resources are limited, as it can quickly fill capability gaps and address emerging challenges before they become significant impediments.

Conclusion

Although development results for the *Te Mato Vai* project will not become evident until the new network becomes operational in 2017, it is clear that the current design will result in significant improvements for both the supplier and consumers, with collateral benefits for the environment and the economy of the Cook Islands. Additionally, the partnership process has not only deepened relations between the partners, but has enabled them to explore other opportunities for development collaboration, be they triangular or otherwise.

6. TRADE AND INVESTMENT

Trade and Investment: The Samoan Experience

Auelua Samuelu Enari
Chief Executive Officer, Ministry of Commerce, Industry and Labour

Distinguished Participants, Ladies and Gentlemen,

It's indeed a great honour that I am presented with this opportunity to share our Samoan experience on matters relating to Trade and Investment with our Chinese partners. Before I start, allow me first to extend my appreciation to the organisers of this important forum; the New Zealand Contemporary China Research Centre; the National University of Samoa and the Sun Yat-sen University of Guangzhou for the excellent arrangements. Allow me also to extend our appreciation to our Chinese partners who have steadfastly contributed to and been actively making pragmatic contributions to the development of Samoa and other Forum Island Countries (FICs).

Chinese migrants have been making the journey to the Pacific since the 1860s and have made a major contribution in almost all walks of life in the Pacific. The Chinese Diaspora is prominent in business, the professions and wider society. This contribution to the country and to the relationship with China is deeply valued. China's opening to the world and its emergence as a major growing industrial power is one of the most significant – and *positive* – global developments of the past 30 years. A prosperous and outward-looking China is a vital component of international security and regional economic prosperity. The rise of China has been rightly described by many as the most important strategic trend of our times in the Asia-Pacific region.

Samoa has consistently always recognised and enjoyed cordial diplomatic relations with the People's Republic of China since 1976. China continues to be instrumental in her support towards development of Samoa's infrastructure which in many ways supports our continuing efforts towards creation of an enabling environment for investment in Samoa. To date, with China's support, we have a modern Sport and Aquatic Centre, excellent conference facilities which were utilised in hosting the recent Small Islands Developing states Conference, an impressive hospital, an x-ray machine and several volunteer doctors, donation of €1,360,000 to Samoa to fund its education policies and other facilities.

At the regional level the relationship with China has been steadily progressing as well, as shown by the commitments of regional leaders. In this regard, on April 6th 2006 at the inaugural China-Pacific Island Countries Economic Development and Cooperation Forum, a guiding framework was signed by China and several Forum Island countries in Nadi, Fiji. The Guiding Framework is an expression of the will of both the FICs and China to build an even stronger economic and trade relation by liberalising trade and investment as well as strengthening development cooperation between the two sides. It also serves as a platform for nurturing China-Pacific relations. The inclusion of Trade and Investment sectors in The Guiding Framework for the China-Pacific Forum is a testimony to the long term vision for greater integration and positive steps.

On November 8th 2013 at the second China-Pacific Island Countries Economic Development and Cooperation Forum in Guangzhou, China announced a new assistance package for the Pacific Islands, potentially worth more than US $2 billion. This package is made up of two loan facilities for use in infrastructure development, of up to US $1 billion each. One is concessional (which is counted as 'foreign aid') and the other is a more commercial loan facility administered through the Chinese Development Bank (CDB). The Government of Samoa submitted projects for consideration under this package that include construction of a new wharf at Vaiusu Bay and new Airport terminal.

Enhancing Trade, Investment and Tourism Relations

With respect to trade, developing exports to the large and rapidly growing Chinese market is both a priority and a challenge for Samoa. While our exports to China are at present minimal we are consistently working towards cooperating with China to expand our export base through strategic partnerships aimed at developing exports in a range of products. Samoa has a very limited number of products that at present can be economically viable to trade with China.

This situation is complicated by the erosion of some preferences resulting from Samoa's graduation from least developed country (LDC) status. China for instance maintains non-reciprocal tariff preferences for groups of LDCs. Samoa previously as an LDC benefitted from the Zero Tariff Scheme of China which allowed 95% of export products from Samoa into China duty free. Upon Samoa's graduation from LDC status, the government of China has generously extended this benefit for another three years. It is our sincere hope that Samoa continues to benefit from this going forward.

The Chinese market is intensely competitive. Samoa faces inherent handicaps imposed by the logistical difficulties associated with her small size and distance from the market, as well as the challenges involved in strengthening our supply capacities. It is vital that wherever possible, Samoa is supported in the process of reducing impediments to our exports posed by trade barriers and specifically associated with infrastructural challenges, so that we are not placed at an additional disadvantage by facing higher trade barriers than competitors from other exporting countries.

Currently, China has been increasing the volume and range of its exports to Samoa and other Forum Island Countries (FICs) and is now one of the *major* sources of FIC imports. This could be rebalanced in the interests of *both* sides by encouraging a balanced expansion of this trade flow.

With respect to investment, although Chinese investment in Samoa is starting from a low base, the potential for investment is very large. This includes both new ventures and taking equity stakes in existing ventures. The capital, the market and the skills that Chinese investors bring could be of benefit in strengthening the development of Samoa. The resource sector and the tourism sectors have held the most obvious potential, but other sectors including fisheries and aquaculture may offer opportunities as well.

Taking for example, existing Chinese investment ventures such as the Chinese-Samoan energy venture company the Green Power Samoa Fuzhou Haohui Ltd, the benefits of such ventures in terms of creating employment for local engineers, potential reduction in power costs for household consumers and local businesses are enormous. The Green Power is investing an approximate US $25 million (WST 57.6 million) for establishment of the entire project that will include building a 3.5 megawatt solar field at Faleolo on a 25-acre property leased from the Samoa Airport Authority. This venture will also be great for the investment outlook of Samoa with cheaper energy rates available. With Green power project fully functional there will be a huge reduction on Samoa's dependence on imported fossil fuels. It will reduce our Electric Power Corporation's enormous imported fuel bill every year. Eventually, considering that solar is a cheap, sustainable and replenishable energy source, there will also be reduction in Samoa's reliance on hydro energy and, more importantly, a reduction in the percentage of foreign revenue used for the importation of oil for its diesel generators.

There are also other companies, especially in the construction sector, that have been contributing their services towards the development of Samoa. These include, for example, Tianjin Construction, which built the Ministry of Justice and Courts Administration building and Tofilau Eti Alesana building at Mulinu'u, and Shanghai Construction Company which will be building a brand new state-of-the-art two storey Faleolo International Airport upgrade, a new and bigger port of Apia at Vaiusu and a 15 storey Government Administration building in Savalalo.

Samoa places great importance on finding ways to stimulate increased investment in our economy and China is a major potential source of increased investment in the future. In addition to the wider goal of promoting sustainable growth and improved living standards, investment from China in export-oriented Samoan industries would be a potentially vital contribution to achieving substantial increases in Samoan exports to China and the world. We would wish to see more and more of value-added processes undertaken in Samoa so that the volume and quality of Samoan made products in collaboration with Chinese technology is more visible. The Samoan Government is also taking further legislative measures to stimulate investment in critical areas whilst offering credible incentives to prospective eligible investors through its various programmes and proposed Citizenship by Investment Bill.

Tourism is the largest and fastest growing sector in Samoa and in recent years there has been a significant growth in the number of Chinese visitors travelling to

Samoa and other FICs. Although development of Chinese tourism to Samoa is in its early stages, good progress is being made in building a platform for sustainable development. This includes initiatives in the pipeline such as direct flights from China being lobbied. This would ease travel arrangements for Chinese tourists and investors without having to encounter the burden of transiting through different countries. Latest statistics from our Bureau of Statistics indicate that there was an increase in visitor arrivals in Samoa by 10.3% compared to the previous year and totaling 15,997 visitors for the period ending 2014. The majority of the visitors were from countries that do not have to encounter any transit burdens including visa-related ones to gain access to our pristine Islands. China's outbound tourism for 2014 was 107million. The recorded numbers for Australia and New Zealand respectively were 413,333 and 222,566. If Samoa could attract 1% of Chinese travelling to these markets, we are looking at 6000 plus additional tourists. This is an area of growth worth exploring.

In conclusion, I am pleased to have been given this opportunity to restate Samoa's commitment to growing the existing strong relationship with China. I am confident that this forum provides an excellent opportunity for all, including our development partners, in strengthening relations that will result in a win-win situation for all and also lay out a road map for future cooperation and development. In this regard, I urge all participants to fully utilise this opportunity and take the next step in formulating a plan of action that will cement trade, investment and enhanced cooperation in the long-run.

China and Natural Resource Developments in Oceania: Feeding the Dragon

Dr Tarcisius Kabutaulaka

Associate Professor, Centre for Pacific Island Studies, University of Hawai'i, Hawai'i

Introduction

This paper provides a broad survey of China's Foreign Direct Investments (FDI) in natural resource developments in Oceania. It focuses on mining, fisheries and forestry. There are three parts to the paper. First, it provides an overview of China's 'resource diplomacy,' outlining the various perspectives and discussions about the connections (and disconnections) between Chinese FDI and its foreign policy. Second, it identifies examples of Chinese investments in resource developments in Oceania. Third, it discusses the implications of Chinese investments for Pacific Island countries.

The increase in Chinese FDI in resource development provides many developing countries – including those in Oceania – with much needed revenue. Chinese investments are also attractive because they are often accompanied with aid and access to credit without the stringent pre-conditions that the governments of Western countries and Western-based international financial institutions attach to their aid and loans. On the other hand, Chinese investors are frequently accused of poor environmental and labour standards, and Beijing's 'policy of non-interference' in domestic affairs of host countries allegedly ignores, and in some cases perpetuates, poor governance and intra-state conflicts. Furthermore, the increasing global presence of Chinese FDI has caused concern, especially among Western countries that perceive it as an extension of Beijing's foreign policy and representing its expansionist strategy. They portray China as a threat to the current global order that is characterised by the dominance of the US and its allies.

In these discussions, Oceania does not feature prominently because China's FDI in natural resource developments in the region is, at present, relatively small compared to those from other countries. However, in the past decade, Chinese investments have increased and are bound to increase further, as China's demand for resources grows and innovations in technology reduce the costs of extracting and processing minerals, and make projects such as seabed mining economically viable. This will have significant impacts on the social and economic development, politics and environment of Pacific Island countries. It could also influence geo-political and geo-strategic relations as global powers tussle for control of Oceania's natural resources.

China's 'Resource Diplomacy'

China's economic growth and emergence as a global power engenders a hunger for natural resources. Consequently, since the 1980s, China has made a concerted effort to access and secure reliable sources of natural resources in other parts of the world to fuel its growing economy.[1] Chinese FDI in resource development increased, especially in Africa, Latin America, Central Asia, Australia and Canada. These were largely investments by state-owned enterprises (SOE) that were '... given the legal and administrative means, preferential access to finance, and diplomatic support...'[2] This was part of Beijing's 'going out' strategy to access and secure resource supply and markets for its growing industries. This intersection between foreign policy and resource extraction is what is referred to as China's 'resource diplomacy.' It allegedly frames the objectives and nature of China's investments, especially in resource development.

There are diverse perspectives on China's FDI and 'resource diplomacy.' Some commentators, especially in the West, have asserted that China's policies and strategies for accessing resources are linked to its foreign policies, foreign aid programmes and its provision of loans, especially to developing countries. China's international relations are, in other words, closely connected to – if not dictated by – its attempts to access and secure natural resources. In commenting on China's increasing investments in Latin America, for example, the vice-president of the American Foreign Policy Council, Ilan Berman, was reported as saying that, 'What we're looking at is not simply an economic play. It's an economic play that also has political and strategic undertones.'[3] This implies that Chinese firms' attempts to access and secure natural resources are part of a state-orchestrated agenda to fuel China's growing economy and establish its global geo-strategic and geo-political dominance.

On the other hand, many developing countries view Chinese investments as a valuable and alternative source of income. It is particularly valuable for countries that have been economically and politically marginalised by Western countries because of their poor records in governance, human rights, or simply because of differences in ideologies. In addressing The Cornel International Law Journal's 2015 Symposium, for example, the Kenyan Ambassador to the United Nations, Macharia Kamau, argues that concerns over China's increasing economic involvements in Africa have been overblown and that 'Africa has embraced the Chinese opportunity.' He went on to say that, 'Not only is China seeking raw materials, but they are also putting their money into manufacturing, infrastructure and construction... In reality, we now see that China has come into Africa and it is having huge transformative impact on the continent.'[4] Chinese investments have indeed contributed to economic improvements in some developing countries. For example, Erik Meyersson, *et al.*, in a study on the impacts of China's investments in resource development in Africa, found that,

A 1% increase in exports to China increases one-year [Gross Domestic Product] GDP growth by 0.2% and three year growth by 0.7%. Exporting [natural resources] NR to China also increases capital formation, investment in value added industries, and decreases labor force participation. This suggests that the increase in GDP is partly driven by increased investment in capital-intensive extractive industries. If China were to completely stop buying NR from Sub-Saharan African countries, on average, one-year GDP growth rates would decrease by 23%, capital formation would decrease by 66%, the value of value added industries would decrease by 21% in levels and by 56% as a fraction of GDP and labor force participation would increase by 9.6%.[5]

China is also an alternative market for exports from developing countries. This is particularly valuable given that many developing countries lost out on preferential trade arrangements because of the push for trade liberalisation. African, Caribbean and Pacific (ACP) countries, for example, lost their special access to European Union (EU) markets as a result of the end of the Lome Convention. This has had a negative impact on the economies of ACP countries because they could no longer sell certain commodities to the EU market with a preferential price and without having to pay for tariffs. Stewart Firth, for example, discusses how this has had negative impacts on Fiji's economy.[6] Chinese investments therefore provide an alternative source of income.

Chinese investments in resource developments are valuable, not only for developing countries, but also for developed countries with resource-based economies. Peter Drysdale and Luke Hurst, for example, note that, 'In 1999, China accounted for less than 5% of Australia's total resource exports, whereas Japan accounted for 23%. In the decade since then, the growth of Australia's resource trade has been entirely focused on China.'[7]

On the other hand, China's critics express concerns about China's FDI in resource developments. There is, for example, the argument that China's attempts to secure and access natural resources are motivated, not only by economic imperatives, but also by a state-driven scheme to exert China's political and strategic influence.[8] As Hongtu Zhao states, 'China is sometimes accused of taking a 'strategic approach' rather than a 'market approach' to resource acquisition by taking resources 'off the market' and conducting a state-orchestrated, worldwide search for energy and resources.'[9] Chinese investments are therefore often portrayed as part of Beijing's agenda to 'take over' global affairs.

The perception that there was a centrally-orchestrated strategy to resource access was fueled, in part, by the fact that a majority of firms involved in China's FDI, are state-owned enterprises (SOEs). In the energy sector, for instance, these include companies such as the China National Petroleum Corporation (CNPC), the China Petrochemical Corporation (Sinopec), the China National Offshore Oil Corporation (CNOOC) and the China National Chemicals Import and Export Corporation (Sinochem). According to Zhao, outside the energy sector, firms such as the China International Trust and Investment Corporation (CITIC Group) and the China North industries Corporation (ORINCO) 'are also getting involved in overseas upstream oil exploration and production.'[10] In the mineral sector there are companies such as Chinalco. It is because of these SOEs that many observers assume that every aspect of China's investments in natural resource development is controlled by the central state and operate within particular policy and operational frameworks dictated by Beijing. Consequently, academic, policy and media discourses, especially in the West, are often framed around the threat discourse: China is out to access and control resources in order to fuel its economic growth and to establish itself as a political and strategic global power.

However, more careful studies of China's investments in resource developments have revealed much more complex – and messy – stories, and that Beijing is not as in control as is sometimes portrayed. These studies have challenged the perception of a centrally orchestrated and monolithic Chinese FDI agenda. Graeme Smith and Paul D'Arcy, for example, argue that we shouldn't assume that there is a 'single China' and that '. . . Chinese people, the Chinese government and Chinese corporations are not monolithic entities; they represent a diverse range of interests, views and values that are shaped by their interaction with other countries.'[11] This echoes the observation of other scholars.[12]

Furthermore, the behavior of Chinese investors is influenced by a variety of factors, including, as Smith and D'Arcy argue, '. . . Chinese domestic considerations, and by legal, cultural and social norms of the host country.'[13] Consequently, the host countries influence how Chinese investors operate, as much as the policies, cultures and demands of China. Others have pointed to the fact that Chinese firms are not static: they are changing and adapting to new situations and requirements. As Drysdale and Hurst point out, 'Corporate governance of China's SOEs is evolving towards a system increasingly driven by market disciplines.'[14]

There is also a challenge to the 'threat discourse' – the perception that China is out to 'take over' the world. *The Economist*, for example, asserts that,

> For all this ambition, China is not bent on global domination. It has little interest in polities beyond Asia, except in as much as they provide it with raw material and markets. Talk of China's 'neo-colonialism' in Africa, for instance, is exaggerated. The country's stock of direct investment there still lags far behind Britain's and France's and amounts to only a third of America's. Though China's influence is undoubtedly growing, its engagement is not imperial but transactional . . .[15]

Another issue that is often invoked as a criticism of Chinese investments in resource development is that it contributes to or exacerbates poor governance, conflicts, environmental degradations and poor labour practices. Critics attribute this to China's 'policy of non-interference' in the internal affairs of the host countries,[16] and point to its investments in mineral and oil extractions in Sub-Saharan African countries such as Angola and South Sudan as examples of this.[17] China invests in resource development irrespective of the host country's internal politics. In its attempts to access and secure resources, Beijing adopts the 'policy of non-interference' in the domestic affairs of the host countries. Consequently, it invests even in countries that are shunned by Western countries. These include, for example, countries such as Venezuela (especially under the late President Hugo Rafael Chávez); South Sudan; Angola; Myanmar (Burma) and Iran. In Oceania – as will be elaborated below – Fiji, for example, has strengthened its relationships with China after Australia, New Zealand, and the European Union (EU) (among others) suspended much of their development assistance to the Fiji Government following a military coup in 2006.[18] In commenting on China's investments in new oil and gas fields around the world, Susan L. Shirk states that, 'The Chinese believe that because the energy supplies in reputable countries have already been claimed by the Americans, Europeans, Japanese and others, they have no choice but to venture into countries that others have shunned as international outlaws.'[19]

However, some have cautioned against the perception that Chinese investments perpetuate poor governance. Debra Braughtigam, for example, insists that there is no evidence that Chinese investments are solely responsible for governance challenges.[20] Meyersson, *et al.* state that,

> ... we find no evidence that diverting [natural resource] NR exports to China causes a slide towards autocracy as measured by Polity IV or Freedom House. Third, exporting NR to China worsens internal conflict and has adverse effects on human rights. To investigate whether these effects are generic effects from trading with a rich and politically powerful country or a fast growing economy, we compare the effects to the effects of exporting NR to the US and exporting to India, respectively. We find that the positive effects on economic growth are unique to exporting to China. Surprisingly, the negative effects on human rights are similar for exporting to China and to the US. For exporting NR to the world at large, we found no evidence of negative effects on economic outcomes but we find evidence of adverse effects on institutional development.'[21]

Others focus on the question of whether or not China's economy, and therefore its appetite for resources, would continue to grow. These discussions present China as a 'fragile superpower'[22] and its economic growth as temporary. Greg Mills, Terence McNamee and Peter Jennings, for example, claim that,

> ... all resource-based economies reliant on exports to China are in the same boat. The end of the good times may not yet be nigh, but China's current appetite for resources will eventually abate – and that could happen with cruel suddenness. The countries that have used their natural resources wisely to develop their human capital, build resilience and diversify their economies will be able to withstand any downturn in Chinese demand. Those that haven't had better start paddling quickly, or the shock may be too much to bear.[23]

This argument is based on the fact that China has enormous internal challenges that are likely to cause it to implode. Central to these challenges is the inability of China's governance structures – specifically the Communist Party – to reform in order to accommodate its changing economy and the changing demands of its citizens. Furthermore, despite its economic growth, a huge percentage of China's population still lives in poverty and lifting them out of poverty will be a challenge. David Shambaugh, for example, argues that, 'Many China watchers, foreign China watchers at least, believe that a kind of tipping point has been reached in contemporary China's development on multiple fronts, and that unless fundamental changes are undertaken, national growth will stagnate. So don't count . . . on the kind of trajectory you have seen in the last three decades.'[24] This is evident in the slowing down of the Chinese economy in the past eight years, more specifically since 2010. This is likely to affect countries, like Australia, that are dependent on natural resource exports to China.

Despite this, for now China continues to invest in other parts of the world, including Oceania. Its investments are important for the economic well-being of these countries. In the next section, I discuss China's FDI in natural resource developments in Oceania.

China in Oceania

China is relatively new to natural resource developments in Oceania, and its FDI is relatively smaller – in terms of value and volume – compared to investors from countries like Australia, France, US, Malaysia and Japan that have traditionally dominated resource development in the region.

That is bound to change as technological innovations make resource extractions economically viable and Chinese firms set their eyes on Oceania. Chinese FDI in Pacific Island countries has generally increased. For example, Yu Changsen points out that the cumulative value of Chinese FDI in the ten-year period from 2003 to 2012 was about USD 689.2 million. The main FDI destinations were Papua New Guinea (USD 313 million), followed by Samoa (USD 252 million) and Fiji (USD 111 million). In 2012, the value of Chinese FDI to Oceania was about USD 148.1m, compared to USD 0.42m ten years earlier (2003). Chinese FDI flow to Pacific Islands countries spiked in 2007 to USD 193.6m compare to USD 33.27m in 2006 and USD 37.94m in 2008.[25]

The value of Chinese FDI on natural resource development is difficult to ascertain, as the available data does not disaggregate this from FDI in general. It is however expected that FDI in resource development would increase as more Chinese firms invest in Oceania. As Terence Wesley-Smith states, 'Oceania is important to China as a source of key resource inputs for its burgeoning economy.'[26] As will be discussed in detail below, Chinese investments in fisheries have grown rapidly since the 1990s. The Chinese have also ventured into the mining industry, especially in Papua New Guinea (PNG) and Fiji. There is also the potential for seabed mining as innovations in technology make it economically viable. Henderson and Reilly claim that, 'China has carried out extensive oceanographic research, including the analysis of the region's seabed minerals' and that the Chinese fishing fleet established a base in Fiji in 2001.[27]

PNG and Fiji have, so far, been the focus of Chinese investments in resource development. In October 2014, for example, 'China's accumulated FDI [in Fiji] increased from about $US100m ($F194m) in 2011 to more than $US200m [F$389m] in 2014.' The report went on to say that, 'In effect, many countries will be playing catchup to match the contribution China has made. This is undoubtedly positive for medium-term growth prospects with potential growth likely to rise with capacity built-out.'[28]

Furthermore, China has increasing high-level political engagements with Oceania. Since 2006, China has held two China-Pacific Island Countries Economic Development and Cooperation Forums hosted in Fiji. The first in April 2006 brought together Pacific Islands heads of governments to meet with the then Chinese President Hu Jintao. In November 2014, the Chinese President, Xi Jingping, again visited Fiji. During that visit, he signed five agreements with the Fiji Prime Minister, Frank Bainimarama, 'with the aim of strengthening economic and strategic ties with Pacific Island nations.'[29] Xi Jingping also had a 'round-table' meeting with Pacific Island leaders, and held bilateral meetings with leaders of Samoa, Vanuatu, Niue, Tonga, Papua New Guinea and the Federated States of Micronesia.[30] These meetings demonstrate China's willingness to engage with Pacific Island countries at the highest political level and Pacific Islanders' inclination to 'look north' to Asia for economic and political partnerships.[31]

The increasing Chinese presence in the region has engendered concerns about Chinese 'threats' to Western dominance and corruption of island politics and environmental degradations. These discussions often portray Pacific Island countries, either as potential victims of a Chinese 'takeover' or as naïve and uninformed about Beijing's 'true' motives.[32] They are reminiscent of the 'threat discourses' about communism and the former Soviet Union that dominated the Cold War era. That led to Western powers' 'strategic denial' policy in Oceania. But, China is an economic and political power in the region in ways that the former Soviet Union never was.

Below, I provide a broad survey of Chinese investments in Oceania, focusing on mining, fisheries and forestry. This identifies the Chinese firms investing in the different sectors, the nature of their investments, and some of the issues and discussions surrounding their involvement.

Mining

In the mining industry, China's biggest investments are in PNG and Fiji, two of its strongest diplomatic allies, and the largest countries in the region, in terms of population and economies.

In PNG, the Chinese SOE, Metallurgical Corp of China (MCC) – a subsidiary of China Metallurgical Group Corporation – owns and operates the USD 1.4 billion Ramu nickel and cobalt mine in the Madang Province. This represents China's single largest mining investment in Oceania to date. Ramu NiCo Mine had a rocky beginning due largely to concerns that its submarines tailings disposal (STD) will pollute the surrounding ocean and poor labour conditions. MCC bought the mine from a string of previous owners. The Australian company, Mount Isa Mines (MIM), originally owned the mine under its subsidiary, Highlands Gold. This company was divested in 1996 before being taken over by Placer Dome in 1997 (subsequently taken over by Barrick Gold). Placer Dome had acquired Highlands Gold for its Kainantu operations, it subsequently bundled the Ramu and Frieda River projects together and sold them in June 1997 as 'Highlands Gold Ltd-noncore assets' to Highlands Pacific. MCC currently owns a share of 85%, Highlands Pacific owns 8.56%, the PNG Government's Mineral Resources Development Corporation owns 3.94%, and the landowners 2.5% on the Ramu Nickel mine.[33]

China is also an important market for PNG's Liquefied Natural Gas (LNG) that is produced by the US Company, ExxonMobil. In December 2009, Unipec Asia Co. Ltd., a subsidiary of China Petroleum & Chemical Corporation (Sinopec) and Esso Highlands Limited, a subsidiary of ExxonMobil Corporation and operator of PNG LNG Project entered into a sales and purchase agreement for the sale and purchase of LNG totaling approximately 2.0 million tons per annum. Under the agreement, the PNG LNG Project will supply LNG to Sinopec's LNG terminal in Qingdao, Shandong Province, for a period of 20 years.

In Fiji, Chinese investment in mining is in the bauxite mine in Vanua Levu. This is owned and operated by the Chinese company, XINFA. This is surface mining, which involves scraping the topsoil for about 3 to 5 meters. The lease is for 20 years. The actual mining on the current site was for 2 years (from setting up to production) and the rest of the lease period (18 years) will be for rehabilitation of the mined area, mostly through the replanting of pines. *The Fiji Times* on February 19, 2015 reports a forecast of exports in 2015 worth F$16 million from 400,000 tons of bauxite ore on the current mine site at Nawailevu in Bua. The company has acquired a second mining site in nearby Lekutu. *The Fiji Times* reports that 'After Lekutu, the company plans to shift its bauxite mining work to Dreketi and discussions have started with the landowners from Nabiti Village.'[34] The main benefits for landowners is through the payment of land lease premium, annual rental, the company's contributions to community development projects such as schools, churches, etc. and compensation for properties that might have been damaged during the establishment of the mine.

Apart from the bauxite mine in Vanua Levu, a Chinese company, Zhongrun, has acquired 66% share of the Vatukoula Gold Mine Ltd., which was formerly held by Emperor Gold Mine. This is the oldest mine in Fiji, and it will be interesting to see how the Chinese firm (with the largest share) operates it.

Apart from the existing mines, Chinese companies are also involved in prospecting in Fiji. In 2014, for example, *The Fiji Times* reported that China Yunnan Metallurgical Company (CYMCO) will carry out exploration worth $5 million on potential manganese deposits in Nasaucoko in the upper Navosa in Vanua Levu. The paper reported that, 'the NLTB has granted a 30 year surface lease to Viti Mining Limited which is exploring in the area,' a partnership with Viti Mining Limited.[35]

There has been a lot of negative publicity about Chinese companies in the mining sector, especially their records in environment, labour practices, and their hiring of Chinese labourers and contracting of Chinese companies, which means much of the benefit goes back to China and there is no development of local skills. However, in his study of the mining sector in PNG, Glenn Banks argues that '. . . the recent hyperbole, fear, and racism that the re-emergence of China on the world stage as a major resource-hungry player may have little foundation this is unlikely to be any different in contemporary Papua New Guinea.'[36] He goes on to say that, 'There is evidence that Ramu as a mining company is already 'fitting' and adapting into the PNG context. . .'[37] In discussing the anti-Asian uprisings in PNG, especially in relation to resource development, Patrick Matbob asserts that Asian companies' tendencies to disregard PNG laws were due largely to the fact that the Papua New Guineans '. . . government has lost effective control of the processes of managing these projects. It has overlooked its own laws and processes, and ultimately the interest of its own people.'[38]

Fisheries

Fisheries in Oceania has long been dominated by countries such as Japan, the US, and Taiwan.

But, according to the Western Central Pacific Fisheries Commission (WCPFC), 'China began to develop its oceanic tuna fisheries in 1988 in the Pacific Ocean and this region is one of the earliest fishing grounds by China tuna fishery.'[39]

There are two types of boats that catch tuna in the WCPFC area: (i) Long-line (LL); and, (ii) Purse Seine (PS). There are four tuna species that are the target: (i) skipjack; (ii) yellowfin; (iii) bigeye; and, (iv) albacore. The Chinese longline vessels operate in both the high seas and the Exclusive Economic Zone (EEZ) of Pacific Island countries. In 1988 they had only seven (7) LL vessels operating in the WCPFC Convention area, with a total catch of 42 metric ton (MT) in round weight. The number of vessels went up dramatically to 457 in 1994, with 14,062 MT of the nominal catch, the highest record level in the 1990s. However, the numbers went down after that. By 2004 and 2005, there were 212 Chinese LL vessels operating in the WCPFC Convention area. They declined slightly to 157 vessels in 2006 and then a dramatic decline to 86 vessels in 2007. But, in 2008 the number of Chinese LL vessels increased again to 199. This fluctuation in the number of LL vessels is also reflected in the volume of catch. Today, China has the largest fishing fleet in the region, accounting for more than 25% of the total tuna catch.

The big concern, especially with the LL vessels, is that Chinese boats are subsidised by Beijing, making it difficult for boats from other countries to compete with them. It also means that they can take fish long after it has become uneconomic for other boats.

This would have a negative impact on the fish stock. On February 11, 2015, Michael Field, a New Zealand journalist wrote an article, titled, "Marine Genocide' warnings over Chinese fishing boats,' expressing concerns about the increasing number of Chinese longline boats in the EEZ of Pacific Islands. He claims that, 'More than 1,300 subsidised Chinese boats are now licensed in the region with plans for a further 300 this year.'[40] He quoted a 'Samoa fish exporter and expatriate New Zealander John Luff' as saying, 'I call it marine genocide, something needs to be done about it soon. . . The whole South Pacific stock is getting hammered and if nothing is done soon, it will be beyond recovery.'[41] At the time of writing this paper, I have not been able to confirm that 1,300 Chinese LL boats were licensed to operate in the region.

Forestry

Forestry is a major industry in PNG and Solomon Islands. In Fiji, the forestry industry is comparative small and focused on mahogany and pines. PNG and Solomon Islands have a larger forestry plantation that involves mostly the harvest and export of round logs from virgin forests. The companies involved are predominantly Malaysian and Korean Companies. The Malaysian companies are owned or managed predominantly by ethnic Chinese Malaysians. In PNG, for example, Rimbunan Hijau, WTK and Cakara Alam are Malaysian companies that control 70% of total log exports. Although these companies are owned by ethnic Chinese Malayans, there is no evidence that they have connections to or supported by Beijing. China is, however, an important market for PNG log exports. As Colin Filer states, 'It does seem that more of these [logging] companies are now Malaysian companies owned or controlled by ethnic Chinese individuals, and this may have something to do with the growing importance of China as a destination for PNG's log exports.'[42]

This is similar to the Solomon Islands where most of the logging operations are by Malaysian and Korean companies. However, since 2000 China has become the major market for Solomon Islands logs, replacing Japan and Korea, who were major markets in the late 1980s and 1990s.

In Fiji, there are standing mahogany plantations that are worth a substantial value. These are managed by Fiji Hardwood Corporation and harvested to supply local sawmills and furniture producers. However, mahogany production has declined in the past few years, mostly because of land issues and the inaccessibility of some of the mahogany plantations. There is a need to build infrastructure in order to access the mahogany plantations. Apart from mahogany, pine is the other important agroforestry product in Fiji. This is produced into woodchips that are exported largely to China and Japan.

As stated above, although Chinese companies are not prominently involved in the production, China is an important market for forestry products. This is likely to increase and could prompt an increase in log production, especially in PNG and Solomon Islands.

Implications for Oceania

China is likely to continue to be a major player in natural resource development in Oceania. In the mining and fisheries industries, Chinese interests have and will continue to play an important role, both as investors and the market for resources. In the forestry sector, China is likely to continue to be the major market for forestry products, especially from PNG and Solomon Islands. Consequently, Pacific Island countries that are resource-endowed will become much more intertwined with the Chinese economy and geo-politics. This is particularly the case as advancements in technology make seabed mining become economically viable and investors compete for seabed resources.

Furthermore, despite the largely negative publicity about Chinese companies, a closer analysis demonstrates that they are generally not very different from investors from other countries. Political and economic forces in Beijing as well as market forces and factors in their host countries are influencing how Chinese companies are organised and operate. Consequently, they are transforming to meet international investment norms.

In natural resource development, China's investments are predominantly in mining and fisheries. China is, however, major market for logs from PNG and Solomon Islands. In mining, Chinese investments are small and few, compared to those from countries such as Australia, Canada and the US. Two Chinese companies are involved in mineral extractions in PNG and Fiji. But, China is a buyer of energy resource, in particular LNG from PNG. Chinese investments in the fisheries industry – especially tuna – are the most influential in terms of impacts on a common resource that all Pacific Islands countries share. There are concerns that Chinese fishing boats will push investors from other countries out of the tuna industry because Chinese boats are subsidised by Beijing and could out-compete others. There are also concerns that the increase of Chinese longline boats could lead to the depletion of tuna resources, especially already endangered species such as bigeye and albacore tuna. Pacific Island countries must therefore make sure that they benefit from Chinese investments while at the same time ensuring responsible corporate practice.

Investments in seabed mining could also engender territorial disputes as Pacific Island countries attempt to secure seabed resources. Fiji and Tonga, for example, have in the past been in dispute over the Minerva Reefs. Consequently, Pacific Island countries must put in place policies, legislation and institutions to ensure that these investments benefit them and their people.

As a result of its increasing involvements in resource development, China will ultimately have an impact on Pacific Island countries' economies and politics, and may even influence geo-politics in the region. This will, in turn, influence how major powers conduct themselves in Oceania. Pacific Islands will therefore need to prepare to deal more with China as an economic and political ally. This will require learning a Chinese language, sending young people to China for school, and understanding how the Chinese government and companies operate. Pacific Island countries will have to learn to manage their relationship with China. The challenge for Oceania is to feed and tame the dragon, and then ride it on the development voyage. That is no easy task.

Notes

1 Drysdale and Hurst point to the fact that, 'While well-endowed with resources in absolute terms, China's per capita endowment is poor, which has led to its rising demand being reflected in increasing purchases from abroad' (2012,16). Note that China's economic growth has slowed down since 2007 and declining since 2010. This causes concern for countries that are economically dependent on China's resource demands.
2 Chris Alden and Ana Cristina Alves, 'China and Africa's Natural Resources: the challenges and implications for development and governance.' : 1.
3 Patrick Gillespie, 'China's big chess move against the US: Latin America.' CNN money. March 4th, 20015. http://money.cnn.com/2015/03/04/news/economy/china-latin-america-relations-united-states/ (accessed on March 4, 2015).
4 Robert Johnson, 'Kenyan ambassador: China offers opportunity in Africa.' In *Cornell Chronicle*, March 3rd, 2015. http://www.news.cornell.edu/stories/2015/03/kenyan-ambassador-china-offers-opportunity-africa (accessed on March 4, 2015).
5 Meyersson, Erik, Gerard Padró i Mequel and Nancy Qian, 'The Rise of China and the Natural Resource Curse in Africa,' (2008): 4.
6 Stewart Firth, 'The Impacts of Globalization on the Pacific Islands.' Briefing paper for the 2nd Southeast Asia and the Pacific Sub-regional Tripartite Forum on Decent Work, 5 – 8 April 2005, Melbourne, Australia.
7 Peter Drysdale and Luke Hurst, 'China's growth and its impact on resource demand and iron ore trade' (2012): 14.
8 Kielmas 2005, 30.
9 Hongtu Zhao, 'China's Overseas Resource Investment: Myths and Realities.' In *Pacific–Asia Partnership in Resource Development*, edited by Paul D'Arcy, Patrick Matbob and Linda Crowl, (Madang: DWU Press, 2014): 110.
10 Hongtu Zhao, 'China's Overseas Resource Investment: Myths and Realities.' (2014): 111.
11 Graeme Smith and Paul D'Arcy, 'Global Perspectives on Chinese Investment.' *Pacific Affairs* 86 no.2, (2013): 218.
12 Ted C. Fishman, *China Inc.: How the Rise of the Next Superpower Challenges America and the World*, (New York: Scribner, 2005).
13 Graeme Smith and Paul D'Arcy, 'Global Perspectives on Chinese Investment,' (2013)
14 Peter Drysdale and Luke Hurst, 'China's growth and its impact on resource demand and iron ore trade' (2012): 32.
15 *The Economist*, 'What China Wants.' (August 23rd 2014): 45.
16 In 1954, during negotiations with India over the Tibet issue, Enlai introduced the 'Five Principles of Peaceful Coexistence': (1) mutual respect for sovereignty and territorial integrity; (2) mutual non-aggression; (3) non-interference in each other's affairs; (4) equality and mutual benefit; (5) peaceful coexistence. This later became the cornerstone for China's foreign diplomacy, aid delivery and its approaches to securing and accessing natural resources (see Braughtigam 2009, 29).
17 Taylor, Ian (2006), 'Unpacking China's Resource Diplomacy in Africa.' Center on China's Transnational Relations, Working Paper 19, (The Hong Kong University of Science and Technology, 2006).
18 Philippa Brant, 'Chinese Aid in the South Pacific: Linked to Resources?' *Asian Studies Review* 37

no. 2 (2013): 167.
19. Susan L. Shirk, *China: Fragile Superpower*, (New York: Oxford University Press, 2008): 23.
20. Deborah Braughtigam, *The Dragon's Gift: The Real Story of China in Africa*, (New York: Oxford University Press, 2009).
21. Meyersson, Erik, Gerard Padró i Mequel and Nancy Qian, 'The Rise of China and the Natural Resource Curse in Africa,' (2008): 4.
22. Susan L. Shirk, *China: Fragile Superpower* (New York: Oxford University Press, 2008).
23. Mills, Greg, Terrance McNamee and Peter Jennings. (2012), 'Introduction.' In *Fuelling the Dragon: Natural Resources and China's Development*, (Australian Strategic Policy Institute (ASPI), Johannesburg: The Brenthurst Foundation, 2012): 10.
24. David Shambaugh, 'China at the Crossroads: The Third Plenum and China's Reform Challenges.' In *China at the Crossroads: What the Third Plenum Means for China, New Zealand and the World*, edited by Peter Harris, (Wellington: Victoria University Press): 38.
25. Yu Changsen, 'China's Economic Relations with Pacific Islands Countries.' National Center for Oceania Studies, San Yatsen University, China, 12 August 2014 (unpublished), p.3. Note that this data is for Pacific Islands Countries: PNG, Fiji, Vanuatu, Samoa, FSM, and Cook Islands.
26. Terence Wesley-Smith, 'China's Rise in Oceania: Issues and Perspectives.' *Pacific Affairs* 86 no. 2 (2013): 362.
27. John Henderson and Benjamin Reilly, 'Dragon in Paradise: China's Rising Star in Oceania,' *The National Interest* 72 (summer, 2003): 103 & 104.
28. Geraldine Panapasa, '$389m input from China.' *The Fiji Times*, 25 October 2014, http://www.fijitimes.com/story.aspx?id=284084 (accessed, 4 January 2015).
29. ABC News, November 22, 2014.
30. Ibid.
31. Ron Crocombe, *Asia in the Pacific Islands: Replacing the West*, (Suva: Institute for Pacific Studies, 2007): vii.
32. See, for example, John Henderson and Ben Reilly, 'Dragon in Paradise: China's Rising Star in Oceania.' *National Interest*, 72 (summer 2003): 94–104; Susan Windybank, 'The China Syndrome.' *Policy* 21 no. 2 (2005): 29.
33. Patrick Matbob, 'We Are Not Anti-Asian – Just Victims of Poor Governance: a Media Perspective.' In Pacific-Asia Partnerships in Resource Development, edited by Paul D'Arcy, Patrick Matbob and Linda Crowl, (Madang: DWU Press, 2014): 60.
34. *The Fiji Times*, (February 19, 2015): 4.
35. Ifereimi Nadore, 'China firm set to mine.' *The Fiji Times*, 16 February 2010, http://www.fijitimes.com/story.aspx?id=140067 (accessed 4 January 2015).
36. Glenn Banks, 'The Origins of capital in natural resource extraction: Does it matter?' In *Pacific-Asia Partnerships in Resource Development*, edited by Paul D'Arcy, Patrick Matbob and Linda Crowl, (Madang: DWU Press, 2014): 41.
37. Ibid.
38. Patrick Matbob, 'We Are Not Anti-Asian – Just Victims of Poor Governance: a Media Perspective' (2014): 60.
39. Western Central Pacific Fisheries Commission (WCPFC) (2009): 4.
40. Michael Field, (2015): 1
41. Ibid.
42. Colin Filer, 'Asian investment in Papua New Guinea's agroforestry sector: some facts and figures.' In *Pacific-Asia Partnerships in Resource Development*, edited by Paul D'Arcy, Patrick Matbob and Linda Crowl, (Madang: DWU Press, 2014): 51.

Dr Tarcisius Kabutaulaka

Patrick Matbob

Foreign Investments and Local Expectations: PNG's Experience with China

Patrick Matbob
Divine Word University, Madang, Papua New Guinea

Introduction

China's presence in the South Pacific has created wide interest in the academic world as studies are done to find out why and what they are doing here. As Pacific people we have also travelled long distances and faced the unknown. While we do not know the reasons for our migration, we do know people are driven away from the comforts of their surroundings by conflicts, conquest, natural calamities, sicknesses, plagues, famines and population growth. We also have experienced the world powers that have gone out in search of riches and resources to power their economies. The people of Madang in Papua New Guinea have experienced such visitors for more than a century. This began in 1871 with Russian naturalist and explorer Nikolai Mikloucho-Maclay who was in search of knowledge, followed by German businessmen of the New Guinea Company led by Otto Finsch in 1884 who came to set up business opportunities in the colonies and to expand their empire. These were the world powers of the time, seeking to dominate and expand their boundaries so they could access vital natural resources to feed their industries and increase their wealth and power.

It was because of the Germans that Papua New Guineans would first come into contact with the Chinese. The Germans had problems dealing with the native Papua New Guineans. They could not convince the local people to provide them with adequate labour to build up their empire, even for wages. So, labourers were recruited from the Bismarck Archipelago, the Solomons, the Dutch East Indies, Singapore and the Chinese treaty ports. Today the world has changed; the Chinese no longer come as labourers but as a world power. With large manufacturing industries that are increasingly hungry for natural resources, the Chinese are expanding their operations into the developing world. They are coming to exploit natural resources of many of the Pacific countries where in the 19th century their forefathers had provided cheap labour for the western powers. The story has not changed, only the characters have. Where there used to be European powers, today we have China. Their mode of operation however, has been different. The Ramu Nickel Project in Madang was the first major Chinese project in the Pacific and both the Chinese and PNG had a lot to learn about each other. This was not the small retail supermarket operation in Madang or Rabaul town that the Chinese are experts at running. And the learning happened for both races, with mistakes made, laws broken, accusations made, and peace brokered. After eight years, the project finally began, but is still not in full operation with the mine's community affairs general manager describing the project as at 70% nameplate load. The company hopes to ramp-up to 80% by end of 2015.

The Chinese have come almost 40 years after PNG became independent. And independence for PNG has meant localisation where locals have and continue to take over from the Australian colonial administration the powers and responsibilities to govern their own country. Papua New Guineans are aware of this trend of foreigners leaving and locals taking over – until recently. The increasing presence of the Chinese however, signals a change. And people are curious and concerned about this change. This is how the people have viewed the increased presence of Chinese migrants in Madang who are not associated with the Ramu Nickel Project. Graeme Smith's ground breaking study[1] helps to explain what the new Chinese are doing in PNG, and should answer some of the concerns about what is going on in the country.

In 2009, groups of young Papua New Guineans in Port Moresby, Lae, Mount Hagen and Madang attacked Asian run businesses in these cities and towns. The violence against the Asians was short lived but drew attention to the strong concerns amongst the local people about migrants from Asia and how the government was dealing with them. While Asians and their businesses became targets of the rioters, anger was also directed equally at PNG leaders, government and the state. Asians are the next biggest population in the country and are actively involved in industries such as logging, fishing, merchandising and the first mining project, Ramu Nickel. Their business successes, Papua New Guineans felt, were possible because they cultivated close relationships with PNG leaders and senior public servants. Ordinary Papua New Guineans had become disillusioned with their leaders and the decisions they were making which were viewed as favouring Asian entrepreneurs and the Chinese Ramu Nickel project[2]. The people perceived that the government was overlooking and changing the country's laws to help the Asians and foreigners become successful.

Yet the state of basic services for the people was very poor, infrastructures nationwide were deteriorating, the education and health systems were failing, and people felt they were not being adequately assisted by the government. The copy of the e-mail petition that was circulated to mobilise the youths referred to Asians owning cottage businesses and tucker shops. Cottage businesses such as tucker shops under the Investment Promotion Authority Act 1992 were reserved exclusively for Papua New Guineans. Seeing Asians involved in tucker shop businesses in Port Moresby angered ordinary Papua New Guineans. Yet they may not have been aware that the tucker shops were actually owned by Papua New Guineans who were renting out the properties to Asians and sharing the profits. An inquiry that was held into the anti-Asian violence also revealed rampant corruption within the Foreign Affairs department with officers being bribed to allow foreigners into the country, and to remain in the country[3]. Foreign Affairs officers also admitted being threatened

Foreign Investments and Local Expectations 237

by senior PNG leaders when trying to deport illegal aliens[4]. In fact, the Inquiry revealed what Papua New Guineans already knew was happening. Not all Asians were targeted in the 2009 violence. The reality is that anyone who is involved in business in PNG, whether an Asian, Papua New Guinean, or any foreigner is equally at risk of being targeted in violent crimes. They all take necessary precautions, and that also involves cultivating good relations with law enforcing agencies.

PNG's education system

PNG's formal education system has long been unequal in catering for a percentage of the population. Large numbers of children have been pushed out at primary school level or have had no access to education at all and left with little hope to cope with the rapid changes happening in the country. The result has been devastating. As PNG progressed economically with growth in extraction of natural resources, agriculture and in service industries, the majority of its semi educated people have been unable to participate in the economic development and/or benefit from it. They remain as subsistent farmers like their ancestors, wanting to be part of development around them, yet being unable to contribute in any way. As expected, not all young people want to be farmers, and many of those who had been raised away from their rural village settings actually do not have a choice. However, without sufficient education and skills to get a job, many turn to illegal activities for survival.

Since the 1990s, PNG began attempts to address this problem by introducing education reforms to ensure universal education for all children[5]. The education reform has created more needs. It means an increase in schools from elementary up to tertiary institutions, it means more teachers and resource persons are needed in all the institutions, it means more resource facilities such as libraries, science laboratories, ICT equipment, etc are needed. And PNG has been struggling up to now to meet the needs. Despite government policies that aim for free education at primary up to secondary level, institutions are having difficulties coping. There are still too few schools, and the number of students enrolling has doubled and tripled. Teachers are struggling to facilitate learning under such circumstances, there are inadequate teaching materials, teachers, classrooms, and the list goes on. Government's direction as part of the free education policy that schools should not charge project fees which are usually collected to fund facilities like classrooms, also do not help as in most cases the government does not provide adequate facilities for all its institutions.

The O'Neill government since taking office has prioritised education, particularly tuition-free education from elementary to secondary level. When the policy was first announced a year ago, it created a huge turn out from interested students, many of whom had been out of school for years. Schools became clogged with people wanting to enrol and were under pressure, and faced threats especially from those who had been out of school for years. Many of these students who missed out on education had failed academically. Teachers struggled to teach classes of up to 60 or 70 students, who competed for the meagre resources such as text books, and desks.

The vast increase in numbers of students in primary and secondary have now created further problems in the 30 tertiary institutions throughout the country. The tertiary institutions can only take in 4,500 out of more than 21,000 who have graduated last year. Those who cannot make it into tertiary education seek employment but without any skills compete for the limited jobs such as shop assistants, security guards, etc. Yet PNG is currently seriously short of skilled workers such as teachers and nurses.[6]

Some impacts of limited formal education

A major impact of limited formal education is that the majority of Papua New Guineans are not in a position to engage in the opportunities brought about by investments in the country. This includes the recent Chinese migrants in their quest to create wealth for themselves[7]. Many young Papua New Guinean women and men find employment in the shops run by Asians as cashiers and shop assistants. Some complain of being paid below the minimum wage level, and have salary deductions if meals are provided for them. The Chinese shop owners keep a close eye on them. A feature in the Chinese run shops is a raised section near the checkout counters where one or more Chinese nationals may be perched keeping a close eye on the cashiers at work. The Chinese are taking no chances with PNG's notoriety as a corrupt and crime-ridden nation. Bags and clothes of workers are closely checked before workers leave. Sometimes, shop owners would provide a basic shelter at the back of the shop so that workers sleep overnight so that businesses can open and close on time. One can understand the concern of the Chinese shop owners. With their limited understanding of *Tok Pisin* and English, and their awareness of corruption within state authorities and law enforcement bodies, they want to be safe rather than sorry if crimes are committed against them.

Informal sector businesses

There is a growing population of PNG entrepreneurs mainly within the informal sector who are creating wealth for themselves like the Asians do. The opportunities are there for the locals after the informal sector businesses had been legalised in the country in 2004. The locals sell items like betel nut, cigarettes, ice blocks, food and snacks and earn regular income on the roadsides or within the boundaries of their homes. While the informal sector businesses are usually on a small scale, earning between K100 to K1000 per week, few locals have been able to grow their operations to bigger enterprises. Most do not know how to. Without appropriate knowledge and skills, they are unable to manage the money they earn. A majority of the women in the informal sector businesses are also supporting their families with their earnings either to supplement, or in place of their husbands' earnings. This has been a major concern for the Bank of PNG which has been trying to ensure that many more nationals become involved in the financial sector and access and use the banking services in the country. In 2013, the Bank of Papua New Guinea committed itself to providing access to a range of financial services for the low-income and rural population in PNG. Part of its financial inclusion and financial literacy strategy[8] is that by 2015, they should educate and include 1 million more low-income people who do not use the banking system. Half of them will be women.

Small to Medium Enterprises

The government's department of Trade and Commerce has also been heavily promoting its Small to Medium Enterprises (SME) policy to encourage more people to become involved in businesses. This is because, according to PNG's National Research Institute (NRI), there is a wealth creation crisis in PNG, and a lack of data on SMEs[9]. NRI reports that 90% of businesses in PNG are foreign-owned while nationals own only 10%. PNG's GDP is generated by large firms and so there is expatriation of profits and the GDP per capita measure does not reflect the incomes for citizens. Governments had encouraged Foreign Direct Investments with large enterprises and informal economic activities for the ordinary people. However, it has failed to support the middle level businesses. There is need for small and medium enterprises (SMEs) to create wealth for citizens, jobs and reinvestments domestically. Only cottage businesses are reserved for Papua New Guineans after the Act known as the Cottage Business Activities List (CBAL) was amended in 1992.

Businesses reserved for Papua New Guineans

Papua New Guineans also feel that certain businesses should be reserved for them. One of the major reasons for the 2009 violence against Asians was that people were aggrieved that Asians were getting involved in businesses that they felt should be reserved exclusively for Papua New Guineans. A copy of the e-mail petition stated:

> The rule of the grassroots will be this and very clear: No more Asians owning Cottage Businesses in PNG by 31 December 2009. Or otherwise, we will celebrate 2010 New Year with bon-fires of all Asian-owned Takka Shops in flames all around the country. That will be the solution. Forget the government. If they can't do it, we will do it ourselves! No need to buy candlesticks on New Years Eve. We can afford to destroy what we can take back and own ourselves but we cannot let what is rightfully ours be stolen from us permanently!
>
> Forward this to all Patriotic sons and daughters of this beautiful nation.
>
> Remember, DATELINE IS 31 DECEMBER 2009! GRASSROOTS WILL ACT! EM MIPLA TOK! EM COUNTRY BLO YUMI!
>
> Cardo Stanzo – Patriot and Pro NGO Activist against Asian Infiltration (28 May 2009)[10]

Cultural factors hinder business growth

PNG cultures which emphasise strong social bonds between families, clans and tribal groups are generally not conducive to capitalist business models that promote competition, profits and individual wealth. Papua New Guineans are well aware of this since their entry into the cash economy, and the successful PNG businessmen and women have to negotiate these cultural obligations, or establish themselves away from their local communities to limit such expectations. Other social business models that include clan or village groups such as the cooperative societies, or ILGs have been encouraged in the country. Few of these group business models have become successful and the country is littered with many failed projects. PNG's favourable natural environment that provides almost all the basic needs for survival for the majority of the population is a major factor in dampening growth in business interest. Also the strong cultural bonds that are built on sharing of wealth or any achievements amongst clan and tribal members also discourage individual pursuits in any activity.

PNG cultures that govern and direct the cycle of life in villages and even in urban settings are recognised as the biggest hindrance to business success amongst individuals. While there are rapid changes going on in PNG, the majority of people who live in rural areas still follow the traditional rhythms of life and activity governed by human life cycles and seasons. The traditions like births, initiations, marriages, deaths, hunting, fishing, planting of gardens, fulfilling family obligations, etc, continue to come into conflict when locals engage in foreign ways and practices of doing things which are introduced to them. When the colonisers in the form of German New Guinea company came to Madang in the 1880s to establish their tobacco, coconut and other commercial plantations, the locals initially helped the colonisers with the tasks, but when continued demands were made to engage them, the natives refused[11]. With no understanding of the western concept of wage employment, the locals turned to their gardens to support their families and attend to their traditional obligations. Ironically, this was the reason why the Germans would look for labour elsewhere thus bringing in the first Chinese labourers (amongst Malaysians and Solomon Islanders) to work on their plantations. More than a century later, Papua New Guineans continue to struggle to participate in the modern cash economy. PNG cultures still require members of tribes or clans, no matter how educated or removed from society, to invest their time, energy, and resources in cultural activities and obligations. Many Papua New Guineans understand and appreciate the power of modern wealth that can acquire goods and services, and a high status, yet for the majority the pathways to accessing and building up the wealth remains a mystery.

Living in environments where food crops grow easily and abundantly, and where there is access to protein and resources for building shelters, the locals have alternatives to wage employment and dependency on cash for basic needs and wants. Therefore, many are unlikely to be driven to be involved in the cash economy to change their lifestyles. A church leader recently described the cultural life cycles as 'building up for a big bang'. Bishop of Bereina Diocese in Port Moresby Rochus Tatamai said Papua New Guineans tend to build up to a celebration or achievement and once that is over, they move on to other things. He said this type of culture does not allow people to invest in and consistently labour and sacrifice over long periods of time to build up wealth before they can enjoy the fruits of their labour. He said family and cultural obligations also impact on any attempts to create wealth. Traditional obligations require Papua New Guineans to give without counting the costs and expectations of immediate reward. This creates conflict between culture and commercial economy. The majority of people today have most basic modern needs that they need money to acquire. These needs are sugar, tea/coffee, kerosene, soap and rice. For a family, the need will include school or health fees for children. Again the practice has been for funds to be raised specifically to meet the need, and then life reverts back to basic existence. Papua New Guineans in the villages who run trade stores also only think and operate on a small scale. They buy stock and sell until stock is finished, then go out and buy more. Without knowledge and culture to manage money, to save and build up capital, and to buy in bulk to cut costs, such operations are often temporary and can cease any time. The businessman however, is not troubled as he can fall back on his gardens to survive.

Papua New Guineans and Asians cultivating business relationships

Today though, the Chinese businessman has turned up on the scene in many parts of PNG. With the skills, knowledge and time to run retail businesses, they are renting and running shops in the urban and rural areas. The relationship may extend to marriage between the Chinese businessman and a local woman cementing long term success for the business.

Successive governments since the colonial times have tried ways of helping Papua New Guineans to be engaged in businesses and to grow wealth over time. However, successes have been somewhat limited and mixed. Cooperative society entities that were introduced into villages were basically designed to work in line with the communal ways that the traditional PNG societies follow. However, none of the societies succeeded. With the experience of the 70s, the cooperative society concept has been revived in recent times by the government. It will take some time before one can judge whether the cooperative societies will be successful after its reintroduction.

The PNG government and aid donors are also helping Papua New Guineans with basic financial training throughout the country to enable them to become involved in business. This is a major drawback for the 80% of people who live in rural areas and follow a subsistence lifestyle. While they have access to traditional land to grow cash crops, or to harvest and sell resources like timber, fish, or pan for alluvial gold, they lack basic knowledge of managing money. The financial education training has been provided since 2003 as a microfinance project aimed at introducing micro-banking. The project has eventually set the Nationwide Microbank now operating in the country. The current project on financial literacy is an extension of the first project and is aimed at educating the grassroots people. For instance in Madang, the project is targeting 120,000 people in the rural and urban settlements who are mainly illiterate to build up their ability to manage their finances.

The new Chinese in PNG have set up shops, or large supermarkets, as well as wholesale businesses. With connections to the cheap Asian markets, they have an advantage over Papua New Guineans and others doing retail and wholesale businesses. This has resulted in a steady growth of the Chinese entrepreneurs who have taken over the control of shops, supermarkets and wholesale outlets that have originally been owned by locals and Europeans. In Madang town up until independence there was a 'China town' with a street lined with small shops run by the old Chinese. By independence, many of the traders had sold or closed down their businesses and moved on, many settling in Australia. No doubt, there was fear of instability in PNG with the withdrawal of the colonial administration. However, this did not happen, and PNG has become attractive again to the 'new' Chinese to do business. The growth of the Chinese entrepreneurs caused concern amongst locals when they saw the ease with which the migrants could acquire licences, land and property to set up their operations. Their involvement in running small trade stores also raised concern as many Papua New Guineans saw that such businesses were reserved for local people by the government. These concerns fuelled the violence after nationalist activists organised protests throughout the country against Asians.

However, not all Papua New Guineans saw the new Chinese as threats. In fact, many local businessmen and politicians saw the business zeal of the new comers as an opportunity to exploit. They were happy to make deals with the new Chinese for them to run their businesses, while the locals get their share from rentals. The business deals with the Chinese also freed Papua New Guineans from their cultural obligations as they were no longer seen as being involved in businesses. However, these arrangements between locals and the new Chinese also raise ethical questions, especially when the local partner is a politician or senior government officer who could be abusing his/her position for personal gain. On the part of the Chinese, having influential support is important when setting up and operating a business in PNG where security is a major issue. The new Chinese try to cultivate good business relationships with key people in authority such as members of the police force, security guards, and government officers. This is done by providing lunches or drinks or gifts such as cell phones to local government authorities and police officers so they can keep in touch. A common practice is for Chinese shops to cash government cheques, on the condition that 10% of the value of the cheque, is spent in the shop. The practice has its advantages helping the Chinese businessman to build relationships with government officers that can be mutually beneficial for everyone.

Notes

1. Smith, G (2014). Fuqing dreaming: 'New' Chinese communities in Papua New Guinea. In P. Darcy, P. Matbob & L. Crowl (Eds) Pacific-Asia Partnership in Resource Development. (pp. 132-139). Madang: DWU Press
2. Eroro, S. (2008, December 23). Court free Chinese miners. Post-Courier, Last retrieved December 2008 from http://www.postcourier.com.pg/20081224/news02.htm.
3. Kolo, P. (2009, November 5). We are bribed. Post-Courier p.1
4. Nicholas, I. (2009, November 5) PNG citizens protecting aliens, inquiry told, The National p.3
5. Department of Education, 2004. A National Plan for Education 2005-2015. Port Moresby. Papua New Guinea Government
6. Philippine nurses to helpout at Port Moresby General Hospital (2014) Retrieved 21. 3. 2015 from http://health.onepng.com/news/philippine-nurses-to-help-out-at-port-moresby-general-hospital
7. Smith, G ibid
8. Bank of Papua New Guinea (2014). PNG National Financial Inclusion and Financial Literacy Strategy 2014-2015. Retrieved 28.3.2015 from http://www.bankpng.gov.pg/images/stories/0NewBPN GWebsite/BSD/Microfinance/PNG_NFI_FIL_STRATEGY_2014-2015_eCopy_pdf
9. Webster, T and Sanida O. PNG unemployment and wealth creation crisis (Powerpoint Slides). Unpublished manuscript, SME Conference, DWU, Madang
10. PNG Grassroots (2009) Retrieved May 20, 2015 from http://asopa.typepad.com/files/anti-asian-propaganda.pdf
11. Sinclair, J. (2006). Madang. Madang: DWU Press.

China's Growing Tuna Fishing Fleet in the Pacific Ocean: A Samoan Fisheries Perspective

Ms Joyce Samuelu Ah Leong

Assistant Chief Executive, Ministry of Agriculture and Fisheries, Apia

Good afternoon everyone. Firstly I'd like to thank the organisers of this conference for inviting me to speak on this topic. I honestly have to say that if I knew this would be the high level of participation, I would not have agreed to this. So please bear with my nervousness. Also, after I was asked to speak on this topic, I found out that it was a very difficult task given that most of the information was confidential. Anyway, as introduced, I am from the Ministry of Agriculture and Fisheries.

For this presentation I will focus mainly on the South Pacific Albacore tuna fishery, or what is commonly known as the longline fishery, mainly because this is the sole commercial tuna fishery for Samoa. I will also highlight the stock status, the Albacore tuna stock status, the fisheries status, highlighting Samoa's fisheries status and also China's flag vessels. And then I will make a few observations on the influence of China on this fishery and how China's interest and involvement can be positively channelled to support the effective management and sustainability of this fishery.

For the South Pacific Albacore fishery (from now on I'll refer to it as the longline fishery), the main fishing gear is longline. The line goes down to depths of 100-300 metres. In the Pacific Islands region, the catches are within the EEZs of most of the South Pacific countries, namely Solomon Islands, Vanuatu, Fiji, Samoa, Cook Islands, American Samoa, French territories, Niue and Tokelau. But there are also notable catches in the high seas pocket which is between the Solomons, Fiji and Vanuatu, east of the Cook Islands, and also north of New Zealand.

The most recent stock assessment for tuna was conducted in 2012. It basically said stocks were in good condition. There was no evidence of overfishing. The maximum sustainable yield calculated then was around 99,000 metric tonnes. Scientific data shows that the biomass is in relatively good condition.

However, it should be noted that longline fishing is very specific. It targets mature individual fish. This is shown by the catches of the last six years. Longline catches normally target Albacore sizes of 80cm to more than 100cm. The longline fishing method does not target the whole range of stock.

In the South Pacific Albacore fishery there are two fishing methods: longline and trawling. I think New Zealand has one of the highest numbers of trawling vessels. But 96% of the catches from the Albacore fishery are caught by longline vessels. In 2013, the most recent calculated overall catch was around 81,000+ metric tonnes. That was 4% less than that of the previous year. That's just looking at the overall annual catch estimates. In 2012 we deployed more than 250 million hooks to maintain those catches so very high effort very recently for the longline fishery.

It should also be noted that more than 50% of total catches of Albacore tuna are from within the EEZs of South Pacific countries. The proportion caught on the high seas increased in 2013 with an estimated total share of 43%. This increase in the proportion caught on the high seas is cause for concern.

Chinese flagged longliners are the biggest catchers. They recorded a total amount of 23,000 metric tonnes. If combined with the Chinese Taipei flagged vessels, they make up more than half of the total catches.

Let me take you back to the Samoan longline fishery. For 2013 we've recorded almost 2,000 metric tonnes from longline fishing and exported around 5500 metric tonnes. But this is looking at the longline fishery in the last 20 years. Samoa's tuna longline fishery once dominated the South Pacific longline fishery. That was before the other neighbouring countries developed their longline fishery, and when they did it was mainly through the licensing of foreign fishing vessels while Samoan longliners were mainly domestic.

I also want to mention the effort over the last five years of our own fishery. We almost doubled the number of hooks just in 2012 to try and maintain the amount of tuna. In fact, there's been a decline in catch rates by the Samoan longline fishery.

I now turn to the Chinese fleet. And when I say Chinese fleet I am referring to the Chinese flag longliners. Records show that longliners from China started within our zones in the 80s but that it wasn't until the early 2000s that their presence started to expand. The expansion involved catches, volumes, and also the area of fishing especially on the high seas. The total catch of Albacore by the Chinese fleet is around 24,000 metric tonnes. The high total catches of Albacore by Chinese longliners, this is not reflected in catches of other species such as Big Eyed Tuna and Yellowfin. But overall there is quite an expansion in terms of catches by Chinese flag vessels.

China's influence in this fishery is significant. They have the largest fishing fleet and a high percentage (25%) of total catches, not only within EEZs but also on the high seas. With this increase of catches there is a possible flooding of the tuna market. Unfortunately, however, there's a lack of operational data from Chinese longline vessels.

Samoa has its own perspective on these issues but, of course, the fishery is not Samoa's alone. The management of this fishery needs a cooperative effort by the whole region, particularly the key players, which in this case very much includes China. The longline fishing region has taken a significant step for this fishery through what is called the Tokelau Arrangement. This establishes a framework for the effective management of the fishery through zone-based catch limits. In our view, the establishment of these catch limits will sustain the Albacore stocks and fishery and also generate maximum economic returns for our countries. It is also our view that a similar arrangement is needed for the high seas. I think that's where China comes in. We need its support and commitment to this effort. They are the key player on the high seas and they need to show their real commitment in ensuring the sustainability and longevity of the fishery.

Perhaps the biggest question is how can China assist us in this? I've sat here through the afternoon session and heard of all the great buildings that China has built for Samoa in particular. Unfortunately that's not what we need in fisheries. Perhaps what we need from China is the commitment to be a more responsible fishing nation. Over-fishing on the high seas is the biggest threat to our fishery. It arises from the less effective management measures for the high seas compared to the more stringent measures we have in force in our EEZ. I think it's fair to say China should be at the forefront of supporting and pushing similar measures for the high seas.

We also need China's assistance in surveillance, monitoring and control initiatives to combat illegal, unregulated and unreported fishing. As you all know, most of the EEZs are owned by very small island countries with a lack of resources to monitor their EEZ. We need capacity building assistance from China as we have from our neighbouring countries and partners. And also from the development perspective, this fishery is the major economic driver for most Pacific Island countries. Hence the need for China's development support through genuine partnership not only through the license fees they are paying small island countries, but also more genuine partnership through the provision of onshore facilities to enable adding value. We need to gain benefits from license fees, generate employment, add value and generally create more revenue for our countries. Moreover, China's assistance is not only needed at a government level through our national management initiatives but also by our own struggling domestic fishing companies.

Finally, we need to remember that the South Pacific longline tuna fishery is seen as one of the last remaining healthy fisheries in the world. The fishery is worth a billion dollars annually. Some Pacific Island countries depend on it solely for their annual budget. And of course, Samoa aims to get a bigger share of the revenue. As I've mentioned, most of the profitable fishing grounds are within our EEZs. Yet we have limited resource and capacity to manage and control or even to monitor what is happening in our zones. We are part of international management organisations and participate in their management measures. But these measures need to be applicable to our situation. Otherwise we will be isolated and put at a further disadvantage.

China is a real player and a key player in this fishery. They are here to stay. And we need them – and their government – to be more effective, more responsible, in the way they manage their fleet not only in our zones but, more importantly now, on the high seas. Yes, we do need China as a true partner to help in promoting and protecting the sustainability of this fishery.

Thank you for your attention.

All materials used for this presentation have been extracted from the Tuna Fishery Yearbook 2013 compiled by the Secretariat of the Pacific Community and from annual reports of Samoa's Ministry of Agriculture and Fisheries.

China and the Sea: Potential for Pacific Partnerships

Dr Paul D'Arcy
Australian National University, Canberra

China and the Sea: Potential for Pacific Partnerships

The open ocean fisheries of Pacific Island nations contain some of the richest fisheries in the world. These fisheries are becoming more valuable each year as other ocean areas have become increasingly overfished to the point of collapse, most noticeably in the North Atlantic. With limited maritime surveillance and policing capacity, and with domestic fishing fleets dwarfed by those of Distant Water Fishing nations (DWFN) from wealthy nations on the Pacific Rim, small Pacific Island nations are forced to rely on renting out access rights to their fisheries to DWFN in which adherence to Pacific Island nation harvesting regulations is largely based on voluntary compliance. Voluntary conservation regimes seeking to persuade fishers that it is in their best long-term interests to comply are the only mechanism able to be applied at present to Pacific pelagic fisheries. The last decade has revealed mounting scientific evidence that this regime is not working, as once prolific fisheries decline substantially. China (the People's Republic of China) is one of the DWFN. China also has the capacity to act as a circuit breaker to redefine a more mutually beneficial and sustainable partnership with Pacific Island nations instead of continuation of existing unsustainable fishery practices and relationships.

International Legal Rights and Economic Realities in Pacific Island Maritime Economies

The 1982 UN Convention on the Law of the Sea (UNCLOS III) forms the basis of ocean governance in Oceania. The Convention substantially extended coastal nations' sovereignty over adjacent waters. This benefited most modern Pacific nations as island archipelagos surrounded by vast expanses of ocean. The outer limit of territorial seas was set at 12 nautical miles (22 kilometers), but coastal states' sovereignty over living and non-living marine resources was extended to 200 nautical miles (370.4 kilometers) from shore in the form of Exclusive Economic Zones (EEZs). Coastal states were also given the right to designate what constituted a sustainable catch within their EEZ, as well as who would get access to harvesting stock in excess of this sustainable catch, and the fee they would pay to the coastal state in return for this access (Articles 55-75, especially 55-59). The new 200 mile (370.4 kilometer) EEZs dramatically increased the territory of Pacific Island nations, particularly archipelagic ones. For example, Fiji's 18,272 square kilometers of land provided an EEZ of 1,290,000 square kilometers, Kiribati's 690 square kilometers of islands translated into an EEZ of 3,550,000 square kilometers, while Federated States of Micronesia's 701 square kilometers of land equated to an EEZ of 2,978,000 square kilometers. Kiribati derives 45% of its revenue from fishing and fishing license fees, while Federated States of Micronesia derive around a quarter of its revenue from these sources.[1]

The potential maritime benefits of political independence have been eroded by economic realities. As small or fragmented political and cultural entities that inherited limited modern infrastructure from their former colonial rulers, Pacific Island nations had limited ability to generate income domestically, and meant that much income was absorbed in providing basic facilities and services taken for granted in more developed nations. Offshore fishing fleets from larger and wealthier Pacific Rim nations regularly violated Pacific Island EEZs in the absence of local monitoring. The same lack of resources to monitor offshore waters also meant that Island nations could not develop effective fishing fleets and were forced into fishing access agreements that returned a mere fraction of the value of the catch at market. The alternatives were forgoing this income and watching the offshore fishery erode through unmonitored fishing by non-citizens, or continued over-reliance on foreign aid from former colonisers.[2] The sea out of sight of land within and beyond Pacific Island nations' EEZs remains beyond the control of the state.

Current Fishery Approaches

The big success stories of Pacific Island fisheries have been sustainable fishery initiatives in neritic (near-shore) fisheries, including Marine Protected Areas (MPA). Their most enduring and successful have been highly localised operations, where communities reliant on harvesting the sea also regulate its use.[3] The Pacific 2020 Background Paper: Fisheries recommends improving coastal fisheries management through community involvement.[4] As well as monetary benefits, local participation in inshore harvesting provides protein sources, import substitution for costly processed foods and local management of marine areas.

Beyond sight of shore, fisheries are managed by national or international legal treaties and regulations signed by largely non-resident foreign signatories from Pacific Island and Pacific Rim governments and administered by government officials and regional fisheries' officials. Such legal frameworks alone are insufficient to guarantee the survival and revival of Pacific fisheries because of the lack of monitoring and enforcement capacity of Pacific Island nations.

The Western and Central Pacific tuna fishery is the largest and most intact tuna fishery in the world, supplying around half of the world's tuna supplies. Data from the Secretariat of the Pacific Community reveals that Oceanic nations' EEZs yield 78% of the Western and Central Pacific Ocean tuna catch. The Oceanic artisanal catch represents less than 10% of the total catch in this fishery.[5]

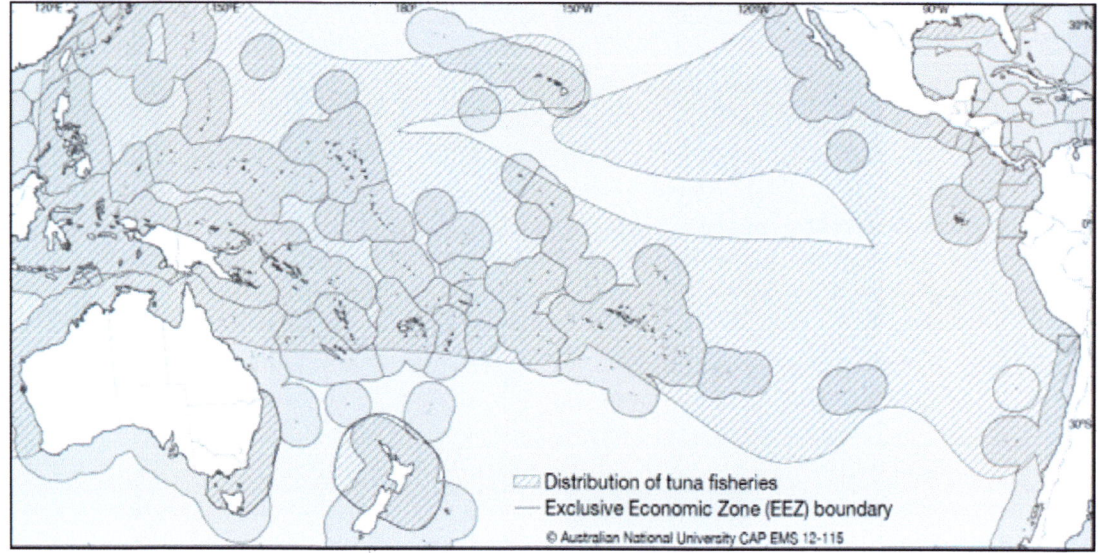

Figure 1: Geographical extent of the Pacific tuna fishery

The wealth of the Western and Central Pacific tuna fishery relative to over-exploited and exhausted fisheries elsewhere has resulted in increased pressure on this fishery. In the last decade, the Secretariat of the Pacific Community has declared bluefin tuna critically endangered and bigeye and yellowfin tuna to be in dramatic decline.[6] The reason is not hard to determine. The total harvest has increased by an average of 5% per year over past 50 years. This average understates the escalating pressure the fishery is under given that the number of boat-days has risen about 10% per year over the period 1970–2000.[7] In addition, illegal, unreported and unregulated (IUU) fishing within this fishery is estimated to take between 8 and 16% of the reported annual catch in the Asia-Pacific region. IUU fishing in Oceania takes the form of unlicensed vessels fishing within EEZs, fishing in closed areas, or misreporting or under-reporting of catches.[8] IUU fishing vessels have lower costs than licensed vessels as they pay less or no fees and are not bound by national or regional fisheries requirements.

Ten DWFNs harvest 86% of the catch sold at market from the Pacific, especially Japan, Taiwan, South Korea and the United States. Despite all major stakeholders bar Japan signing a Multilateral High Level Convention (MHLC) on the Conservation and Management of Highly Migratory Fish Stocks in the Western and Central Pacific Ocean in Honolulu in 2000, DWFN continue to prefer bilateral relations to multilateral ones when dealing with Pacific Island nations.. The exception has been the United States whose multilateral agreement with Pacific Forum nations produced terms more favourable to island nations than most bilateral ones with DWFNs.[9] Bilateral agreements tend to be less restrictive on DWFN operations than protocols Pacific Island nations collectively agreed to in the FFA. The latter are perceived as also potentially compromising bilateral aid which is seen by DWFN donors as a potential tool for access to fishery rights on terms desired by them.

China as Circuit Breaker: New Possibilities for Sustainable Pacific Fisheries

As a major Distant Water Fishing Nation, China can be viewed as both part of the problem facing Pacific Island nation maritime interests, but also as part of the solution of a sustainable fishery and future. Two propositions are central to this new relationship. The first is that the ultimate purpose of aid should be to free the weaker party from the need for aid by building sustainable economies and ecologies controlled by the host nation. The second is that long-term perspectives beyond domestic election cycles and even the lifetimes of incumbents in decision-making offices are vital for planning for sustainable futures. What is the Pacific we want for our children and our children's children? To be truly sustainable, we need to adopt a big picture framework in planning for sustainable fisheries in 30, 40, 50, 60 years and beyond

A number of reports since 2012 have suggested that while China is currently not the predominant DWFN in the globe, its rising population, their increasing purchasing power, and the overfishing to the point of exhaustion of China's own EEZ, mean that the Chinese market and China's fishing fleets will play an increasingly central role in the fortunes of the world's fisheries. These reports have criticised China for providing unfair subsidies to their vessels which means that more vessels go to sea than would otherwise be economically viable in a no-subsidy environment. Specifically, Chinese tuna boats have been accused of having an unfair advantage in getting government fuel and other effective subsidies that mean they have lower operating costs and therefore have a competitive advantage over Pacific fishing nations and other fleets. Cheaper costs means more vessels can go to sea in circumstances where there are already too many vessels for fishing to be sustainable. Chinese vessels have also been accused of participating in illegal and undeclared fishing operating under Sir Lankan flags. China has rigorously denied these accusations and the scale of these behaviours has proven hard to quantify by foreign researchers. In China's defence, it should be noted that few if any nations have the capacity to rigorously police and regulate their fishing vessels on the high seas.[10]

The influence of China has risen rapidly in the Pacific Islands since 2000. As many academic commentators and Pacific Island leaders have noted, this new and rising economic and diplomatic presence provides an alternative to the so-called Washington Consensus for Pacific Island nations frustrated by the latter's insistence on rigid rules of governance and fiscal restraint in terms of how aid is used. In contrast, the so-called Beijing Consensus is seen as more respectful of Island nation internal sovereignty in how aid is used.[11] However, as noted above, the USA has led the way in its tuna fleets' adherence to Pacific Island nations' desired fisheries policies as voiced through the Forum Fisheries Agency.

China can do the same. Working in partnership with Pacific Island nations' wishes and aspirations, China can be even more influential and beneficial to Pacific Island nations as it becomes more and more important over time as a market for and fisher of Pacific Island marine resources. China has consistently and unequivocally committed itself to respecting Pacific Island nations' rights to control their resources sine they became independent. Former New Zealand diplomat to China and Fiji, Michael Powles notes that the PRC has been a responsible and early participant in regional forums seeking to establish sustainable tuna regimes.[12] China's actions elsewhere also give cause for optimism. China has consistently adhered to observing the Law of the Sea concerning disputed resources in the South China Sea that have far greater national and strategic relevance to it than any interests it might have in the Pacific Islands region.[13] While Taiwanese fishing fleets have been less cooperative, it is unrealistic to believe Taiwan is not sensitive to regional criticism when set against its chief rival's official support of international maritime conventions. As relations between China and Taiwan continue to improve, and former Pacific colonial powers realise the new approaches of Asian aid donors are providing welcome alternatives to their own ways of operating, praising China for its adherence to international maritime conventions and Pacific Island nations' preferred fisheries management principles opens the way for all party cooperation on maritime issues.

The key short-term requirement is to restrict fishing. The main tactic used at present is to try and reduce the number of fish being taken. The only fishers that comply are not the problem – the illegal and undeclared excessive catch takes are the problem. In effect, what current policy is doing is trying to get the people who already comply to reduce their yield while the illegal fishers in poorly policed high seas' fisheries can carry on regardless. Sadly, experience demonstrates that the more people think the fishery is near to collapse, the more they increase their take so as not to miss out before the fishery collapses, especially if they feel they have no direct stake in a particular fishery as many DWFN perhaps do. Reducing the fish catch is problematic for Pacific domestic fleets as well which need minimum catch to guarantee market demands in larger, more viable markets.

How might China begin a transformation away from this self defeating regime of poor policing and enforcement, voluntary compliance and rising prices, and towards sustainable futures for Pacific fisheries? I want to propose two solutions – one for the near shore, one for the offshore fishery. They relate to things that have been consistently observed and advocated throughout this conference. The first is that we hear many groups say that what the nation state does on behalf of its Pacific citizens does not trickle down into the villages. Some Pacific nation states place control of near-shore fisheries in the hands of those with the greatest stake in their sustainability – local communities. The near shore fishery is very productive. Kiribati shows that local communities in alliance with government fisheries scientists and advisors can make a substantial amount of profit from the near shore fishery. A way to empower local communities is to give them neritic sovereignty – the sub-sovereignty to ensure sustainable near shore fishing. China can assist in directing part of its aid towards this end. Such community-based sustainable fisheries may also be combined with marine-centered eco-tourism.[14] China can also assist in providing privileged market access for community-based sustainable harvests, and tourists, especially among its burgeoning and increasingly environmentally aware middle classes. The potential for this link is suggested by the virtual collapse of the shark fin market in wealthy parts of coastal China in response to marketing campaigns in recent years.

Further offshore, where the real crisis in Pacific fisheries occurs, the most immediate pressing need is for some form of improved surveillance and enforcement capacity to protect the offshore fishery from illegal distant water fishing fleets. The most commonly suggested means are the use of satellite monitoring to pinpoint locations, more fisheries officers on vessels to monitor catch, and giving DWFN a stake in reviving the MPAs such as exclusive access rights to them until such time as the fishery has recovered sufficiently to allow commercial fishing to be resumed. The real circuit breaker I would like to finish with is the proposal that the most effective way China can secure a sustainable fishery for its domestic market is for its fleets to work in partnership with Pacific Island domestic fleets. Pacific Island nations must set the terms.

China should not assume these terms will be poor, given that the best deal Pacific Island nations get at present involves receiving less than 10% of the sale price for fish legally taken and nothing for those illegally taken in excess of defined sustainable catches. More joint venture Chinese and Pacific vessels in an EEZ means more policing of the fishery by those setting the sustainable limit of the catch, and also benefitting the most from sustainable limits. In return for guaranteed market access to a booming market, China can ensure privileged and long-term access to a fishery it has a direct stake in. Technological transfer to boost the Pacific domestic side of the joint venture can be linked to Pacific expertise in reviving near-shore fisheries in China's depleted EEZ. Long-term market access will stabilise prices and enable better long term planning and budgeting, and means aid to boost Pacific domestic fleet returns direct benefits to China in the form of long-term supply chains.

Conclusion

Pacific Island nations face major challenges in seeking multilateral solutions to oceanic issues confronting them. Their collective thinking is reflected in the Pacific Islands Regional Ocean Policy (PIROP) produced by a Marine Sector Working Group of the Council of Regional Organisations in the Pacific in response to a request from Pacific Island Forum leaders in 1999. The PIROP seeks to 'ensure the future sustainable use of our ocean and its resources by Pacific Islands' communities and external partners'.[15] The PIROP outlined five guiding principles for ensuring this objective: improving understanding of the ocean; sustainable development and management of ocean resources; maintaining the health of the ocean; promoting the peaceful use of the ocean; and creating partnerships and promoting cooperation.

Laurence Cordonnery ends her insightful commentary on the practicality of implementing the PIROP by noting its two major challenges – one within Oceania and one concerning DWFN. 'Within the region, political leadership and the willingness to commit and raise adequate resources will be essential if the foreseeable implementation difficulties outlined in this article are to be overcome. This challenge will determine whether the Policy can be used as a model in ocean governance as it promises to be. For regional powers within the Pacific Rim who were not part of the inception and endorsement phases of the PIROP process, their commitment to PIROP will be determined by Pacific Rim nations' willingness to act as partners and to cooperate with PICs in the implementation process'.[16]

Over the last decade, China has set a new agenda in how aid is delivered in the Pacific Islands. While not without its criticisms, these new approaches and alternatives have largely been welcomed by Pacific Island nations. China has the capacity, foreign policy philosophy and means to set a bold new agenda in partnership with Pacific Island nations to avoid the ecological disaster that engulfed Atlantic fisheries. This approach can provide a circuit breaker on unsustainable development and rewrite the textbooks on aid, cooperation, and developing sustainable marine economies and ecosystems. The still realisable end point will be a guaranteed fish stock; viable maritime economies, and national partnerships for our children and our children's children.

Notes

1. United Nations (1992) *The United Nations Convention on the Law of the Sea*, New York: Division for Ocean Affairs and the Law of the Sea, United Nations, (n.d.) (available at http://www.un.org/Depts/los/convention_agreements/texts/unclos/closindx.htm); Ron Crocombe, *The South Pacific*, Suva: University of the South Pacific, 2001; and, F.R. Thomas, 'Fisheries Development in Kiribati: sustainability issues in a 'MIRAB' economy', *Pacific Studies* 26 (1-2), 2003, 1-36.
2. Crocombe 2001, 368, 377-378, and M. Jacobs, 'Spoiled Tuna: A fishing industry gone bad', *Micronesian Counsellor*, 40, 2002, 1-15.
3. A. Anderson (Ed.), *Traditional Fishing in the Pacific*;. Bernice P. Bishop Museum: Honolulu, HI, USA, 1986, Paul D'Arcy 'The role of the tuna fishery in the economy of Federated States of Micronesia', *Pacific Economic Bulletin* 21(3), 2006, 75-87, and Tamatoa Bambridge and Paul D'Arcy, 'Large-scale Marine Protected Areas in the Pacific: Cultural and Social Perspectives', in F. Feral and B. Salvat (eds.), *Enjeux politiques et écologiques de la création des grandes aires marines protégées dans le Pacifique*, Edition Presse Universitaire de Marseille, Marseille, 2014.
4. L. Clark, *Pacific 2020 Background Paper: Fisheries*; Commonwealth of Australia: Canberra, Australia, 2006.
5. P. Williams, and C. Reid, *Overview of the Western and Central Pacific Ocean (WCPO) tuna fisheries, including economic conditions – 2005*. WCPFC-SC2-2006/GNWP-1. WCPFC – Scientific Committee Second Regular Session, Manila, Philippines, 7–18, August, 2006 (available from: http://www.wcpfc.int/); S. Chand, R.Q. Grafton, and E. Petersen, 'Multilateral governance of fisheries: management and cooperation in the Western and Central Pacific tuna fisheries,' *Marine Resource Economics*, 2003, 18, 329–348, 331-332 and Laurence Cordonnery, 'Implementing the Pacific Islands Regional Ocean Policy: How difficult is it going to be?' *Victoria University of Wellington Law Review*, 36 (4), 2005, 723-731.
6. Forum Fisheries Agency (FFA), *Proposed Outline of Regional MCS Strategy Projects and Strategy:*

Development of an Integrated Regional MCS Strategy, Honiara, FFA, 2008.
7   T. Kompas, Q.R. Grafton, and T.N. Che, 'Bioeconomic losses from overharvesting tuna,' Conservation Letters 2010, 1–7, 1-2.
8   Food and Agriculture Organization of the United Nations (FAO), *International Plan of Action, to Prevent, Deter, and Eliminate Illegal, Unreported and Unregulated Fishing*, FAO, Rome, 2001 (Available at http://www.fao.org/fi/website/FIRetrieveAction.do?dom=topic&fid-16007; Marine Resources and Fisheries Consultants (MRAG) and University of British Columbia (UBC), *The Global Extent of Illegal Fishing*, MRAG, 2008, available at http://www.Illegal-fishing.info/uploads/MRAGExtentGlobalIllegalFishing.pdf; and Marine Resources and Fisheries Consultants (MRAG), Review of Impacts of Illegal, Unreported and Unregulated Fishing on Developing Countries, Synthesis Report, MRAG, 2005, available at http://www.imcsnet.org/imcs/imcs/docs/iuu_fishig_synthesis_report_mrag.pdf.
9   J. Van Dyke, and C. Nicol, 'US Tuna Policy: a reluctant acceptance of the international norm,' in D.J. Doulman (ed.), *Tuna Issues and Perspectives in the Pacific Islands Region*, Honolulu: East-West Center, 1987, 105-132; S. Tarte, 'Negotiating a Tuna Management Regime for the Western and Central Pacific: the MHLC Process 1994-1999', *The Journal of Pacific History*, 34(3), 1999, 273-280, and Cordonnery 2005, 725.
10 'Scrapped IPO offers lens into China's tuna fishing and shows how financial levers can influence conservation', in FFA TRADE AND INDUSTRY NEWS Volume 7: Issue 6 November-December 2014, https://www.ffa.int/node/1443; Justin Pearce, 'The Status of Fisheries in China: how deep will we have to dig to find the truth? *Scientific American*, 3 June, 2013, http://www.scientificamerican.com/education/science-in-action/; and Gwynn Guilford, 'China's government is subsidizing your sushi – and driving other countries' fishermen out of business', *Quartz*, 14 August 2013, http://qz.com/114596/chinas-government-is-subsidizing-your-sushi-and-driving-other-countries-fishermen-out-of-business/.
11 Terence Wesley-Smith and Edgar A. Porter (eds), *China in Oceania: reshaping the Pacific?* (New York and Oxford 2010), 235–236. The Washington Consensus is more often portrayed as compliance with good governance requirements such as accountability and transparency, and less as adherence to free market ideas hostile to 'excessive' government control of development agendas, national expenditure, and business legal frameworks.
12 Michael Powles, 'China Looks to the Pacific', in Paul D'Arcy (ed.), Chinese in the Pacific: Where are they now?, Special Issue of Chinese Southern Diaspora Studies, May 2007, 43-55, 50.
13 Greg Austin, China's Ocean Frontier: International Law, Military Force and National Development, St. Leonards, N.S.W., Allen and Unwin, 1998, 4, 71ff.
14 Papahānaumokuākea Marine National Monument, http://www.papahanaumokuakea.gov/, n.d.; and Sahiban Kanwal, 'Speaking out on the marine park,' *Cook Island News*, 4 August 2013, http://www.cookislandsnews.com/2013/August/Wed14/environment.htm.
15 Pacific Islands Forum Secretariat, *Pacific Islands Regional Ocean Policy*, Marine Sector Working Group, Council of Regional Organisations of the Pacific, Pacific Islands Forum Secretariat, Suva, 1999 (available at htt://www.spc.int.).
16 Cordonnery, 2005, 731.

7. THE FINAL FORUM

Professor Yu Changsen and Dr Tarcisius Kabutaulaka

Professor Jon Fraenkel

Overview of the Final Forum – drawing the strands together

Michael Powles

The Final Forum was Chaired and Moderated by Jon Fraenkel, Professor of Comparative Politics, Victoria University of Wellington, assisted by by Leasiolagi Professor Malama Meleisea, Director, Centre for Samoan Studies, National University of Samoa, and Associate Professor Yu Changsen, Executive Director, National Centre for Oceania Studies, Sun Yat-sen University, Guangzhou.

A main purpose of the conference was to encourage dialogue between academics and officials from China and from the Pacific. Bringing together academics and officials (and in this case politicians as well) is not uncommon in the Pacific and it was widely felt to have been successful in Apia.

Discussion and dialogue were features of the whole conference and the Final Forum on the third day of the conference was structured to provide an extended opportunity for discussion. Many participants took advantage of this opportunity and there was both examination in depth of propositions raised earlier in the conference and discussion of issues which particular participants felt had received insufficient attention.

The Final Forum more than achieved its aims. Discussion focused on:

Security and the threat discourse
The argument, loudly advanced at conferences earlier in the decade, that China posed a security threat to the region was not pursued vigorously at this conference. While there were real concerns about aspects of China's involvement in the region and these concerns were raised and debated, Pacific participants in particular clearly saw no major cause for alarm arising from any threat to regional security due to China's rise and increased presence. At the same time, the reassuring view of some observers that 'the Pacific was big enough for all' was criticised in relation to both the region's security and its sustainable economic development; in relation to security there was concern that it could seem an open invitation for outside powers to involve themselves militarily in the region, or increase present involvement.

'Pacific Island Agency' and the 'China Alternative'
The increased confidence of Island leaders, even assertiveness, indicated a new determination to exercise Pacific Agency. Current examples included pressures to adjust the region's cooperative arrangements to better suit the wishes of Island

leaders, including the further development of sub-regional groupings; strengthened Island assertiveness on issues like climate change and development partnerships; signs of resistance to the assumption that progress (or 'wellbeing') should be judged by western rather than local criteria; and Fiji's charting of its own international course. China's increased presence in the region had not created all this but its presence and the notion of a 'China alternative' had opened up new options for Pacific leaders, even though China itself did not seem to have promoted the concept of China being an 'alternative' to the western models and practices followed since World War II.

Chinese in the Pacific

It was recognised that the role and influence of Chinese in the Pacific was a major factor. There were at least two categories: early Chinese migrants, badly treated originally but today respected and wholly integrated, whose descendants, today often called the 'old Chinese', fill many influential positions, particularly in Samoa and Fiji (the paper on the subject given by Samoa's Attorney-General, Tuatagaloa Aumua Ming Leung Wai, was regarded as invaluable); and recent Chinese migrants, the 'new Chinese', come to buy and run small businesses, work as labourers, and the like. Pacific communities and leaders reported real concerns regarding some members of this second group. Some were regarded as insensitive to local tradition and customs, unwilling to mix with local people and greedy in taking over small businesses from locals and doing labouring work which otherwise might provide employment for locals. Local concerns had led to rioting in several countries and tensions in others. Potential outcomes, some with possible security ramifications, were discussed at some length.

The aid scene

Development cooperation is of course a major aspect of China's presence in the Pacific region and inevitably the subject was a major feature of this conference. Pacific Island participants in the Final Forum generally welcomed China's aid. They particularly approved the absence of conditions attached to China's aid (except of course the assumption of consistency in maintaining diplomatic relations with Beijing), the readiness to fund major infrastructure projects and the opportunity, where Chinese aid is available, of avoiding the good governance conditions and what were described by some as an increasingly aggressive neo-liberal (or 'retroliberal') approach on the part of the Pacific's traditional Western development partners, often relying on 'universal' norms and structures considered by some Pacific participants to be inappropriate. The 'China alternative' opened the way to alternative options.

Nevertheless, concerns were raised in several areas: the use of imported Chinese labour on China's aid projects instead of available local labour which sometimes was desperately seeking employment; the designing of projects in Beijing rather than in the partner country, resulting in inappropriate design features in some projects; a

Michael Powles, Conference Organiser

lack of transparency in the inability or unwillingness of Chinese officials to provide information regarding their projects; and the dangerous debt levels being reached by some Island countries as a result of Chinese concessionary loans.

Chinese officials and other participants pointed to signs of improvement in some of these areas of concern and it was emphasised that where Island countries were clear and forthright with their Chinese counterparts about their requirements in the aid field those requirements were usually achieved.

Some participants asked about the possible evolution of the international development regimes as a result of the growth in China's aid. Responses suggested that while China was not setting out to create an alternative system, the days of the tight DAC Club within the OECD were over. Of course the one major new institution China had created, its Asian Infrastructure Investment Bank, was prompted by the Chinese perception that the existing institutions had unreasonably failed to give China decision-making power consistent with increases in its contributions.

Access to resources

Again there was a focus on the 'big enough for all' saying; most Pacific participants were critical, one saying that it implied a feast to be shared by all comers, a virtual invitation to outsiders to exploit Pacific resources; a Chinese academic strongly endorsed it, denying any special rights for Pacific Islanders.

Several participants emphasised the need to eliminate corruption in local governments and to design and enforce more rigorous governance systems. There was discussion of the tourism resource and a suggestion that, looking into the future, the availability of unused labour, particularly in Melanesia, could become a valuable resource for the region.

Security and the threat discourse

Several participants noted the significant change in thinking that had occurred in the several years since the subject of China in the Pacific had first attracted attention. At that early stage the emphasis of Australian and American observers, and some New Zealanders, was on the problems associated with a growing Chinese presence, including likely security threats. Pacific Island leaders and commentators were more circumspect but, understandably perhaps, did not dispute this Western line. Gradually attitudes changed and at this Apia conference comments on China and its increasing role in the region, while still cautious, were more positive.

There was little discussion of the reason for the change. It was acknowledged that Chinese diplomacy and the accessibility of its leaders were factors. One Pacific leader (a western-educated minister of finance) told the Forum that he was far more comfortable managing a relationship with China than one with the United States or other countries:

> ... because I have a lot of engagement at the political level with counterparts from China. The US has been out of the Pacific for a number of years, particularly our region of the eastern Pacific. So we don't really get a chance to have a relationship.

The minister explained that because of his relationship with Chinese counterparts he was able to gain their concurrence in the employment of local contractors and local labour – a point of interest to other participants for whom the importation of contractors and labour from China had been a matter of concern.

Several factors contributed to a positive atmosphere in the Final Forum and, indeed, in the Apia conference overall. First, there was no suggestion of a specific Chinese security threat to the region. Second, Pacific leaders and officials, as well as academics, displayed confidence in their capacity to negotiate and deal with China on the issues which concerned them. Finally, Chinese academics and, most notably, officials (in the form of China's ambassador to Samoa and her deputy) displayed a willingness to engage with Pacific participants even on sensitive aspects of China's involvement in the region.

It was pointed out, and was accepted by participants, that it would be foolish to counter the negativity of the 'threat discourse' of the past with a celebration claiming that everything was now wonderful and beneficial from a Pacific viewpoint. That would be quite wrong. Pacific Island governments and people did have real concerns about aspects of China's involvement and role in the region. Several of these were raised and discussed throughout the conference and especially during the Final Forum. The atmosphere in these discussions was positive, not least because there was little underlying sense of tension in the security field.

Concerns raised that were relevant to regional or national security involved unplanned consequences of policies or practices designed for non-security purposes. For example, strong concern was expressed about the levels of recent Chinese migration into the Pacific and the ease of acquisition of small businesses. The fear was that these developments and the resentment they have caused among local populations could contribute to the kinds of disturbances that have occurred in the Solomon Islands (2006), Papua New Guinea (2009) and Tonga (2009). (Since the Apia conference a further disturbance involving the arson of businesses has been reported in Port Moresby.)

It was emphasised that some at least of these disturbances, including the Tongan arson, were not aimed at Chinese or their businesses. But as one participant said, in Nukualofa while the riots may not have been anti-Asian in origin, they certainly took an anti-Asian turn and targeted Asian businesses in the end.

It was also suggested that Chinese immigration could exacerbate inequalities which themselves contributed to instability and could threaten security. Tensions were also aggravated by the perception, discussed more fully later, that new Chinese immigrants, unlike the long-established and now well-integrated Chinese communities, made insufficient effort to integrate with the local population in their new countries of residence.

Broader security issues were barely discussed at the conference. One participant from China mentioned the American pivot or rebalancing, arguing that it increased China's sense of containment – the perception that China's move towards the Pacific Ocean was being 'stymied by the invisible hands of the alliance between the United States, Japan and Australia'. The subject was not mentioned by Pacific participants. This was presumably a consequence of the pivot or rebalancing having little practical impact among the independent countries of the Pacific Islands region.

One Pacific participant commented that the average Pacific Islander did not see China as a geopolitical power, a major trading partner or an influential player in the region. Rather, the average Pacific Islander saw China as the family selling from the shop down the road, or the company that has dug a big hole in the middle of their island and was taking the profits away to a faraway place. A reaction of resentment on the part of local communities has had the occasional security consequence. One participant argued strongly that while geopolitical issues were not of interest to ordinary people, when considering the parameters within which China had to operate in the Pacific:

If you just base those parameters on geopolitical issues and discussions, you only understand half the parameter. If you don't base it on what ordinary people think, you're only going to understand half the rules, half the boundaries within which China has to play. Even though it is the dragon and is a powerful country, there is agency in the Pacific. There are parameters that Pacific governments *and people* establish and within which China has to play. And if we don't believe that, we just have to look at PNG, at Honiara and at Tonga. When the ordinary people see China hasn't observed the parameters, then 'we'll show them what the parameters are'.

There was some discussion of the possibility of China intervening in some way in the Pacific Islands region. The discussion involved questions and suggestions, but there were no alarmist predictions. One suggestion was that they might do so if they felt that their citizens were under threat; another that the growing Chinese economic presence could, through some unforeseeable incident, lead Beijing to intervene. Would that be in soft or hard ways? It was suggested that it was hard to imagine a big Chinese military engagement in the region but not so difficult that China might want 'to put its hands more firmly on the tiller of a government they did not trust'. It was a valid question whether the recently increased Chinese assertiveness in the South China Sea might eventually be seen in the Pacific.

A respected Pacific academic was unhappy with the security implication of the oft-repeated mantra that the Pacific was 'big enough for all of us'. He said that in relation to the foreign military presence in the region, 'I think what we need to do is try to shoo out some of the military presence in the Pacific, not bring in more . . . I wouldn't like the Pacific to be a flashpoint for military demonstrations . . . ' (The resource and economic ramifications of the 'big enough for all' mantra are discussed in the final section of this chapter.)

'Island agency'

Decolonisation in the Pacific, led by Samoa's independence in 1962, opened the way for leaders and governments to exercise what has been called 'island agency'. Early on, it involved the assertion of fundamental sovereign rights, many of which of course are now simply taken for granted.

An aspect of island agency that was a focus of discussion at the Forum involved the relationship between island countries and their development partners. One experienced observer of the Pacific development scene said that some island countries had been assertive in defining their development objectives with donors in saying, for example, 'this is what we're about; these are our development objectives; deal with us on these terms'. Pacific countries that had been consistent in their engagement with donors in this way (Samoa and the Cook Islands were cited as good examples) had benefitted enormously.

It was emphasised that success in exercising island agency in this field was as much attitudinal as procedural. Processes and procedures were indeed important but attitude, particularly confidence, was more important. In fact, the one element of this conference which clearly distinguished it from earlier similar meetings (particularly those in Canberra and Japan nearly a decade ago) was the evident confidence shown by Pacific participants vis-à-vis, particularly, their development partners. Good natured talk about feeding and taming the dragon was followed by a half-serious suggestion that the dragon might be trained to tame the kiwi, the kangaroo and the bald eagle. This suggests the possibility of increasing islander agency in relation not only to China, the major newcomer to the Pacific Islands region, but also the traditional donors of Australia, New Zealand and the United States.

The sense of increased confidence was picked up by a senior participant from the Pacific Islands Forum Secretariat who spoke of the need for the Secretariat itself to be a bit more robust and courageous in the advice it gives to Pacific leaders. Clearly this could lead to increasing 'regional agency'.

Similarly, possible new and more assertive directions were suggested in a discussion of the need to examine existing institutions adopted at independence. A participant from Melanesia suggested that they inadequately reflected the needs and values of the peoples of Melanesia. The sub-regional organisation, the Melanesian Spearhead Group, had initiated a study designed to define and articulate Melanesia's own indicators of wellbeing, several of which were quite different from the western assumptions that had shaped institutions designed and built at the time Melanesian countries achieved independence. Discussion of this complex issue is likely to appear on the agendas of future Pacific conferences.

One participant pursued a different aspect of island agency. He argued that it should not be regarded as a phenomenon in the hands of only governments and their leaders and officials. Business interests were obviously important in this regard. Ordinary people and communities could also exercise power and should be encouraged and supported as they did so.

The exercise of island agency by people themselves and by community groups depends for its effectiveness on the availability of information. A participant from Fiji spoke of the over-arching importance of the information issue and a leading Samoan academic said there were examples of situations in the Pacific where 'ordinary people' (a term used frequently in the Forum discussions) became frustrated with their governments because of the lack of access to information, particularly about various aid projects in their countries:

> You cannot educate your people and then keep information from them. That's a contradiction in policies . . . Some people provide explanations as to why information is not available: for example, there are not enough people in the Pacific to provide requested information. Well, I do not think you can do things that impact on people's lives, on people's values and resources, and then say you are not going to tell them why you are doing these things. If you do that, you will have a huge internal security problem . . .

The availability of information regarding aid projects was particularly important to several participants. Without it, people could not exercise their agency, even through influencing their own governments, and were deprived of their right to agency in this area. It was suggested that China was particularly unforthcoming in providing development information. But two development experts suggested that China was not being deliberately secretive. Rather, its administrative processes were such that information in the form some people wanted it was often simply not available. One New Zealand development expert acknowledged that while New Zealand's development system was theoretically transparent, a lot of digging was often necessary to unearth needed information. Another expert said it was a problem for some observers that information regarding China's aid was often not collected in a way that observers have come to expect from the region's traditional donors.

It was emphasised, however, that Chinese practices were changing and that more information was becoming available. A Chinese representative said she doubted the Chinese statistics system was very effective but it would improve.

Criticism was also made of the failure of Pacific Island governments to collect and make available relevant information. This impaired the rights of their own citizens. Sometimes this failure was attributable to administrative incapacity; sometimes, according to a former Pacific minister, because

> too often, Pacific governments are like a collection of warring tribes with ministries trying to outdo each other, trying to bypass procedures, trying to get resources . . .

The 'China Alternative'

Mention of a 'China alternative' suggests a global contest between superpowers in which China is actively promoting itself as an alternative to the United States – politically, militarily or economically. Some commentators supporting this thesis have in the past painted an alarming picture of a struggle for global leadership. But there was no suggestion in the wide-ranging discussions at the Forum, or indeed in the course of the conference as a whole, that there was evidence from the Pacific Islands region supporting such a thesis. China was of course a subject of the conference and could be expected to be at the forefront of discussion. Even so, an interesting feature of the conference was the almost total lack of mention of the United States. (And interestingly, unlike China, Australia, Japan, New Zealand and the European Union, all of whom were represented at the conference by the heads of their diplomatic missions in Samoa, several of whom participated in discussion, the United States took comparatively little interest.)

In line with the focus of the conference, much of the discussion was on China and China's role and presence in the Pacific. Concerns on several aspects were raised and discussed. But overall most participants indicated they were reasonably relaxed with China's increased presence in the Pacific. As noted above, one Pacific participant, a minister, spoke warmly about his personal relations with Chinese ministers and counterparts and said that he had never met the equivalent Americans. And while clearly there is some American aid in the Pacific, it was not mentioned once during the discussion.

The clear implication was that the United States was not interested in competing with China, at least in this part of the Pacific, despite all that was being said about the American 'pivot' and 'rebalancing'. (Participants would have known about American statements regarding its pivot towards Asia, about the growing military base on the island of Guam, not far away, and about the basing of American forces, possibly even long range bombers, in Darwin, making this indifference curious. Perhaps strategic geopolitics was felt not to be very relevant to today's Pacific. The late Epeli Hau'ofa of Tonga, who was quoted several times by participants, once said, 'Conquerors come, conquerors go, the Ocean remains, mother only to her children.')

In many respects the term 'China alternative' was used as a shorthand for the changes taking place in the region, including China's rising presence and influence, which together created a situation in which island governments could more easily exercise their agency than they could before. Of course, in one or two areas there would sometimes be a real 'China alternative' – in the form, for example, of development capital for infrastructure projects – but the term mostly related more generally to the greater freedom of action which Pacific governments now have.

The light-hearted reference during the Forum to feeding and taming the dragon, and then later to training the dragon to tame the kiwi, the kangaroo and the bald eagle, mentioned above, nicely captured the sense of a new freedom with wider options that China's rise had helped bring.

Discussions in the Final Forum, and indeed the papers delivered to the full conference, tended to acknowledge that overall China's presence in the region was welcome but that there were specific concerns that needed to be addressed. (Aspects of this attitude are discussed in almost all of the parts of this chapter dealing with individual topics.) No participants specifically predicted a Chinese threat to the region or the Island countries in it. But several participants did not rule out the possibility of a security threat in the future. Moreover, conflict between China and one or more of its neighbours over territorial and resource disputes could disrupt at least the geopolitical atmosphere in the more tranquil South Pacific. Actual conflict between the United States and China might be unlikely (and no-one at the Forum mentioned it as a possibility) but it cannot be wholly discounted at a time when Chinese and American armed forces are patrolling in close and unfriendly proximity. Such conflict would likely have enormous impact on the Pacific Islands region.

An observer at the Final Forum would undoubtedly be left with the sense that earlier fears caused by China's rising power and increasing involvement in the Pacific were no longer widely shared in the region. At the other extreme, the concerns clearly held by numbers of participants about particular aspects of China's involvement in the region also make any sense of euphoria unsupportable.

Chinese in the Pacific

It was a significant theme of the conference, and one well reflected in discussion at the Final Forum, that attention needs to be paid to the concerns and needs of what one participant called the 'ordinary people'. Principally, of course, these are the indigenous Pacific Islanders of the region but it also includes the many Chinese in the Pacific Islands, both descendants of early migrants and also more recent immigrants.

Early in the conference, the paper delivered by Samoa's Attorney-General, Tuatagaloa Aumua Ming Leung Wai, had focused in depth on what some observers call the 'old' Chinese, as opposed to newer migrants. Several participants referred to the successful integration of descendants of early Chinese migrants into modern Pacific communities. (One mentioned in passing that the ethnic Chinese Archbishop of Fiji had conducted a Chinese mass in Suva the previous week.)

The process of integration for the 'old' Chinese had been painful and difficult at times in the past. Gross injustices were inflicted on members of this group of early Chinese migrants and their immediate descendants. Today, however, the established Chinese communities appear to be embraced as valued members of Island country communities. Inter-marriage in Polynesian countries became common and it was noted in the course of the Forum that in Samoa, for example, inter-marriage had resulted in many leading politicians and others sharing part Chinese ethnicity. (And New Zealanders were reminded that their revered former All Black captain, Tana Umaga, was of part Chinese descent.)

No participants in the Final Forum criticised the 'old Chinese' in the Pacific. There was, however, a focus on concerns regarding new Chinese migrants to the region. A participant from Fiji emphasised:

> The average Pacific Islander did not see China as a geopolitical power, a major trading partner or an influential player in the region. The average Pacific Islander saw China as the family selling from the shop down the road, saw China as the company which had dug a huge hole in the middle of their island and was taking the profits to a faraway place.

The most pressing concerns described by participants related to the influx of traders and the ease with which they could, and did, take over small businesses. In Fiji, Tonga, Samoa, Solomon Islands and Papua New Guinea, Chinese migrants were said to be increasingly displacing locals in small businesses. Increasing inward migration was said to be encouraged by the ease with which business permits and even land could be acquired, often because of local corruption. In some cases, local businesses could not easily compete with the newcomers because of the cultural demands placed on locally-owned businesses.

Other concerns raised in the Forum discussion included rising real estate prices and, a point elaborated in the final section of this chapter on *Resources,* the evident degradation or depletion of natural resources, particularly fisheries.

The complaint was also made that the new Chinese community was 'very closed, very insular'. Whereas the old Chinese had inter-married with locals, there seemed to be little inclination to do so on the part of recent arrivals. Numbers of the new Chinese had come to Pacific countries to work as labour on Chinese-funded aid projects. With high local unemployment, these new Chinese immigrants aroused considerable resentment. Immigrants from lower socio-economic backgrounds were also looked down on, despised even, in China, according to one participant. This made them vulnerable and marginalised both in their new homes and their old.

Another participant reported on a 'more middle class Chinese migrant' coming to the Pacific recently:

> People who practice yoga, do meditation, follow the latest American soap operas; quintessentially middle class and cosmopolitan. But they, too, seem to have little interest in developing deep ties with local communities.

The history of disturbances and riots in the course of the past decade in Solomon Islands, Papua New Guinea, Tonga and, since the conference, again in Port Moresby, was clearly on participants' minds. (There was also passing mention of the horrendous discrimination, brutality and even slaughter suffered by Chinese in the late 19th century and mid-20th century in Southeast Asia.) It is not surprising several participants regarded the situation of new Chinese immigrants as serious and needing attention. But ideas or proposals for improving the situation were few. One participant pointed out that with rising labour costs in China, the use of China-based labour on aid projects overseas would probably decrease over time. But that still left the issue of small businesses which Chinese migrants were acquiring so readily.

A participant from Melanesia said that the Chinese were in the region to stay. The challenge was understanding their presence and learning how to manage that. She recounted how chiefs in a part of her capital city managed Chinese migrants there. When there was a rapid increase in Chinese coming in and opening up retail shops, the chiefs said 'that's it, we're not going to have any Chinese in our area'. But of course there were competing interests at play: there were locals who had loans to pay off but were unwilling to open businesses because of the local culture and family obligations. At the moment there were no Chinese shops in the area, but there were ongoing complaints by locals who needed money. She commented that it would be interesting to see how these competing interests played out.

A Chinese official participating in the Conference pointed out that for the past 200 years, Chinese communities in the region had lived peacefully with local people and had contributed significantly to local development. He referred to a 'gap of assimilation' between new Chinese migrants and local populations, saying 'it was not surprising at all to see some degree of clashes of civilisations'. He acknowledged that issues relating to Chinese migrants in the Pacific were very important both for development and also as a regional security issue. He had been responsible in

Beijing for drafting talking points on the subject 'but this issue never came to the front'. Nevertheless, he believed that with time and education the problem would be solved. As mentioned earlier, the Chinese government tried to persuade Chinese migrants in the region to fully respect laws and customs in Pacific Island countries:

> This is true. This is not just a diplomatic discourse. Every year we hold a Chinese Spring Festival function. One important task for our Ambassador is to appeal or implore our Chinese communities: Please, you should fully respect the local custom and try to learn more to mingle with local people.

He hoped that time and education would see the problems solved – and he could have emphasised of course how historically brief and recent China's present engagement with the region has been.

Development Issues and the Aid Scene

China's aid to Pacific Island countries was a major focus of discussion in the Final Forum of the conference. Overall, speakers made it clear that China's aid was welcome in the region and for many diverse reasons. One of these, raised principally by academic participants, was a perceived increase in the national badging of aid from traditional donors and increased unwelcome promotion of what was called 'retroliberalism'. As well, the conditionality attached to aid from traditional donors had never been popular – and one participant questioned whether 'good governance' conditionalities had actually been effective. A participant from China asked rhetorically why China was criticised for the lack of conditionality of their aid. And the point was made that the machinery necessary to provide the accountability and oversight of aid from traditional donors used up a significant proportion of that aid.

Concern was also expressed about the hypocrisy of some traditional donors. An example given related to Australian and New Zealand condemnation of what they had both called 'cheque-book diplomacy'. Yet it was claimed that this was something both of these two traditional donors engaged in: Australia was said to have given increased aid to Papua New Guinea and Nauru in exchange for the establishment of detention centres in both countries and New Zealand was said to have cut aid to Tonga because of disagreement over civil aviation issues.

The aspect of China's aid that was most criticised was what was perceived to be its lack of transparency. As discussed earlier in the section on 'Island agency', the point was made that without adequate information about China's aid it was very difficult for Island countries to exercise 'Island agency' in relation to development cooperation. As with most other concerns regarding China's aid, the view of one informed participant was that China's practices were improving:

> We are starting to see greater transparency around China's aid programme and I think that will continue. We are also starting to see a little bit more forward thinking in the planning of China's development assistance . . .

A significant area of concern in Pacific Island countries has also been China's importation of its own Chinese labour for many of its development projects. Also that the designing of projects by Chinese engineers and architects within China often resulted in Pacific conditions and requirements being inadequately reflected in the end result. In both areas, participants reported signs of improvement. It was suggested that the answer lay in the Pacific development partner being well organised and forthright in insisting that its requirements for the project be met. Projects which had been handled in this way and were successful as a result were said to exist in Samoa and the Cook Islands. And one participant suggested that the rising cost of labour within China would discourage their use on overseas development projects. (A participant also suggested that, looking well into the future, it was possible that the labour resource in Melanesia in particular would be a considerable asset: 'Maybe a future scenario would see relationships between local economies and peoples in Melanesia changing fundamentally from one based around extraction of natural resources to one around the engagement of the human resource.')

The relationship between China's aid and the systems within which it operated on the one hand and traditional western aid systems on the other was raised. Was there divergence or convergence between the two? It was suggested there were

Liu Yang, Deputy Head of Mission, Chinese Embassy, Apia

elements of both. One participant suggested that what was really interesting was that China did not appear to be trying to establish an alternative global development regime. It was argued this was so despite the creation of the new Asian Infrastructure Investment Bank which followed Chinese frustration with the slow pace of reform of the World Bank, IMF and Asian Development Bank. Specifically, revised voting rights commensurate with China's increased financial contribution were blocked by the United States.

The point was made that until recently the DAC club within the OECD effectively controlled global development systems. China's entry into the field had changed that and it was suggested there could now be no return to the 'old tight DAC club'. A looser and more inclusive aid environment was likely with more diversity in the way it operated.

The debt levels of some of China's development partners in the Pacific cause significant concerns. Tonga was in the most difficult financial situation. The apparent ready availability of soft loans from China's Exim Bank had resulted in a Tongan debt-to-GDP ratio said to be around 50%. Participants had heard a Tongan speaker earlier in the week lament that the influence of China in Tonga today 'basically revolves around finding ways for Tonga to be able to repay its loan to China. It is a debt collector's influence, and Tonga has no option but to satisfy the demands of its debt collectors'.

In the development field the forgiveness, or cancellation, of soft loans is not uncommon. China has done this in the past. It was implicit in comments regarding Tonga's situation that the forgiveness by China of at least some of Tonga's debt would not only assist Tonga itself but would also boost China's reputation in the region.

A former finance minister of Tonga told the Forum that while indeed Tonga had probably borrowed too much, following the riots which had destroyed much of Nukualofa's commercial district in 2006, a loss equivalent to 10% of Tonga's GDP, there was a strong political imperative. Tonga had approached its traditional donors regarding the rebuilding of so much of Nukualofa. There were no positive responses so when the Chinese announced a $3 billion soft loan facility in 2006 the Tongan Government had no alternative take advantage of it and, indeed, was pleased to be able to do so. The former minister said that looking back on the negotiations with the Exim Bank of China it was clear that the Tongan government had very little knowledge of China's policies or processes. He believed that was something that needed to be addressed if Pacific governments were to be able to engage effectively with China. He also echoed the words of a previous participant in the Forum who had said many Pacific governments behaved like a collection of warring tribes and ministries, all trying to outdo each other in bypassing normal procedures in efforts to get their hands on resources.

The Cook Islands Minister of Finance explained that concerns about long-term debt were also in his mind when he negotiated with both China and New Zealand regarding the Cook Islands water supply project. The total cost was approximately $60 million but of that, the Chinese loan was only $23 million. There had also been concern in the Cook Islands that the Chinese might be coming in and 'taking over jobs'. But the Cook Islands government had prepared carefully and knew the terms it wanted to negotiate with China. It succeeded in negotiating an arrangement whereby local Cook Islands contractors would be used.

Other participants expressed interest in the unique trilateral (Cook Islands/China/New Zealand) feature of this particular project. Would that be the way of the future? Or would the administrative and management costs required because of the complexity of trilateral projects prove prohibitive?

There was also interest in the success of the Cook Islands in negotiating with China. It was suggested it was attributable to the development of good bilateral relations between counterparts from both governments and the clear development and articulation of the Cook Islands' policy requirements. One participant from Melanesia commented that the success of the Cook Islands, one of the very smallest Pacific Island countries, contrasted with the difficulties of the comparatively huge Papua New Guinea. The difference lay in the development of systems in the Cook Islands which enabled them to engage effectively with China.

It was suggested that Samoa had also developed effective systems to both develop and negotiate its development policies and negotiate them with donor partners. Tonga was moving towards this situation. The point was made that the requirements were not only procedural and institutional, they were also attitudinal: 'It's being assertive and being prepared to say 'no' and being prepared to say 'this is our time and these are our objectives' and so on.'

It was also important, according to one participant that the Pacific partner government make a real effort to ensure it was satisfied with the initial designs for the project. All the better if it could get agreement for it to have the designs done by its own professionals. Chinese companies as principal contractors varied in quality. There had been concerns about competition between companies seeking to out-bid each other causing a 'race to the bottom' which would bring the quality of projects down. But there were encouraging instances of the reverse happening. Chinese companies were conscious that to get more work from the Chinese government, the local government and possibly even the Asian Development Bank they needed to demonstrate good quality. Some were influenced by considerations like these.

Resources and sustainability – enough 'for everybody'?

Many participants were unhappy with the suggestion that, so far as its resources were concerned, the Pacific was 'big enough for everyone'. One said this implied 'a feast which could be shared with everyone, as if inviting the great powers to a healthy rapaciousness as regards the exploitation of the Pacific's resources'. The reality was that native forests were close to exhaustion and the fishery resource was struggling. Carpet-baggers from several countries had had a serious impact. And while decolonisation had enabled Pacific peoples to exercise sovereign rights, at least to some degree, in practice it was extremely difficult to protect major natural resources.

Another participant deplored the consequences of a 'feeding frenzy' in the Pacific. He suggested the dynamics of that feeding frenzy would continue to be a very important topic in the future.

It was also suggested that it would be very much against the interests of Pacific peoples to accept the suggestion that the Pacific was 'big enough for everyone'. He commented that a similar phrase had been found by the Waitangi Tribunal in New Zealand to be an argument for depriving Maori of their particular rights: 'One of the ways they took things from the Taranaki Maori was by saying that it belonged to everyone.'

In that regard, one participant from China caused some surprise by suggesting that the resources of the Pacific belonged not to the indigenous people of the Pacific but to Almighty God. (Of course, Pacific leaders recently (2014) agreed: 'Pacific peoples are the custodians of the world's largest, most peaceful and abundant ocean, its many islands and its rich diversity of cultures.' The late Epeli Hau'ofa, author of 'Our Sea of Islands' and quoted several times at this conference, would have strongly endorsed the concept of Pacific peoples being *custodians* of the Pacific.)

An official from China strongly defended China's role in relation to Pacific fisheries and its long history of responsible association with the Western and Central Pacific Fisheries convention and, today, sustainability regime. He detailed China's positive actions in defence of the sustainability of the Pacific tuna resource, in particular. Not all participants agreed that China's role had been entirely positive but the discussion was potentially constructive.

Several Pacific participants argued that for the preservation of Pacific resources (as well as for so many other reasons) stricter and better co-ordinated governance was need in Pacific Island countries themselves. (One participant from Melanesia commented that he had a couple of relatives who were as bad (in illegal extraction of natural resources) as any outside companies.)

Finally, there was reference to a report suggesting that 50 years hence the only remaining large pools of labour globally would be in Sub-Saharan Africa but there would be a small secondary pool of surplus labour in Melanesia. Perhaps a future scenario would see relationships between economies and peoples in Melanesia changing fundamentally from ones based around extraction of natural resources to ones around the engagement of globally scarce human resources.

Leasiolagi Professor Malama Meleisea and Tony Browne

Editor's Acknowledgements

The National University of Samoa's generous hospitality and cheerful efficiency were principally responsible for the conference's success. Vice Chancellor Fui Le'apai Tu'ua 'Ilaoa Professor Asofou So'o took a close and supportive interest. Many NUS staff were involved, including Deputy Vice Chancellor Letuimanu'asina Dr Emma Kruse Va'ai, Leasiolagi Professor Malama Meleisea, Director of the Centre for Samoan Studies, who supervised the NUS team arranging the conference and was a leading participant in the conference itself. Ms Measina Meredith, of the Centre for Samoan Studies, was in charge of organisation on the NUS side. We cannot speak too highly of her, not least her efficiency, enthusiasm and indeed tolerance of occasionally unreasonable requests. Other staff of the Centre for Samoan Studies assisted in many different ways. Mohammed Sahib put in long hours meeting and greeting participants at Faleolo Airport and assisting generally. A group of graduate and senior students provided invaluable assistance during the conference itself, as did NUS technical and support staff.

Our warm appreciation also to the team of academics who came from China, co-ordinated by Associate Professor Yu Changsen, Executive Director, National Centre for Oceania Studies, Sun Yat-sen University, Guangzhou. He and his colleagues from Sun Yat-sen University played a key role in the conference, as did the several senior academics from Peking University, Beijing, and Liaocheng University, Shandong. Professor Yu was enthusiastic and cooperative in the planning for the conference and at the conference itself. The team from China was helpful throughout. Our warm thanks to them.

The conference was made possible not only by the practical collaboration of the three universities involved but also by the support of the New Zealand Ministry of Foreign Affairs and Trade, the New Zealand Ministry of Defence, the New Zealand Defence Force, the Confucius China Studies Program and the Confucius Institute at Victoria University of Wellington. Their support was much appreciated.

Organisation of the conference depended heavily on a small group associated with the New Zealand Contemporary China Research Centre and at Victoria University in Wellington. Tony Browne, the Centre's Executive Chairman was engaged throughout, Brian Moloughney, Pro-Vice Chancellor Humanities at Otago University and an Associate Director of the New Zealand Contemporary China Research Centre, was involved from the start, Jon Fraenkel, Professor of Comparative Politics at Victoria University, provided invaluable advice and input during preparations for the conference, including on Pacific Island participation and during the conference itself, not least in chairing and moderating the Final Forum which occupied the last day of the conference. Jason Young of Victoria University provided invaluable advice. And none of this would have been possible without the efficient and helpful involvement throughout, not only in Wellington but also in Apia during the conference, of Lai Ching Tan, Administrator of the New Zealand Contemporary China Research Centre at VUW.

Index

access agreements (fisheries), 248–249, 250–251
adaptive capacity, 154–155
Africa (China's involvement in), 99, 193–194, 195–196, 222–223
agriculture, 64–65, 125, 133, 134, 197–198, 199
Ah Ching, 74
Ah Leong, Joyce Samuelu, *244*
Ah Mu, 74
Ah Sue, 74
aid. *see* developmental assistance
All China Women's Federation, 191
American Foreign Policy Council, 222
Antarctic scientific expeditions (China), 91
ASEAN/China relationship, 70
Asia in the Pacific Islands: Replacing the West (book), 46
Asian Infrastructure Investment Bank, 177, 261, 272
assimilation, 80–81, 83, 135, 137, 148–149, 269–270
Australia-China Development Cooperation Memorandum of Understanding, 106
Australian Studies (in China), 56
'Ava welcome ceremony, *10, 14, 22*

Bainimarama, Frank, 105, 190, 191, 227
bauxite (Fiji), 228
BBC World Service Poll (perceptions of China), 70
Berman, Ilan, 222
bilateral relations. *see* diplomatic relations
Blue Book of Oceania (book), 36
Bo Zhiyue, *67*
Bougainville truce support, 116
Brant, Philippa, *174*
Browne, Tony, *33, 275*
business sector (Papua New Guinea), 236, 238–242

Cairns Compact (2009), 104

Chen Shuibian, 71
chequebook diplomacy, 47, 93, 94, 100, 129, 181, 270
children, Chinese-Samoan, 78, 83–84
'China alternative.' *see* development assistance, China alternative
China in Oceania (book), 48–49
China Scholarship Council, 150–151, 152
China-Caribbean Economic and Trade Cooperation Forum, 99
China-Pacific Island Countries Economic Development and Cooperation Forum, 31, 35, 43, 71, 95, 98, 140, 182, 195, 217–218, 227
'China's Emergence: Implications for Australia' (report), 146
China-US Strategic and Economic Dialogue meetings, 196
Chinese Association of Western Samoa (formerly the Chinese Club), 82
Chinese Civil Engineering Construction Corporation (CCECC), 211–213
Chinese Communist Party leadership, 67–68
Chinese companies, overseas activities of, 104, 106, 168, 187, 273
  in natural resource development, 223–224, 227–232
  in Samoa, 132, 219
Citizenship Investment Bill (Samoa), 136, 219
Clark, Helen, 196
climate change, 26, 35, 45, 107, 154–155, 157, 204, 207
Clinton, Hillary, 35, 102, 106, 157, 198, 203
Compact of Free Association agreements (Micronesia), 44, 116
Confucius Institutes, 63–64, 95
construction contracts, 99, 219
contract labourers. *see* indentured labourers
Cook Islands National Sustainable Development Plan, 204

Cook Islands water scheme. *see* Te Mato Vai
cooperative societies (Papua New Guinea), 240–241
'core interests' (China), 68–69, *69*
corruption, 136, 236–237, 238, 262, 268
crime, 44–45, 126, 145, 147, 238, 242
Crocombe, Ron, 35, 46, 125
cultural obligations (implications for business), 132, 240–241, 242, 268–269
cultural tolerance, 84
culture, importance to Samoa, 135
customary land rights, 128, 136

Dai Bingguo, 198
D'Arcy, Paul, *47*
debt cancellation, 98
debt concerns, 43–44, 104, 141, 179, 183, 186–187, 192, 261, 272
debt position (Cook Islands), 204
defence strategy (China), 90, 91–92
democracy (in Oceania), 130, 136, 156–157
Deng Xiaoping, 68, 157
Denghua Zhang, *193*
development assistance. *see also* infrastructure projects; Te Mato Vai (Cook Islands water scheme)
  as % GNI, 113
  and adaptive capacity, 154–155
  from Australia, 102–103, 106–107
  'China alternative,' 42, 48, 103, 105, 130, 156–157, 181–182, 187, 196, 251, 259–260, 266–267, 270
  China conditionalities, 37, 41, 104, 166, 168, 187, 260, 262, 269, 271
  China overview, 31, 43, 95, 117, 190–191, 195
  Chinese-funded projects in Cook Islands, 169
  components of Chinese foreign aid, 195
  criticisms of, 37, 104, 162–163, 165–166, 224–225, 270–273
  distribution of Chinese foreign aid, 196
  features and patterns, 163–164
  in Fiji, 190–192
  finance management, 205–206
  future aims, 32, 157–158, 183, 187–188, 253
  and global economic downturn, 48, 166–167
  implementation issues, 185–186, 202
  inequalities, 164
  information sources, 173–174
  major donors, 36, 94, 112–113, 175, 189
  mapping tool, 173–175
  ODA to the Pacific region by donor, 165
  policy reforms, 166–167, 169–171
  quality assurance, 187–188, 206, 213, 273
  rapid growth of, 99, 156, 177, 194
  in Samoa, 128, 133, 185–188
  and Secretariat of the Pacific Community, 64
  'shared prosperity' approach, 167
  by Taiwan, 93
  total aid to all regions, 163
  Western conditionalities, 48, 131, 161, 196, 221–222, 260
Development Assistance Committee, 161–162
development cooperation, 162–164, 168–169, 170, 183, 188. *see also* trilateral cooperation
development effectiveness, 42, 161–163, 167–168, 191, 199
development partners (Cook Islands), 203
development strategy (China), 70, 71–72
Diaoyu Islands (Senkaku Islands), 48, 69–70, 101
diaspora. *see* ethnic Chinese
diplomatic relations (China)
  with Cook Islands, 201
  with Fiji, 32
  history of, 31, 34, 41–42, 54–55, 71, 89, 90, 94
  and international image, 99
  political impact of, 35, 58, 98, 100, 103, 105
  time and energy accorded the Pacific, 35
  with Samoa, 26, 32, 131, 184, 217
  with Tonga, 139–140
diplomatic relations (Cook Islands), 201, 211
diplomatic relations (Taiwan), 42, 93, 100, 139

discriminatory laws, 79–80, 125–126
Distant Water Fishing Nations (DWFN), 248, 250–251, 253–254

East China Sea Air Defense Identification Zone, 69, 101
economic and technical cooperation agreements (Samoa/China), 185
economic development
 as aid priority, 166–168, 247
 in China, 30, 53, 182, 198–199, 225–226, 264
 in Papua New Guinea, 237
 in Samoa, 25–26, 124
economic equality issues, 130
economic influence (of China, in Pacific), 36, 43, 177–179
economic security, 113
education, higher, 55–58, 63–64. *see also* international students; scholarships
education issues (Papua New Guinea), 237–238
embassy, Chinese (in Papua New Guinea), 145–146
Enari, Auelua Samuelu, *216*
energy resources, 99, 155–156
Enhanced Cooperation Programme, 118
environmental protection, 155–156
ethnic Chinese
 business interests, 34, 46–47, 128, 140, 230, 263, 268–269
  Papua New Guinea, 50, 144, 147, 236, 242
  Samoa, 74, 76, 81–83, 131–134
 community studies, 49–50
 early migrants, 25, 26, 34, 50, 54, 73–74, 76, 260, 268
 intermarriage, 49–50, 268
 overview, 46
 political success, 50, 83
 recent migrants, 34, 46, 50, 81–82, 127, 131–132, 236, 238, 242, 260, 263, 268–269
 in Samoa, 73–84, 124–125, 131–137
 sporting success, 83
 in Tonga, 140

as vehicles of China outreach, 36, 94–95
Eti, Tofilau, 131
Exclusive Economic Zones (EEZ), 229–230, 245–247, 248–249, 250
exports. *see* trade

financial literacy issues (Papua New Guinea), 238–239, 241–242
fisheries
 in East China Sea, 101
 geographic extent of the Pacific tuna fishery, 250
 illegal, unreported, unregulated (IUU), 250–251
 imports (China), 99, 178
 management, 36, 63, 115, 231, 248–254
 near-shore, 249, 252–253
 overview, 226–227
 in Samoa, 244–247
 subsidies (China), 229–230, 251
 sustainability, 229–230, 268, 273–274
Fong Toy, Andie, *14*
Fonua, Pesi, *143*
food (of Chinese origin), 83, 125, 127
Foreign Investment Act 2000, 82
foreign policy
 Australia, 182
 China, 30–31, 58–60, 68–71
forestry, 64–65, 230, 273
Forum Fisheries Agency, 62, 63
Forum on China-Africa Cooperation, 99
fossil fuels (import reliance), 219
Fraenkel, John, *258*
Framework for Pacific Regionalism, 45
France (as colonial power), 114
Free Papua Movement (OPM), 118
free trade agreement (China/NZ), 59
Free Trade Areas, 177
Fujian province, 34, 146
Fuqing migrants, 50, 146–148

'Gang of Nine' (scholars), 56
geopolitical interests, 41
geo-strategic competition, 114
global economic downturn, 48, 166–167

global objectives (China), 33–34, 35–36, 177–178
grading system (Chinese universities), 151–152
grants, 64, 185–186, 195, 202–203
Green Power Samoa Fuzhou Haohui Ltd, 219

High Level Forum on Aid Effectiveness, 204, 210
higher education policy (China), 55–57
homogeneity (of Samoan society), 135–136, 137
Hou Weirui, 56
Hu Jintao, 58, 68, 193, 227
Hu Wenzhong, 56
Hu Yaobang, 54, 71, 190
Hu Zhuanglin, 56
Huang Yuanshen, 56
huayi, 46. *see also* ethnic Chinese, recent migrants

Iati, Iati, *129*
indentured labourers, 73, 76–78, 82, 124, 125, 130, 131, 235, 240
India Pacific Summit, 177
indigenous agency. *see* Pacific Island agency
infrastructure projects
    China's priorities, 36–37, 91, 102, 166, 168, 195
    commercial influences, 104–105
    in Cook Islands, 202–203
    in Fiji, 192
    overview, 44, 95, 177
    in Samoa, 134–135, 185, 217, 219
    in Tonga, 141
integration (with Australia, New Zealand), 177, 179
intermarriage, 49–50, 241
    Chinese/Samoan, 78, 79–80, 83, 125–126, 127, 131, 133–134
international students, 55–58, 150–153
investment
    by Chinese companies, 43, 98
    Chinese FDI in Oceania, 43, 179, 226–227
    criticisms of, 224, 229
    growth, 31, 36
    in Papua New Guinea, 144
    in Samoa, 219
    in Tonga, 140
investor behavior (Chinese), 224

Jian Yang, 35–36
Jiang Zemin, 58, 68, 146

Kabutaulaka, Tarcisius, *234, 258*
Kamau, Macharia, 222
Kavieng Declaration on Aid Effectiveness, 103
King Tàufa'àhau Tupou IV, 140
Kruse Va'ai, Letuimanu'asina Emma, *10*

Laban, Luamanuvao Winnie, *75*
land reforms (in Samoa), 136
Laupepa, Malietoa, 74
Leung Wai, 73, 79, 82
Leung Wai, Tuatagaloa Aumua Ming, *75*, 125, 260, 268
Li Keqiang, 194
Li Yanduan, *27*
liquefied natural gas (Papua New Guinea), 228
Liu Shusen, *53*
loans
    commercial, 43, 99, 218
    concessional, 37, 43, 99, 104, 140–141, 166, 175, 179, 185, 186–187, 194, 195, 211, 218
    Cook Islands, 203
    preferential, 98, 185
    renegotiation of, 188
loli (sea slug), 123–124, 127
Lyu Guixia, *189*

Ma Ying-Jeou, 94, 100
MA60 aircraft (gifted to Tonga), 141
malaria control project, 197, 199
Malielegaoi, Tuilaepa Lupesoliai Sailele, *24*
Mao Zedong, 68, 71
mapping tool, 173–175
Marine Protected Areas (MPA), 249, 253

maritime navigation security (China), 90–91, 96
Maritime Silk Road of the 21st century, 59, 72, 91
maritime surveillance, 246–247, 248, 249, 253
Marles, Richard, 106
Matbob, Patrick, *234*
Melanesia, vulnerability of, 183
Melanesian Spearhead Group, 107, 118, 265
Meleisea, Leasiolagi Malama, *10*
migrants (Chinese). *see* ethnic Chinese
migration (Chinese)
   ancient Neolithic Era, 54
   illegal, 145, 146–147
   importance to Samoa, 125
   motivations for, 148
   recent increases in, 34, 133, 263
migration (in Oceania), 113
military assistance, 44, 115, 116
Millenium Development Goals, 161, 170
mineral resources, 99, 227–229, 231
mining. *see* mineral resources
Ministry of Women (Fiji), 191
MIRAB (Migration, Remittances, Aid and Bureaucracy), 113
motivations (of China), 49, 99–100, 190–191, 194, 198–199

national resilience, 113
natural resources (China's search for), 99–100, 221, 235
naval aspirations (China), 92, 101
naval visits (to Tonga), 141
neoliberalism, 162–163, 260
neostructuralism, 162–164, 169–170

Obama, Barack, 68, 70
Oceania
   historic external influences, 112
   natural resource developments, 221, 226–232
   ocean governance, 248–249
   relationships with former colonial powers, 114
   State relationships, 114–118

Oceanian Studies (in China), 60, 89
One Belt, One Road initiative, 60, 177
One-China Policy, 26, 32, 94, 103, 139, 184, 187, 191, 201
opium smuggling, 126
Overton, John, *160*

Pacific Asian Partnerships in Resource Development (book), 49
Pacific Island agency, 105–108, 127, 178, 180–181, 183, 204, 207, 259–260, 264–266, 270
Pacific Islands Development Forum, 107
Pacific Islands Development Programme, 63
Pacific Islands Forum, 94, 102, 104, 106, 107, 114, 118, 179, 211
Pacific Islands Forum Cooperation Fund, 155
Pacific Islands Forum Secretariat, 41, 42, 62, 63, 103, 265
Pacific Islands Leaders Meeting, 117
Pacific Islands Regional Ocean Policy, 253–254
Pacific Islands Trade and Invest Offices, 43, 63
Pacific Loans Facility, 186
Pacific Plan, 63, 64, 103, 107
Pacific Power Association, 62
Pacific Transnational Crime Network, 118
Paris Declaration of Aid Effectiveness, 161–162, 165, 167–168, 170, 188, 199
Passport Sales Scheme (Tonga), 139
People's Daily (newspaper, China), 68–69
political equality issues, 130
Post Forum Dialogue (PFD) partners, 45, 63
poverty alleviation, 161–164, 166–167, 170, 198, 226
Powles, Michael, *261*
Prasad, Biman, *176*
prospecting, 228–229

Qian Jiaoru, 56

racism, 79–80, 81–82, 84, 125–126, 135
Ramu nickel mine (Papua New Guinea), 36, 43, 49, 99, 179, 235–236

labour practices during construction, 104
ownership history, 227–228
reform agendas, 102–103, 106–107, 183
reforms, China, 30
regional agencies, 62
Regional Assistance Mission to the Solomon Islands (RAMSI), 107, 164–165
regional integration (Pacific Island countries), 45
repatriation, 76–79, 131
resource diplomacy, 221, 222–226
retroliberalism, 167, 170, 270
reunification of China, 90, 93, 94, 101
riots, 34, 47, 84, 115, 128, 130, 144, 145, 229, 263, 269, 272
  reconstruction costs (Tonga), 140–141
  underlying issues (Papua New Guinea), 236–237, 239, 242
rivalry
  China/Japan, 47–48, 69, 70, 100, 102, 117
  China/Taiwan, 42, 47–48, 71, 89, 90, 93–94, 96, 100–101, 129–130, 145–146, 157, 178
  China/United States, 25, 47–48, 69–70, 92–93, 98, 101, 102, 129–130, 192, 221, 263, 266–267
Rolfe, Jim, *111*

Salesa, Toeolesulusulu Damon, *122*
Sapolu, Patu Tiava'asu'e Falefatu, *75*
scholarships, 31–32, 37, 43, 59–60, 63, 95, 141, 150–153
Secretariat of the Pacific Community, 62, 64–65
Secretariat of the Pacific Regional Environmental Programme, 62, 63
security issues, 27, 60, 103, 113–118, 154, 259, 262–264, 267
Senkaku Islands (Diaoyu Islands), 48, 69–70, 101
Simi, Peseta Noumea, *184*
Smith, Graeme, *143*
Somare-Brash, Dulciana, *180*
So'o, Fui Le'apai Tu'ua 'Ilaoa Asofou, *10*

South Pacific Tourism Organisation, 62, 63
south-south cooperation, 42, 60, 117, 168–169, 170, 188, 196, 205, 209
Southwest Pacific Network, 92
Standard and Poor's rating (Cook Islands), 204
status symbols (in China), 148
strategic interests (of China), 32, 44, 49, 89–90, 92, 96, 223
Strategic Partnership, 35
subsidies (Chinese fishing), 229–230, 251
sustainable development, 30, 95, 205, 211, 219–220, 273–274
  fisheries, 229–230, 246, 248–254, 268

Taiwan, recognition of, 42, 47
Taylor, Meg, *14, 40*
Te Mato Vai (Cook Islands water scheme), 37, 42, 44, 106, 196, 273
  collaborative approach, 201, 204, 213
  financing, 205–206
  governance group, 206, 212
  implementation, 212–213
  international tendering process, 206
  overview, 204, 209–210
  peer review process, 202
  private sector inclusion, 206
  project delivery structure, 210
  project design, 211
  quality assurance, 206, 213
  strategic approach, 202
  sustainable development, 205
  transparency, 204–205
threat discourse perspective, 25, 30, 48, 128–130, 224, 227, 259, 262–264
timber, 99
Tokelau Arrangement (for fisheries management), 246
Tong, Anote, 105, 107
TongaSat, 140
tourism, 63, 113, 205, 219–220, 253, 262
trade
  Australia/China, 223
  barriers, 218
  Chinese exports, 178
  early Asian links, 123–124

growth, 31, 36, 94, 98, 99
imbalance, 140, 178, 218
liberalisation, 223
and marine transport, 90–91
partnerships, 41
regional programmes, 65
Samoa, 218
statistics, 42
tariffs, 43, 59, 95, 178–179, 218, 223
vulnerability, 113
training opportunities, 31–32, 188, 195
transitions (in Melanesia), 181
Trans-Pacific Partnership, 177
transparency, 192, 194, 204–205, 261, 265–266, 270
trilateral cooperation, 37, 42, 188, 196–214, *197*, 273
tuna fishing, 229–230, 231, 244–247, 249–252, 274

UN Convention on the Law of the Sea (1982), 248
United Nations, 71, 94, 107, 161
University of the South Pacific, 62, 63–64
US-China Global Development Dialogue, 198

Utoikamanu, Fekita, *62*
'Utoikamanu, Siosiua, 141

visits
by Chinese leaders, 26, 31–32, 35, 45, 54, 58, 59, 71, 156, 190, 227
by Pacific leaders, 35, 95, 100, 140, 190
by Samoan leaders, 26, 131

Wang Yang, 35, 98–99
Wen Jiabao, 35, 36, 58, 71, 98, 100, 106, 190
Wesley-Smith, Terence, *111*
Western powers, dissatisfaction with, 107–108
White Paper on Foreign Aid (China), 155, 157, 190, 193, 194
worker mobility, 124–125
Wu Bangguo, 58

Xi Jinping, 26, 31–32, 35–37, 44, 45, 59, 67–72, 95, 99, 155–156, 157, 227

Yu Changsen, *88, 258*

Zheng He (early explorer), 54